heard it was the best match he played.

Little Smart gushed tears at that scene and used it as source material to write another BL story. It received tens of thousand of views in less than half a day when she posted it to a certain fujoshi forum. Publishers even contacted her asking if she had any plans on publishing it.

I didn't participate in any of the celebratory events, including receiving awards, because I was too tired. After the excitement had passed, I realized I was faced with a severe problem.

I might have won the match, but I lost the bet with Niu ShiLi. I wasn't someone who would go back on my words, so as long as Niu ShiLi mentions it, I would down an entire bottle of Fu Yan Jie.

But it looks like Niu ShiLi completely forgot about it. Niu ShiLi followed the class leader's orders and hung up the number one basketball team in the grade award on the back wall of the class and began discussing the match with other classmates.

Niu ShiLi, who won the Fu Yan Jie bet, exchanged looks with me. I reminded him with my gaze: "Aren't you forgetting something?", but he didn't respond.

I was even a bit worried that Niu ShiLi was purposely leaving me hanging, to make me anxious about when he would make me suffer.

At this time, Sun Yu, the one who contributed the least and always headed to the infirmary, walked in front of me with a brand new bottle of Fu Yan Jie.

"Hehe, Ye Lin, you can't go back on your words." Sun Yu said with a smile, "The school doctor heard about the bet and donated a brand new bottle of Fu Yan Jie& or are you going to go back on your words as our class' PE committee member?"

The class leader had been called away by teacher Yu. Xiao Qin, who was sitting next to me, clenched her fists like she wanted to punch Sun Yu to death, but she couldn't do anything because of her androphobia.

All sights landed on me once Sun Yu brought up the bet.

Xiong YaoYue waded through the crowd and stood in front of me in protest.

"Hey, Ye Lin is exhausted after bringing our class to victory, but not only do you guys not thank him, you still keep bringing up the Fu Yan Jie bet. Do you guys have any humanity?"

"That's right." Loud Mouth said, "Sun Yu, you didn't even play more than 10 minutes in all three matches combined. Why are you bringing this up when everyone is already happy?"

Sun Yu looked a bit awkward, but he didn't give up. He placed the Fu Yan Jie on my table and said in defiance.

"This is completely different. I'm also happy our class won, but you have to keep your words if you made a bet, otherwise no one is going to believe what the PE committee member says anymore."

Xiong YaoYue and Loud Mouth wanted to continue to defend me, but I stopped them and stood up from my seat. Other than Niu ShiLi, everyone around me seemed a foot shorter.

Sun Yu took a step back and put up a guard in case I hit him. He looked around towards the other basketball team members for support, but didn't get any response.

The other team members already viewed me as a comrade after our victory in the life or death battle and I was glad.

It might be possible to muddle past this incident, but a man always keeps his word. I looked at Sun Yu with disdain (he retreated even further). Then I opened up the bottle of Fu Yan Jie and began to chug it.

If anyone wants to know what Fu Yan Jie tastes like, I can personally attest it's sour and sweet with a hint of a taste of pregnancy.

As Director Cao said, it might smell nice but it tastes extremely strange. It made me think it's a combination of czar wine and an archaic vinegar.

"Ye Lin classmate, don't!" Xiao Qin let out a sad cry and covered her face because she didn't want to see my twitching facial expression.

My actions stunned everyone around me. Xu LiJun stuck up his thumb and spoke with praise: "Ye Lin is a real man, respect."

Respect my ass, I drank half the bottle and already wanted to vomit. I think I'll get pregnant if I drank anymore.

But I couldn't give up halfway. No matter how painful it was, I had to endure it.

Suddenly, I felt someone grip the bottle of Fu Yan Jie and it was snatched away from me.

Even if I was exhausted, the only one who could easily snatch it from me in class 2-3 was the stocky Niu ShiLi.

I was confused on why Niu ShiLi snatched the bottle away. As I was about to question him, I heard him say:

"The one who made the bet with Ye Lin was me. I'm sorry I dragged the other members of the team into it." he paused then said, "It was an arduous journey and there might be unsatisfied people if there isn't a proper resolution."

Niu ShiLi then increased the severity of his tone and stared at Sun Yu. It only made Sun Yu feel more isolated.

"A lot of credit goes to Ye Lin for today's match, you could even say he deserves half of the credit. Someone even told me if Ye Lin didn't pass the final ball to me, then the one who would be drinking Fu Yan Jie now would be me."

The words weren't beautiful or rhetoric, but it was powerful and it touched me.

Niu ShiLi and I looked at each other. We used to be like fire and ice, but now our eyes were brimming with camaraderie.

"That's why.." Niu ShiLi said loudly, "A man always keeps his promise. Since they are people expecting one of us to drink Fu Yan Jie, then I'll let Ye Lin drink the first half and I'll drink the rest."

Niu ShiLi opened his mouth and chugged the rest of the bottle until it was completely empty.

Everyone watching was stunned.

Niu ShiLi wiped his mouth and placed the empty bottle on the table. He had a fierce expression that said 'come over here if you weren't satisfied'.

Who would even dare go over. You're battle power is already off the charts for finishing that half bottle of Fu Yan Jie so quickly.

Just like the scared water Korin gave to Goku in Dragonball, it's practically a poison! You can only become a true master after drinking that disgusting liquid.

What& is this power? I could also feel myself getting a bit stronger. Is it because of the Fu Yan Jie or is it all in my head?

Oh, it was all in my head. I felt bad for drinking Fu Yan Jie, so I wanted to trick others to drink it too. If someone actually fell for it, then I'm sorry, but isn't it an interesting experience (LOL)?

I was especially touched after Niu ShiLi helped me finish the rest of the Fu Yan Jie. As I expected, friendship between men is much simpler. You don't have to talk a lot nor do you need to whisper sweet words, sometimes you can already recognize each other as friends with a simple glance.

It was a friendship created by drinking the same bottle of Fu Yan Jie. The feeling can't be understood by outsiders unless you drink Fu Yan Jie too. (Really, just one gulp. As Chinese people we've already eaten Sudan Red and gutter oil, so what harm can a little Fu Yan Jie do?)

Of course, there's also the issue of Niu ShiLi not wiping the bottle opening when he drank the Fu Yan Jie. In theory, that's what we can an indirect& indirect kiss&

Luckily, Little Smart wasn't here, or who knows what kind of scary BL story she would have created.

That's when I realized Sun Yu had also run away. He acted like a nasty person, but only made the friendship between me and Niu ShiLi become apparent.

Even though Niu ShiLi and I both kept our words, we still paid the price. Neither of us were able to eat lunch.

The most annoying was after Xiao Qin determined I wouldn't die, she asked curiously:

"Ye Lin classmate, does Fu Yan Jie taste good?"

What do you think? I rinsed my mouth 50 times and I still couldn't get rid of the taste in my mouth. I also want to barf every time I burp.

Niu ShiLi was pretty much in the same state. We had a deeper sense of camaraderie after seeing each other's miserable state.

I heard that if you had heavy metal poisoning, you could drink milk to somewhat neutralize it. Fu Yan Jie might not be a heavy metal, but it is a heavy flavor, so I asked Xiao Qin to help me head to the school convenience store to get me a carton of milk.

What was unexpected was Xiao Qin even bought one for Niu ShiLi even when I forgot to ask,

"Ye Lin classmate, I have a good impression of Niu ShiLi since he drank half of the Fu Yan Jie for you. But I'm still afraid of boys and can't apologize to him, so can this milk count as my apology?"

Seeing as I refused to reply, Xiao Qin pleaded with tears in her eyes, "If one carton of milk isn't enough, then I'll use my allowance to buy a lot of milk to apologize. Ye Lin classmate, please forgive me for the fact I beat up Niu ShiLi before."

If I think about it, it wouldn't be right forcing Xiao Qin who has androphobia to apologize to Niu ShiLi. I can't guarantee she won't continue to force He Ling to be Niu ShiLi's girlfriend, but if she's willing to buy milk for him, that means she's at least feeling a bit apologetic.

Xiao Qin relaxed after I said I won't keep pressing the matter.

I held the straw in my mouth as I passed the other carton of milk to Niu ShiLi.

"You didn't eat anything either, right? Drink some milk or you might be too hungry in the afternoon."

Niu ShiLi was stunned and didn't immediately accept it. I joked: "What, you can't drink milk because your surname is Niu?" (TN: Niu = Cow)

Niu ShiLi laughed out loud, "Nonsense, milk is originally for cows to drink."

He grabbed the milk and began drinking and we both looked at each other and smiled.

Don't misunderstand, we don't have any kind of intimate relationship. It's simply because milk is delicious when compared to Fu Yan Jie.

You would always smile if you starved for ten days and then suddenly get to eat until you were full.

I looked forward to the girl's volleyball match in the afternoon. I heard the class leader's vision wasn't in great shape, she still had to play to defend their crown.

It meant I would finally be able to see the class leader play in volleyball shorts! How lucky, it seems Fu Yan Jie is a lucky medicine. (If there's anyone reading who's down in luck, I recommend you to give it a try)

I had a simple desire to see the class leader in volleyball shorts, but life isn't fair. 20 minutes before the volleyball match started, it& actually began to rain.

It was a downpour. Since 28 Middle didn't have an indoor court, the match had to be delayed.

Xiong YaoYue rejoiced over the outcome.

She sat in the classroom watching the storm from out the window with a big smile.

"Hahaha, I was just worrying about what to do if the class leader can't play at her best, but then the match was delayed by the rain. It was the right decision for me to do good deeds."

The rumbling sounds of thunder came along with the storm. Eunuch Cao and Gong CaiCai were both pale with fright.

Eunuch Cao must have made some vow involving being struck by lightning. As for Gong CaiCai, it was simply because she was timid and I can't think of anything that she's not afraid of.

Xiong YaoYue might have held back from teasing Gong CaiCai for a period of time, but old habits die hard. She crept up next to Gong CaiCai and suddenly shouted in imitation of lightning, "zzz&BANG, BOOM."

Gong CaiCai almost jumped up with her chair. It took almost half a minute to calm her down and she said unhappily to Xiong YaoYue:

"Why are you scaring me when you already know I'm afraid of thunder? My lifespan must have been shortened again&"

"Noo, no." Xiong YaoYue hugged Gong CaiCai and apologized, "Someone as cute and kindhearted as you will definitely live to a hundred, and your dreams might even come true."

I reckon since Xiong YaoYue thought rain came to delay the match because she did good deeds, then Gong CaiCai, who's always willing to help others (letting other people copy her homework), will have her dreams come true.

Gong CaiCai lowered her head in thought after she heard Xiong YaoYue talk about her dreams, then she said sullenly: "I have no idea what I'm going to do in the future, but if would be great if I could turn into a conch&"

Eh, what a strange dream? Why would you want to be a conch? Or is it some strange magical girl setting where your original body is a conch?

"Why?" Xiong YaoYue had the same question as me.

Gong CaiCai said softly, "If I was a conch, I could hide in my shell if I was in a scary situation."

So it's the mindset of an ostrich to run away when you run into something scary? Shells aren't as safe as you think. I once saw a video where a fish hit a clam against a rock until it cracked and it was able to eat delicious meat.

That's why I'm a firm believe of 'a good offense is a good defense'. If Gong CaiCai met something who wanted to smash the shell, then she would definitely be eaten.

When Xiong YaoYue heard Gong CaiCai wanted to be a conch, she asked:

"Huh, if you shut yourself inside the shell wouldn't that affect your claustrophobia?"

Gong CaiCai's face turned pale after suddenly being reminded of this fact. She sobbed and pummeled her fists at Xiong YaoYue.

"It's all because of you that my only dream is shattered."

Xiong YaoYue laughed without evading as if she enjoyed Gong CaiCai's soft strikes.

The class leader's plan was disrupted due to the rain.

Loud Mouth suggested that our whole class should celebrate at a buffet if we won both the basketball and volleyball matches. Loud Mouth was a senior member in a certain food review website, so she could use her points to buy coupons. If everybody if our class bought one, we would be able to save a lot of money.

But since the volleyball match was delayed, that plan was also put to the side for the time being.

A lot of students didn't bring an umbrella because the weather forecast said it wasn't going to rain today. Luckily, the rain began to slowly die out before school ended and it eventually stopped.

It might be due to the sudden rainstorm that prevented them from filming, so Auntie Ren drove over to pick up Xiao Qin. Xiao Qin asked her mom: "Can we take Ye Lin classmate home too?"

Auntie Ren took out her anger of my dad at me and didn't agree, then she forcefully dragged Xiao Qin on to the car.

I started to head home by myself. To be honest, I wanted to find the class leader to get my free food, but she disappeared right after school ended, so she might have been tied up with school duties.

As I was thinking about where to eat tonight, I suddenly heard the crisp ring of a bicycle bell from behind.

I turned around and saw the class leader had caught up to me on her bike. She stopped the bike and supported herself on one leg and smiled.

"You can come to my house for dinner if you don't have any other plans."

I perked up right away when I heard I could get free food tonight and asked:

"What's for dinner?"

"I can make whatever you want as long as I can buy the ingredients from the food market. But it can't too much time, those dishes needs to be reserved a day ahead of the time."

Huh, so based on what she said, she already acknowledges I can eat meals at her house for a while! Based on our agreement, I can eat until before the start of summer break! That means I don't have to worry about my dinner for over twenty days, it was worth it drinking the Fu Yan Jie!

I said I wanted to eat red braised pork. The class leader nodded and said: "It's not hard to make, but I need to soak the meat in cooking wine for an hour. Are you willing to wait that long?"

"I am." I agreed, "I can definitely wait an hour for a good meal."

The class leader smiled and said to me, "Then I'll head to the market first on my bike. You can head to my home first. Xiao Zhe is at home, so he'll open the door for you."

So in the end, I was still walking by myself, but my mood was completely different than earlier.

I thought about the time it would take the class leader to buy groceries and cook. If I went early, I could only chat with Shu Zhe, so it would be better to help out at the hospital. I was the one who persuaded the class leader to not volunteer here anymore, so I feel a bit bad for Dr. Zhao and Xiao Ding.

"Out of the way, the main force is here." I said half-jokingly as I walked in.

Dr. Zhao and Xiao Ding both had happy expressions. At this moment, I played a bigger role than the class leader.

Five boxes of medical supplies that had to be moved to the surgery room was moved by me and Xiao Ding in less than ten minutes.

After I helped, I apologized about the fact the class leader might not be able to volunteer anymore and hoped they would understand.

Dr. Zhao was puzzled: "Shu Sha just came over."

I paused: "Why did she come here?"

Dr. Zhao scratched his stubble, "Shu Sha asked what we did with the little black dog's body and said she was already fine. She said she would keep volunteering here and take care of the dogs like before even when she knows there's a high chance stray dogs would die of illness."

After experiencing death, she still chose to get closer to those close to death and take care of them while being prepared to lose them at any time.

The class leader was braver than me.

Just like how she wanted to be a police officer. She always chose the more difficult path, the path filled with thorns.

Why couldn't she choose the simple path?

I felt a bit unwell after chatting with Xiao Ding.

I already had a slight cold and headache when I woke up today morning, but I held it back because of the basketball match.

Since we already won the match, I had no more pressure and the sickness began to spread.

It was also really cold inside the hospital because of the AC. It was just raining earlier, so they should learn to save energy.

I felt chills all over my body, but I didn't tell Dr. Zhao (plus he's a veterinarian), and left the pet hospital.

I was muddleheaded after arriving at the class leader's house. I couldn't even hold a proper conversation with the class leader and Shu Zhe. The food the class leader made smelled delicious, but I didn't eat a lot and I felt sorry.

The class leader asked numerous times if I was sick. I kept saying I was fine until I began to tremble. The class leader put her hand on my forehead to test my temperature and I didn't even have the strength to avoid it.

"So hot." I heard the class leader say as I was in a daze.

"39 C, you should go to the hospital for a drip. Ye Lin, can you walk with me and Shu Zhe supporting you?"

I replied in a daze: "It's fine, I never eat medicine or get shots. I'll get better after I sleep."

I'm not sure if they believed me or if I wasn't being cooperative and it was difficult to bring me to the hospital. All I knew was when I awoke, I was lying in an unfamiliar room on top of a soft double bed,

The class leader helped me change wet towels many times. I couldn't see clearly, but I was sure this was the class leader's parents' room. Since it was usually empty, it would also be used as the guest room.

I felt my body and it seems all my wet clothes were removed. I was wearing nothing but my underwear while under the cover.

Did the class leader tell Shu Zhe to help me take it off? But he's pretty weak, so it would be hard for him to remove my clothes while I was unconscious.

Or was it a cooperative effort from the two of them?

It was shameful just thinking about it.

I was still in a bad state and switching between states of being dizzy and being clear-headed. I felt the class leader feed me water and something bitter.

The class leader took care of me until late into the night and it was completely dark outside. I didn't want to let them see me in a weak state, but it looked like I couldn't avoid staying over night.

The class leader fed me water many times, but my throat was still parched.

But I understood my own body. It was my great immune system battling with the sickness. My cells entered an all out war, so that's why my body burned up. As long as I keep the covers over me and sleep to the next morning, I would be completely healed. That method has never failed me.

But I was faced with a problem I never encountered before.

I couldn't fall asleep.

It's not like I was like the Princess and the Pea where I can't fall asleep if I change beds. I could even sleep on the floor as long as I had a pillow and a body pillow.

That's right, as I've said before, I had a habit of hugging a pillow when I sleep. If I don't have a body pillow, it would take me an extra two hours to fall asleep.

The desk lamp was still on and I could see the class leader's shadow walk back and forth. I felt bad since I could fall asleep if I had a body pillow and the class leader didn't need to stay here anymore.

As for Shu Zhe, of course he already went to sleep. The class leader wouldn't let her brother stay up overnight.

I couldn't really say anything with my hoarse throat, but even if I could, it would be too embarrassing to ask for a body pillow.

I flipped around the bed and tried hugging the pillow under my head, but it didn't work.

My breathing was heavy and my chest was on fire. In my drowsiness, I finally found something that I could hug.

Ah, what a soft pillow. I think I hallucinated a scene where the pillow struggles and tried to escape, but I never let go.

I still had quite a bit of strength even when I was sick.

I held the pillow in my embrace and slept soundly through the night.

The desk lamp that was in the room was still on when I woke up.

A faint beam of light came through the windows, so it should already be morning.

That's strange, did the class leader forget to turn off the light after she gave me a body pillow?

Regardless if it's to save energy or to let a sick person have a better rest, it doesn't seem like something the class leader would forget to do.

Or was it because she was too tired from taking care of me? I cause way too much trouble for the class leader.

As expected of a Spartan.

If it was Shu Zhe, it would have been an awful sickness. But for me, all I did was sweat it out and have a good sleep, then I was completely fine the next morning.

My dad used an analogy where your immune system was a country's army, regular medicine was supplemental army provisions, and antibiotics was mercenaries.

If you relied on mercenaries too often, then your own immune system will suffer.

As for me, who didn't take medication or shots and stayed of from antibiotics, each of the cells in my immune system was strong enough to fight against ten enemies.

That's why the first thing I had to do after recovering was to wear my clothes and express my thanks to the class leader for taking care of me. Then I would try and see if I could get some breakfast, since I still might be sick.

But then my body pillow opened its eyes.

Ahhhhhhhhhhhhh scared me. What's going on? Am I hallucinating?

No, wait, I've seen these eyes before. The pupils were jet black and it felt like it would suck you in if you came too close.

Who else could it be but the class leader? When did the body pillow turn into the class leader?

Did I accidentally take the class leader as a body pillow last night?

Now wonder it was much softer than a regular body pillow. There was only a single layer of thin fabric between the class leader, who was wearing a pair of blue pajamas, and me, who was in my underwear.

I was face to face with the class leader. Since I mistook as her as a body pillow, it couldn't be helped that I didn't take her into consideration and she currently had her chest unwilling pressed against my chest.

Once I recognized those two soft lumps, I really wanted to move my chest up and down, but the class leader's deathly glare dispelled those thoughts.

I remember the class leader talking last night about how she only needed to wear the eye patch outside, that's why she took off her eye patch for dinner. Currently, her two bright eyes were sending chills down my back.

If you're asking why I was so afraid, it's because it was inevitable for my two hands to be behind the class leader when I used her as a body pillow.

My left hand was fine since it was on the class leader's back, but as for my right hand& It was on her butt!

If it was Gong CaiCai, she definitely would have started cry while yelling 'I can't get married anymore'. With her frail body it's possible I might have even hugged her to death in my sleep.

So I was still a bit glad the one I hugged was the class leader, since she could handle it.

I could kind of guess what happened last night after I hugged onto the class leader.

Her first reaction must have been to break free, but it wouldn't have been possible because I couldn't even hear what she said and I had a strong desire for a body pillow.

The class leader must have been afraid I would move on to the next steps, and she probably thought about if it would be wise to call Shu Zhe for help.

Even if you called over the weak Shu Zhe, it would be like delivering meat into a tiger's mouth.

Of course, I had no interest in a trap. The class leader was simply worried I would hurt her little brother.

But the class leader quickly realized I had no idea what I was hugging onto. My breathing quickly calmed down after I hugged her and I fell into a peaceful sleep.

The class leader then reminded herself that I was sick. Since I didn't have any plans to take any further actions and the class leader was unable to break free, she could only endure it silently.

She endured it all the way until the next morning.

I had subconsciously moved my right hand on the class leader's butt in the middle of the night. It can't be helped, since it's natural for humans to like soft things.

"Move your hand."

The class leader finally spoke.

She was staring at me to determine if I had recovered. If I was still sick, she might have been a bit more polite.

But I guess her words were polite enough towards someone who was groping her ass without her consent.

My hand quickly jumped off the forbidden area.

"Move your other hand too."

The class leader must have been certain I was fine seeing how I was able to nimbly move my hand.

I let my hand go, but since the class leader was still on top of my arm, I couldn't pull my hand out for the time being.

After I released my hands, she rolled out of the bed at an unimaginably fast speed.

I've always had a poor sleeping posture since I was a kid, so the blanket that was covering me had slid to my waist. My upper naked body was exposed.

The class leader might have not wanted to see my upper body anymore. She put on her slippers and walked out without looking back.

My feelings were complicated after hearing the class leader washing up in the bathroom.

My actions might have been involuntary, but the truth was we still slept together on the same bed for a whole night.

I wonder what the class leader thought about it. She was nice enough to take care of me, yet I forcefully hugged her for an entire night.

I hope the class leader wasn't hiding in the washroom while using the sound of running water to mask her crying. I don't think the class leader was someone that weak, plus she would never waste water.

I placed my hand over the spot where the class leader was sleeping. I could still feel the warmth and smell a sweet fragrance, but my male body odor made me feel ashamed.

I was only concerned with my own well being and used the class leader as a body pillow for the whole night. The class leader was constricted to the point where she had troubles breathing, and she had to endure my body odor, I feel sorry.

In order to take care of me as a sick person, she didn't really resist. She still had a chance to escape if she was protesting violently as if her life depended on it.

In order to help me recover, she still let me use her as a body pillow. What an admirable feat, they should give her the Florence Nightingale Medal for being an exceptional nurse.

I jumped off the bed and quickly wore my clothes.

As I put on my pants, I was glad I didn't have a morning erection because I was sick or it would have made it even more awkward.

After I put on my clothes, I hid in the room and was afraid to go out. I was waiting for the class leader to criticize me.

Should I say it was unexpected, but the class leader didn't return. Instead, she went back to her own room.

I then remembered to check the time. It was 5:20, so it was reasonable for the class leader to go back to sleep.

When it was time to normally get up, I heard the sound of the microwave in the kitchen. After the ding, the class leader called Shu Zhe up for breakfast and also called me.

As I ate breakfast with the class leader and her brother, I didn't really feel like her attitude towards me has changed. What's even stranger was that Shu Zhe wasn't shocked at all about how I recovered in one night.

"Can you still go to school?"

The class leader asked after she collected all the dishes.

I really wanted to use my sickness as an excuse to skips school for a day, but that would mean I would stay at the class leader's home alone which wasn't really suitable, so I said:

"It's already, I already recovered. Let's go to school together."

The class leader suddenly had a displeased expression like she was mad when I said I already recovered. Didn't she want me to recover, wasn't she willing to be my body pillow so I could recover? Why is she mad? Or was it because she found out I had amazing self-recover ability and she was worried for nothing last night.

"I'll go to school first on my bike, you can go with Xiao Zhe."

The class leader then left by herself.

After Shu Zhe confirmed his sister had left, he poked my with his elbow and said:

"Bro Ye Lin, you're a huge pervert."

"What did you say?"

Shu Zhe made an expression as if to say 'stop pretending' and said:

"You were really sick last night, but you still pulled my sister on to your bed. It seems you would rather than than give up lust."

I panicked and asked: "How did you know, what did you see?"

"I noticed your room door and light was still open when I went to the washroom last night. I was curious so I took a peek and I saw the two of you hugging each other in your sleep."

Damn& it, so he saw everything? Based on his usual behavior, did he take pictures and plan to use it to blackmail me?

But this time it's different (last time was the picture of when I was smelling the class leader's legs). This time the class leader already knew I was hugging her, so it doesn't matter if Shu Zhe took pictures.

Shu Zhe spoke while packing his bag:

"I originally thought I was mistaken, but I rubbed my eyes and it was true. I thought it was because the two of your was alone and couldn't hold it back, but my sister was still wearing her clothes&"

"Based on my analysis and your expression at the time, you must have mistaken my sister as a body pillow. I already heard a rumor that you couldn't sleep without a body pillow, but I didn't expect it to be true."

Damn it, if you already heard that rumor, you should have gotten me a body pillow. Then your sister didn't have to be forcefully hugged for an entire night.

In the end, it was still Shu Zhe's fault. He's basically an expert at screwing over his sister. If I had a brother like him, I would have choked him to death.

It rained throughout Thursday and Friday.

The girl's volleyball finals was pushed back to at least next week.

The class leader's eye had recovered in these two days. Her eyes exuded confidence after she took off her eye patch.

But the way she looked at me was a bit strange.

And she didn't invite me to eat dinner these past two days either. Since she didn't invite me, I was too embarrassed to ask.

I mean she had to cook for me and act as my body pillow. I don't even think her husband would get that kind of treatment.

On Saturday, I went to film city to film the Bloody Battle of Jin Ling.

Director Cao was waiting for me in front of a restaurant freezer with six other casually dressed employees to film the freezer scene.

Seeing me, the lighting technician was the first to yell:

"You look really similar to Wu Sheng, are you guys biological brothers?"

I don't have such a melancholic brother. I later heard that since Wu Sheng moved to Switzerland, their suicide rate for that increased by 4%, but not sure if it was related to Wu Sheng.

Since short films are short in time, the plot is condensed. My only job today was to dress up as Jin Ling young thug and fight a couple times in the freezer with 'righteous' martial artists (The masked justice men are cameos by the owner of the restaurant and the head chef. Apparently Director Cao gave them the opportunity to appear on film to pay for the venue).

Director Cao told me to go easier on the people I was fighting since they were the ones who owned the freezer. I thought that Wu Sheng would have never agreed since he's a good actor who pays attention to a character's traits.

But I don't really care about the results of the short film series, so I agreed.

The most important part was Director Cao told me to put on a gold Rolex and instructed me to purposely raise my arm when the fight starts to reveal the watch.

I also readily agreed since it was still Wu Sheng's name in the credits.

Previously, shooting was always delayed due to Wu Sheng's opposition of inserting advertisements. Now, everyone rejoiced and celebrated after Director Cao had finally found an actor like him who had no integrity.

Everyone cooperated flawlessly and was able to finish shooting the scene in 15 minutes.

Later, I realized the reason everyone was so focused was because they didn't want to stay inside the freezer that reached a temperature of -30 degrees Celsius. Even if everyone had down jackets, we would still be trembling after staying inside for too long.

One of the people caught a cold because of the sudden shifts in temperature between hot and cold and had to go to a clinic like Wu Sheng. I just caught a cold recently and was more careful, so I was fine.

Director Cao was beaming since everything went smoothly. He told me he would still pay me according to Wu Sheng's contract. The pay was probably not as high as what I was paid in the American set, but it was better than nothing.

I finished work early, so I wore my casual clothes and walk towards the Magic Cauldron set to go see Ai Mi.

Unexpectedly, I met her on my way there.

Ai Mi, who had her ponytail tied up with a red ribbon, was holding Obama on a leash while standing in front of a street fruit vendor.

Ai Mi was like a food inspector carefully inspecting the pears, watermelon, lychee, and mango in front of her and she didn't notice me.

004 and 005, who were guarding Ai Mi from afar was the first to notice me.

The owner of the fruit stand was a middle aged auntie. She frequently sets up her stall near film city, so she was used to foreign tourists. The auntie wasn't timid, nor did she show any signs of showing preferential treatment to the foreigner, she only said lethargically:

"What are you looking at, just put the fruits in a bag. Do you know how to speak Chinese, if not, #@@*&*&@@####@@@%, @#$&^$*@*@##$#$$#$&"

What the hell was she saying? Based on my limited knowledge on English, I think she was speaking English. I can't believe a fruit seller auntie even spoke better English than me. I should just crash into and kill myself with one of those watermelons.

Ai Mi wasn't impressed with the auntie's strange English and frowned: "I know how to speak Chinese, do you sell cola here."

Why are trying to do the impossible by buying cola at a fruit stand? Even if the auntie did have cola, there's no way 004 and 005 would let you buy it.

The auntie was shocked when she realized the blond loli in front of her spoke fluent Chinese and couldn't help but ask"

"Eh, where are you from? Are you not a tourist?"

Ai Mi didn't respond as if she didn't hear the question. Then the auntie realized there was another urgent issue that had to be taken care of. Obama had stuck out his long tongue and was licking one of the apples on the stand.

Was Obama going crazy from hunger that he would even eat an apple?

"Hey, hey." The auntie made a shooing motion, "Stop your dog from licking my fuji apples, I can't sell them anymore."

"Did you hear that?" Ai Mi said sternly to Obama, "Stop licking it. The apples in China are all covered in pesticide, so now you need to get your stomach pumped when we go home."

Then Ai Mi lowered her voice and asked again like she was trying to buy drugs: "Do you sell cola here?"

The auntie was baffled after being stared at Obama, she shook her head and said: "We don't sell cola here, it's full of chemicals. My fruits are way better than cola."

Ai Mi lost interest once she heard they didn't have what she wanted, she clicked her tongue and said:

"What kind of store is it if it doesn't even have cola."

Then she left the Auntie and turned to leave.

She saw me right when she turned around.

"Huh, manservant, are you following me?"

It was a coincidence. It's hard not to notice you when you have blond hair and you're walking a large dog.

"It's nothing to feel embarrassed about." Ai Mi said complacently, "Since you're a lowly manservant who loves me and you're also the slave I love."

"Here, you hold the leash for a while."

Ai Mi handed over control of Obama to me. We both walked down the spacious street with the afternoon sun shining brightly on us.

As we were chatting, I suddenly realized Ai Mi was gone. I looked around and found her hiding behind me to avoid the sun.

"Manservant, when can you get as big as Peng TouSi so that your shadow can completely cover me."

Ai Mi didn't seem pleased that my shadow could only cover a part of her.

I'm sorry, but there's no way I would ever get as large as Peng TouSi, he's nearly the same size as the Hulk! Or are you willing to expose your brother to gamma radiation just so you can hide from UV rays?

"Oh right, Kyle has been playing clap clap clap recently."

Ai Mi suddenly said.

Clap clap& isn't that a slang for intercourse? I mean Kyle is already over 18, so I don't care who he has sex with, but don't cause negative influences to my sister.

"He's absorbed to the point where he would do it whenever he has nothing else to do on set."

I could understand getting absorbed, but what do you mean on set? XXX on set? The open mindedness of Americans is completely changing my worldview.

"Kyle not only plays with himself, but also keeps recommending it to others as a way to reduce stress. He even asked me yesterday if I wanted to do it with him&"

Shit, does he want to die? I'll give Xiao Qin a call and tell her to let the triads kidnap him!

"Hmph, there's no way I would play such a childish game with him. I can also reduce stress by eating chips and drinking cola."

As expected of my sister to thoroughly reject him, but to think chips is better than clap clap& most people can eat chips first before they are allowed to clap clap&

"But after Kyle left, I was a bit bored and played it with myself a bit and it was quite fun."

Wait& wait, what did you say? What do you mean played it by yourself? Don't you need at least two people to play?

Or are you& did you DIY it yourself in the RV? That's way too much information.

"Now I feel empty without clap clap clap for a day&"

Now you're addicted? No need to tell me, because there's nothing I can do for you.

"Hey, manservant, you look a bit off."

Ai Mi gazed at me curiously.

That's because of the topic you're talking about!

Ai Mi got happier the worse I looked. She covered her mouth and snickered:

"Are you jealous because Kyle and I are playing clap clap clap by ourselves without calling you? How about we play together next time."

Stop& how can you mention a taboo so casually. I never knew I had such a shameless sister.

Ai Mi kicked a pebble that was on the street.

"Oh right, you can't play without the proper tools."

Ai Mi reached into her pocket and pulled out something.

I can't look. If it's a tool for that, then it has to be a condom! I can't believe my sister has already degenerated to the point where she would casually carry around condoms. Where did it all go wrong?

What Ai Mi took out was actually a folded sheet of bubble wrap. Over half of the bubbles on one side had been popped.

"Here's the trending clap clap clap game. Every time you pop a bubble, it sounds like a clap. Do you want to give it a try?"

Stop giving games random names! This childish game is usually something we only played in kindergarten!

Back in the days, the Little Tyrant would sit on my back with a sheet of bubble wrap on the back of my head. She would pop it for an entire afternoon and now my head hurts just hearing that sound.

I was almost certain Ai Mi called popping bubble wrap as clap clap clap simply for her own amusement.

I shouldn't have fallen for it. I could tell because I saw her familiar smirk as she was pranking me.

It was the same smirk I had when I pranked the class leader (like how I tricked the class leader to bark like a dog).

My dad, Ye YuanFeng, isn't a boring person, but he doesn't have a habit of pranking others. It's because he used to be a teacher and he had to pat attention to his actions.

Even if I didn't like it, I could guess the smirk for Ai Mi and me was inherited from our mother, Ai ShuQiao.

But it's just Ai ShuQiao likes to commit crimes rather than play pranks. How we both have the same smirk as that monster isn't something to be thankful for.

Peng TouSi came to pick up Ai Mi after we walked the dog a bit. He said the director needed to discuss some last minute changes to the script.

Ai Mi returned unwillingly with Peng TouSi. I couldn't attend even if I went with her, since it was an internal meeting. I decided to stay outside of film city for the time being and told her I would visit her later.

I could have also followed them back and spent my time in the RV while sampling the French chef's desserts, but I felt I've been lazing around too much lately and that's why I caught a cold. I shouldn't always think about enjoying myself, but instead, I should challenge myself and put my body through trials to become a true fearless man.

I began to walk briskly along the road outside film city to train my leg muscles.

I walked a kilometer like a racewalker (TN: Just found out it's a sport lol). The scenery around me gradually began to turn into vegetation and I would often see underbrushes half the height of a person on both sides of the road. There were even horse drawn carriages that passed by and the smell of horse feces was spread around in the dry and hot air.

Since film city was constructed on the outskirts of Dong Shan city, the further I walked the more desolate it became.

I didn't want to end up in place where I couldn't even buy water when I was thirsty, so I turned around and decided to head back.

That's when I saw a person squatting in the brushes.

I thought it was Xiao Qin's cousin, Ren Peng, aka the Prince of the Brushes. The one who's addicted to LOL and would always squat in a brush to think about his life.

Then after taking a closer look, I realized it was a boy who was 8 or 9 years old. He had a bald cut with a large vest and he looked identical to Ren Peng when he was squatting inside the brush.

I felt like it was a serious problem if the future of our country was already addicted to web games.

They all say there's a lot of grade school students who play LOL. The number one LOL player in our city is even called 'Red Scarf Hero'. But it was the first time I saw a grade school student who was so addicted he was squatting inside a brush like Ren Peng and preparing to jump out and passersby.

Luckily, I was the first one who passed him. He might have thought my face too scary, so he didn't jump out, but I couldn't say the same if it was someone else who passed by instead of me.

I was just feeling ashamed because I carried criminal blood inside me, so I felt a sudden sense of responsibility when I realized I could prevent an accident from occurring and leading the future of our country onto the right path. I walked near the boy and said to him:

"Little boy, do you know hiding in brushes doesn't actually make you invisible in real life?"

The little boy looked up at me. Surprisingly, even though he was scared of me, he didn't immediately jump away.

Even though he didn't move away, he quickly lowered his head as if to deny my existence.

Damn, is this a sign that he was way too addicted to games? I once pulled an all-nigher playing Dota with Xiao Ding and the next morning, when I left the net cafe, I thought everyone had HP bars over their heads.

Does he think I would ignore him if he doesn't respond? I have to wake him up and prevent him from becoming even more addicted!

I cleared my throat and continued to lecture him like an elder:

"Little boy, you shouldn't only play video games, you should play outside more. Of course, it's completely unnecessary for you to play these cosplay games outside. Is that a wooden stick you're holding in your hand? You will be arrested by the police if you hurt someone."

The little boy still didn't say anything, but he appeared to be in distress.

I realized the item he was clenching in his right hand was a roll of newspaper and not a stick. I guess it was fine it was newspaper since he couldn't hurt anyone if he hit people with it, but it might be bad if he gave seniors heart attacks.

"Ahem, when I was your age, I would play outside every day. I would play hide and seek, go on the slide, or play with mud. I still cherish those memories right now."

I actually don't cherish those memories at all. When I played hide and seek, I would get a beating if the Little Tyrant caught me. When I was playing on the slide, I would get a beating if the Little Tyrant saw me. When I was playing with mud, I would get a beating if I made something better than the Little Tyrant.

What's wrong with my childhood, why can't I remember anything fun? It's like a compilation of me getting a beating and it's not worth cherishing at all. If computer games were as developed as it was now, then I definitely would have stayed at home gaming every day.

My words of advice really moving and the little boy finally raised his head in embarrassment, he said:

"Big brother, I'm not addicted to games, I& I'm taking a poop."

No wonder it stinks! I even thought it was horse feces earlier, but it was actually child feces! So that means you're holding newspaper to wipe your ass? Use toilet paper! There's lead in newspaper print, so it's definitely not healthy for a child's butt.

I felt really awkward and I gave the little boy the tissues I had on me for him to wipe his butt, then I turned and left.

On my way back to film city, I met three men dressed in striped suits.

The left one was really skinny, he had a devious expression and his hair drooped down in front of his eyes like snakes. The right one was really fat, he wore shades and kind of looked like Sammo Hung.

The man in the middle was tall and sturdy. He was austere man wearing an eye patch and only revealed one of his eyes.

No, it's a temporary eye patch like the one the class leader wore, but a real black eye patch like the one Sagat from Street Fighter wears.

I immediately made a connection between him and the one-eyed uncle Xiao Qin mentioned. I heard he was the one in charge of the triad members sent by Xiao Qin's father to protect her.

Didn't you guys kidnap Fu ShiJian a few days ago? If I didn't tell you guys to let him go, were you really going to bury him alive? What a bunch of ruthless and cold-blooded triad members.

Why are you guys blocking my way? I mean I just gave a little boy a pack of tissues to let him wipe his ass, but it seems like doing good things doesn't really make good thing happen to you.

"You're Ye Lin, right?" Uncle Long (one-eyed uncle) pointed to a black sedan parked by the street, "Get on, we have something to tell you."

I looked inside the black sedan and there didn't seem to be anyone inside, but I don't think it's smart getting onto a car with triads.

I wanted to run, but that's not manly and it's not guaranteed I would be able to get away since they have a car.

I stuck my hands in my pockets: "Why would I get on just because you told me to?"

The skinny man on the left aimed at me with something in his pocket and threatened:

"Shut up, I know it's you, get on the car."

The fat man also made the same actions as the skinny one.

I might be a Spartan, but I'm not Superman, I don't have the confidence to go against two handguns.

Even if they didn't have a gun, I can't really go against three triad members.

A wise man knows better than to fight when the odds are against him. I pretended I was unperturbed as I followed them on the car.

I knew they wouldn't do anything since they listened to Xiao Qin.

The fat man was responsible for driving. Uncle Long was smoking silently, but the skinny man was quite talkative.

He sat next to me in the backseats and he looked at me with picky eyes as he mocked me.

"Hmph, your appearance doesn't look any different than triad members."

"Why did the boss' precious daughter take a fancy to you? It seems like you don't even know you have it blessed. We know about the things you did to our boss' second miss (TN: using second miss for second daughter)."

"When the second miss just transferred, you bullied her a lot and we couldn't take it anymore. If she didn't stop us, we would have already turned you into a cripple."

"If you dare&"

I didn't say anything back, but I thought about his words.

"Second miss referred to Xiao Qin, but why was it second and not first? Dores Xiao Qin have an older brother or sister? I remember Auntie Ren only had one daughter, Xiao Qin!"

As the car got on the highway, I questioned where they were taking me. But not only did they not answer my questions, they even confiscated my cellphone and blindfolded me with a black cloth.

I didn't make any sudden actions when faced against the barrel of a gun. I thought even if Xiao Qin instructed her men to kidnap me, it would at most be a prank. It's not like they would bury me alive, right?

After about an hour, they removed my blindfolds and took me out of the car. I was surprised to find we were at the foot of a deserted mountain.

Apparently someone was waiting for me in the pavilion at the top of the mountain.

The barren mountain in front of me was referred to as 'Duck Butt Mountain' by the elders in Dong Shan city. Based on its name, you could tell it doesn't have an elegant appearance.

They didn't really have to blindfold me if they were planning on taking me here, or is it because it's an action of habit for them?

A certain municipal leader once tried to transform the mountain into a scenic area, but after they repaired the stone steps up the mountain and the pavilion at the top, the mayor and deputy mayor were detained by the CCP and never heard from again.

Some superstitious elders said there was a god residing in the mountain. They said the two people got retribution for making the mountain god mad.

I'm not sure if it was because they were afraid of the mountain god, but none of the successive leader decided to continue remodeling 'Duck Butt Mountain', so the half finished project was abandoned halfway.

I was always curious about the appearance of the god of Duck Butt Mountain. Is it a duck like Donald Duck? If it's a duck, why not live by the river instead of on a mountain? I don't think a mortal like me could comprehend the thoughts of a god.

The three triad members escorted me up the mountain. Uncle Long and the skinny one was fine, but the fat one was panting after ascending 250 steps.

I guess he only looks like Sammo Hung, but doesn't have his stamina.

After we arrived on the relatively flat mountaintop (the area known as the duck butt), Uncle Long pointed towards the broken down pavilion in front of us and told me to walk over alone.

I strolled over to the pavilion in large strides. I noticed there was a stone table and four stone stools after I entered. A gloomy middle aged man was sitting on one of those stools.

He was wearing a custom fit suit and had a fountain pen in the pocket of his jacket. It was a luxurious good based on its appearance.

He may have been a handsome man before, but now his cheeks were sunken in and he was thin like he was deathly ill. He would occasionally cough and it would resound clearly on the quiet mountain top.

I had a rough guess of the identity of the man. I wasn't afraid of standing up against power, so I sat directly across from him and waited for him to speak.

The man sized me up from top to bottom like a general sizing up his soldiers or a father-in-law sizing up his son-in-law.

"You're Ye Lin?"

His Mandarin had a heavy Cantonese accent, but I could understand since I watched a lot of Hong Kong films when I was younger.

He clearly already knew my identity, but he had to waste the time to ask again.

I didn't answer pointless questions, so I asked: "You're Xiao Qin's father?"

As the head of the Ju Ying Sect in the triads, Huo ZhenBang, could not help but show a light smile at the corners of his mouth seeing that I was so young but so bold, as if mocking me for being a calf and not fearing a tiger.

"Young people should have proper manners. Answer my question first."

"I am Ye Lin. Are you Xiao Qin's father?"

Huo ZhenBang nodded, "That's right, I'm Xiao Qin's father. I came to the mainland to set up arrangements for Xiao Qin and her mother."

I inevitably cursed silently in my mind: He chased Auntie Ren away by frequenting brothels, but now he wants to set up "arrangements" for them on his own accord?

Huo ZhenBang coughed twice again and then took out two capsules from a small box. He ingested the capsules with the bottle water that was on the stone table and continued to speak:

"I heard you're Xiao Qin's childhood friend and that she's always liked you."

If her violent actions towards me could be described as 'liking me', then that's right.

I nodded.

Huo ZhenBang expressed a bitter smile. He covered his heart with his hands and said:

"I defiled many of girls back in the day and now my own daughter has a boyfriend and it's an unbearable feeling."

I didn't really know how to answer, but there's an old saying that goes: Those who lust after other people's wives and daughters will have their own wives and daughters lusted after, but obviously it's not appropriate to say.

"Why does your subordinate refer to Xiao Qin as the second miss?" I raised my doubts.

A hint of sorrow flashed through Huo ZhenBang's eyes. He froze in place for a while then slowly said:

"Before Xiao Qin, I had a son with a dancer. He was really similar to me and I was raising him as my successor. But last year, he got into a fight with the mafia when he was in America and was assassinated with poison."

There's nothing more painful than seeing one's children pass away first, so now the grizzled white hairs on his temples made more sense.

"I will never rest before getting revenge for my son. But you should also understand that means Xiao Qin is now my only child."

Huo ZhenBang made a finger gun and pointed it at me.

"I understand men very well. If you dare treat my daughter poorly, I'll take care of you."

I definitely didn't treat Xiao Qin well at the beginning of the semester, but I didn't know Xiao Qin's father was part of the triads at the time! If I think about it now, I was basically playing with fire. I could have been kidnapped at any time and never heard from again!

"I, I'm already treating Xiao Qin better&" I explained in a hurry.

Huo ZhenBang squinted his eyes in disbelief, "If my daughter felt she was mistreated by you in any way and she voices her concerns to me, I'll have you buried alive."

I shuddered and subconsciously looked around the duck butt mountain top to see if there were any already dug out pits.

If Xiao Qin didn't complain about me when I was bullying her, then I shouldn't get buried alive since my attitude towards her is much better.

Huo ZhenBang then said sternly as if he read my mind:

"It's your duty to be nice to her, but you can't take advantage of her because your relationship is stronger. If you bed my daughter, then I'll break your third leg."

I was so shocked I almost covered the lower half of my body with my hands. I was one step away from bedding the daughter of a triad boss!

It's the same as when Auntie Ren said she would crush my dad's nuts if I got Xiao Qin pregnant, but Huo ZhenBang actually has the capability and the determination to break my third leg! He's already lost a son, so he's madly in love with his daughter!

I lied with a pale face: "We're only middle school students and we expend our energy through sports, we definitely won't taste the forbidden fruit."

"Stop lying. I could even see your lustful face, do you think I wouldn't know what a 14 year old man is thinking about everyday? Tell me, did you touch Xiao Qin yet?"

I could only lower my head and admit: "Once&"

Huo ZhenBang had an 'as expected' expression. He never asked where I touched his daughter, but he did ask: "Which hand did you use."

I answered honestly: "Both hands&", then I suddenly realized he might have been planning to chop off the hand that touched his daughter. If I knew earlier, then I wouldn't have answered honestly.

Huo ZhenBang held his chin in silence for a bit then snorted:

"The fact you did that means you already know you're going to marry my daughter in the future, right?"

I paused, "Um&"

Huo ZhenBang abruptly changed his attitude, "What, you don't want to take responsibility? Do you think the daughter of the triads is somebody anybody can touch?"

I could only lower my head as I didn't know what to say back.

A gust of wind blew by. Both of Huo ZhenBang's eyes were bloodshot as he coughed twice again.

"You guys will get married after you graduate high school." Huo ZhenBang arranged for us.

"But you can't touch her before you get married. If you want to take advantage of her then leave, and something happens to my daughter, I'll kill your entire family."

What, I don't think I'm rotten to the point where I would take advantage of Xiao Qin then abandon her. Besides, if you want to kill my whole family, Ai ShuQiao, who's in America, is a direct relative! It will be quite a scene when the American underworld collides with the Chinese underworld.

"You're also not allowed to date any girl other than Xiao Qin before or after your marriage. If you can't treat Xiao Qin wholeheartedly, then I don't think I need to repeat what will happen to you."

Eh, the self-proclaimed father-in-law is quite rude and unreasonable. You were a playboy both before and after marriage, yet you want your own son-in-law to be a saint? My youth has just begun, so don't set my future for me.

I couldn't help but feel a sense of rebellion.

"Xiao Qin calls my dad Uncle Ye, so I'll call you Uncle Huo. Uncle Huo, may I ask if Xiao Qin knows you kidnapped me here?"

"Xiao Qin doesn't need to know. She doesn't even know I'm in mainland right now."

"So that means you're making these decisions by yourself? Even if Xiao Qin is your daughter, you don't have to decide everything for her. Shouldn't you leave us a bit of freedom of choice?"

Huo ZhenBang suddenly lunged across the stone table and grabbed my collar. He stared at me with a very frightening look, and said slowly word by word:

"If I tell you to marry Xiao Qin, then you will get married. And your first born boy will take my surname of Huo. I have to let him inherit my family business."

"Wh- why?" My collar was being pulled to the point it was uncomfortable, but the atmosphere was even worse.

"Because, it's impossible for me to have children anymore."

Huo ZhenBang hollered at me with a voice filled with sorrow.

"I frequented nightclubs to deal with the pain of losing my son and I ended up catching AIDS from two foreign girls. It's difficult to get healthy offspring with this illness and it's impossible for me to get remarried to Hong Li anymore. Can you understand my feelings now?"

Damn, you're spitting all over my face! I know there's pretty much zero chance of getting AIDS through normal contact, but it still makes me feel gross! No wonder there are fewer people coming to 28 Middle looking for trouble ever since the rumor of me having AIDS got spread.

Huo ZhenBang threw me backwards and said:

"I have a lot of money, so AIDS is more of a chronic disease for me. Since the former NBA star, Magic Johnson, fought against AIDS for over 20 years to the point where it's almost undetectable, then I might not die from it. Even if my constitution isn't as good as Johnson, I could still at least live another ten years, so&"

He pointed to his own eyes, then pointed at me.

"As for my remaining years of life, other than getting revenge for my son, it will be used to arrange a good home for Xiao Qin and her mother. Anyone who dares to bully Xiao Qin or Hong Li will be going against me and I'll make sure they have a painful death."

I was suddenly worried about my dad's safety. Does making Auntie Ren have an unexpected pregnancy count as bullying her? But if Huo ZhenBang has AIDS and can't get remarried to Auntie Ren, wouldn't it be good to let her marry someone who will treat her well?

Although that's what I thought, I obviously didn't say it and hoped Huo ZhenBang wouldn't find out for the time being.

Huo ZhenBang's admonition to me was no less than the ten commandments. I felt like I was bound by invisible shackles after I was released.

I turned on the phone Uncle Long had returned to me and saw there were three unread messages.

The first one was from Ai Mi: "Damn manservant, where did you go? Why aren't you picking up my calls?"

I replied: "Something urgent came up and I had to go home. I'll visit you at Qing Zi Academy another day."

The second message was from a scammer: "Dad, I got caught visiting prostitutes and my cellphone was confiscated. Please transfer 50,000 for bail to the card 622XXXXXXXXX&"

Nowadays scammers will do anything for money like pretend to be your son or even your grandson.

The third message was from Xiao Qin: "Ye Lin classmate, the crime syndicate finally return Brother Optimus Prime to me. If you come to my house right now, I can let you taste my cooking skills I worked hard to practice and you can take Brother Optimus Prime home with you."

Nonsense, the crime syndicate was clearly with me. Brother Optimus Prime has always been in your hands!

Ever since I forcefully hugged the class leader, I felt embarrassed to go to her house for free food. Xiao Qin's skills might be far off from the class leader, but it's still better than mines.

The most important thing is Xiao Qin agreed she would return Brother Optimus Prime! Although I can't fully believe her, I still can't pass up this opportunity!

But what should I do? Should I go or not? If Xiao Qin called me, that meant Auntie Ren wasn't at home. If she took this opportunity to seduce me, then would I be able to resist? Her father warned me that If I sleep with Xiao Qin before marriage, he would castrate me!

"My mom won't be back before 10pm tonight."

Xiao Qin said to me as she was preparing dinner for me in the kitchen.

I checked my watch and it was only 6:20. Which meant I still had a bit over 3 hours of alone time with Xiao Qin.

But there was still a high chance of Auntie Ren coming home early.

"What's Auntie Ren doing? Is she working overtime?"

"No, she went to visit a classmate."

"Classmate?"

"Yeah." Xiao Qin used her spatula and clumsily flipped around the chicken, "It's my mom's high school classmate, she's now a gynecologist and she's a bad person&"

"How can you say that about Auntie Ren's classmate? If Auntie Ren went to her, then maybe she&"

I swallowed the rest of my words. Maybe Auntie Ren went to her gynecologist classmate to get an abortion and that's not good news for my dad.

"She's a bad person." Xiao Qin pouted, "Do you remember when I stayed over at your house the night you agreed to be my girlfriend? My mom came over the next morning and suspected we did that, so she took me to her classmate's place where I got tied me to medical stirrups to part my legs and gave me an embarrassing inspection."

I do remember something like that happened. Now it was Auntie Ren's time to be in the stirrups and I guess it would be her retribution.

"Ah!" Xiao Qin screamed out in shock.

"What happened?" I jumped up from the sofa and ran to the kitchen to check on her.

"It's nothing&" Xiao Qin put the wok on the stove and covered a section of her thigh, "I, I got some hot oil on me&"

I already said your apron was too short and it's nowhere as practical as the class leader's apron since it barely covers your leg! Plus, when your cooking skills aren't up to par, you would get burned sooner or later.

Xiao Qin endured the pain and wanted to keep frying the chicken, but I stopped her and turned off the gas. I pulled her to the sofa, so she could treat her injury.

"Where do you keep the band-aids?" I asked.

Xiao Qin was touched by my concern and she said with sparkling eyes: "I don't need band-aids, I only need Ye Lin classmate to kiss my injury and it will heal instantly."

She said as she lifted up her skirt to reveal the area of her thighs around the hem of the apron which had a small red spot that was burned by the oil.

My kiss doesn't have healing abilities, it's more likely to give you an infection!

As a teenage girl sitting so closely to a boy while lifting her skirt and closing your eyes& please don't be so perverted, do you want me to be castrated by your dad?

I cooled myself off, "I can also make fried chicken. If you don't want a band-aid, then wait here and I'll cook."

Xiao Qin said in a hurry: "No, I can't let Ye Lin classmate cook for me. I'm going to go to my room to grab some equipment, then I won't be afraid of getting burned."

Equipment, do you think you're playing an online game?

I followed her with my eyes as she went back to her room. She didn't close the door and pulled something from her dresser and began wearing it on her bed.

It& it was a pair of white stockings! Is she using it to increase the defense around her legs?

But why are you making seductive poses when you're wearing it? She even began groaning and grunting when the sock seemed to tight for her.

After Xiao Qin put on the stockings, she bounced up and down twice before walking towards me confidently.

"(*^__^*) Hehe& now I won't be afraid of being hit by oil."

The silk white stockings was thin in certain areas and I could make out the color of her skin.

For example, areas like Xiao Qin's knees and heels combined with the stockings to make a cute light pink color.

I didn't really notice those areas when she wasn't wearing stockings, but why do I notice it more after she's covered it? Why do I feel like I'm such a pervert?

"It seems like Ye Lin classmate really likes stockings."

Xiao Qin stood in front of me with a smile.

"Nonsense." I blushed and averted my gaze rather than admit it.

"Hehe, you actually haven't seen the cutest part of these stockings."

Where, I've already seen all around it.

Xiao Qin sat down on the sofa and proudly showed me the bottom of her feet.

"Do you see it~~~ the cutest part of these stockings is here meow."

If you ask why Xiao Qin suddenly ended her sentence with a meow, it's because there was a special design on the bottom of her feet.

On the bottom of her feet were pink cat paws. Xiao Qin even bent her toes to make the pattern move and make herself appear cuter.

Damn it, it's clearly incomparable to the class leader's elegant and seductive black stockings, but why does that cuteness make me want to touch it. It must be because I'm a person who loves animals.

In order to prevent Xiao Qin from getting carried away, I resisted the urge to touch the bottom of her feet. I only looked at them a couple more times before I went to the kitchen to fry some chicken to calm down.

Xiao Qin followed behind me like a tail and kept asking me questions:

"What do you think? How is it? Do I get any extra points?"

I kept my silence.

"I also bought a different pair of black stockings where the cuff is shaped like a cat's tail. How about I wear it for you later?"

I still kept my silence.

"I also have a matching pair of long gloves where the palms also have a cat's paw on it. I felt like I actually turned into a cat after I wore it."

As always, I remained silent.

"Oh right, I also have a matching cat's tail, but I never figured out how to wear it&"

Wait, that's already outside the scope of being a normal outfit. Why does it sound like something we would sell in our family's adult good shop? Any uniform that comes with a tail is always secured into the butt. It would be a big problem if Xiao Qin did figure out how to wear it.

"Damn it, where did you but those clothes?" I said angrily, "Throw the tail away. It would be bad if Auntie Ren found it."

Xiao Qin blinked in confusion, "It was the first link that came up when I searched cat uniform. What's wrong with a tail? Cats that don't have tails don't look good. Or do you not like tails because you think it would get in your way?"

"Throw it away immediately. If you don't throw it away, then you can't be my girlfriend anymore."

I threw out my trump card.

"Okay&" Xiao Qin lowered her head and said: "But can I keep the stockings and gloves?"

"Yeah, you can keep those." I had a strange feeling of expectation for some reason.

For dinner, we had the fried chicken Xiao Qin and I made together, along with a steamed egg custard that Xiao Qin made.

Xiao Qin also wanted to make a Beef Bourguignon, but I thought it would take too much time. If we took too long, then Auntie Ren might be back before I could get Brother Optimus Prime, so I stopped her.

To be honest, another reason was because she lacked the skills necessary to properly prepare that dish.

I already ate that dish prepared by a French chef at Ai Mi's place, so no matter how hard Xiao Qin tries, it would never match up. So it would be better if we ate a simpler meal together.

As a certain philosopher once said, a simple life is a good life.

I felt a simple happiness as I ate the fried chicken and the steamed egg with rice.

As we were eating, Xiao Qin stepped on my feet.

Since Xiao Qin had carpet in her house, neither of us wore slippers. My athletic sock feet had intimate contact with her stocking feet.

It might be fueling Xiao Qin's recklessness, but it's really comfortable being rubbed by a girl's feet and it's hard for me to resist.

"Ye Lin classmate, does the steamed egg taste good? I was only able to make it after I failed 20 times."

Xiao Qin asked in high spirits while rubbing my feet under the table, but she didn't show it on her face.

"It's okay." I felt like ever since I almost pushed Xiao Qin down, I've been conceding to her more and more. I can't let her take control since she was the one who bullied me first. If I'm too soft-hearted, it would go back to the old days and she will bully me as my girlfriend.

There are too many boyfriends being bullied by their girlfriends nowadays.

Thus I suddenly moved my left foot and clamped Xiao Qin's feet between my left and right foot.

She was flustered for a bit, but she didn't resist. It seems she enjoyed it as her cheeks turned red.

"Huh, why aren't you eating?" As payback, I asked while pretending nothing was wrong.

Xiao Qin said bashfully: "Ye, Ye Lin classmate, it's too tight. I can't pull it out&"

Wait, isn't that what the man is supposed to say? Why are you saying that line?

I got straight to the point after dinner and told Xiao Qin to return brother Optimus Prime along with the other robots.

Xiao Qin widened her eyes, "Huh, didn't I already tell you? So you didn't have to carry it all home, I already sent brother Optimus Prime via courier service. It should arrive at your house tomorrow night at the latest."

You never mentioned it before, and how can you give something so previous to a courier? And who can prove if you actually delivered it or not?

I glared at Xiao Qin with bloodshot eyes.

Xiao Qin trembled as she cowered in a corner of the sofa and asked weakly:

"Is it okay if I apologize? To show my sincerity, I'll even take off all my clothes."

My phone vibrated in my pocket after it received a text.

I took out my phone and Xiao Qin also came over to see what it said.

She completely regarded herself as my girlfriend.

"Hey, I need to have some privacy. If you keep acting this way, don't blame me when I fire you as my girlfriend."

Xiao Qin sniffled her nose.

"When you say you're going to fire me as your girlfriend, does that mean& you're going to abandon me?"

"That's right." I pretended to be more serious and said, "I already said you could only be my temporary secret girlfriend, but you've become more presumptuous as of late. Are you not afraid of me anymore because you have the triads backing you?"

My logic was really strange because Xiao Qin already had the triads backing her for a while, but I only found out recently.

"If& Ye Lin classmate doesn't like me getting involved with the triads, then I'll cut off the relationship with them right away. I'll never meet the people from my dad's side anymore, is that okay?"

She had an eager and inquiring look in her eyes.

I might be opposed to having connections with the triads, but it's not like Xiao Qin can choose her own father. Huo ZhenBang might pass away at any time due to his AIDS, so it would be sad if his only daughter also cut off her relationship with him.

I couldn't bear it, so I didn't push Xiao Qin any further.

I suddenly wanted to ask Xiao Qin if she knew she had a half-brother and that he died in a mob fight.

"Xiao Qin, do you know why Uncle Long and the others refer to you as the second miss?"

"Maybe because Uncle has an older cousin, I'm not sure either. I got brought over here when I was still really young, so I don't know all the relatives from my dad's side of the family."

As expected, Xiao Qin doesn't know about her half-brother. Huo ZhenBang didn't have any reason to let Auntie Ren and her daughter know about his son. Even if Auntie Ren found out, she doesn't have any reason to tell Xiao Qin.

Which means Xiao Qin never knew about his brother and about how he's already gone.

I had complex feeling and wasn't sure if it was right to keep her in the dark.

That dancer's son might take his anger out on Xiao Qin because Auntie Ren married Huo ZhenBang and stole his mother's status. If the two of them knew each other, they might not even be on good terms.

There's also the fact that Xiao Qin has androphobia.

But I felt it was unfair to Xiao Qin that her brother, who should have been in her world, disappeared without a trace.

They might not have the same parents, but aren't Ai Mi and I close?

Since the relationship between Xiao Qin and me has been restricted, then regardless if my dad or Auntie Ren gets married, I will treat Xiao Qin as my younger sister for the time being.

I'll replace the brother Xiao Qin should have had. The care she should have received from her brother will be carried out by me instead.

If I treat her as my sister, then I won't be tempted when she says she would 'take off her clothes as an apology' at every turn, which means I won't be castrated by her father.

I only have the confidence to overcome my lust if I treat her as my sister, it was proven effective with Ai Mi.

"Ye Lin classmate, Ye Lin classmate." Xiao Qin brought me out of my thoughts and back to reality, "What are you thinking about with such a sinister expression, are you thinking about how you're going to abandon me?"

Who had a sinister expression! I was clearly seriously thinking about our relationship.

Xiao Qin whimpered and tried to put on a pity act.

"Uh& if Ye Lin classmate hates me, it's fine if you fire me. But just let me know one day beforehand by text."

"Why do I have to tell you a day beforehand?"

"Uh& I'll kill myself after I receive the text, that way I can die while I'm still your girlfriend. I'll choose to die of carbon monoxide poisoning and I'll make sure to dress myself up. When someone discovers my corpse, they will see my face full of happiness&"

"Stop your delusions! I'm going to get nightmares just thinking about you smiling while committing suicide."

I'm holding back our relationship because you always keep mentioning suicide. If I get too intimate with you, I'll get castrated. If I alienate you, then you will commit suicide& it looks like I have no way out.

I guess the best option is to keep you as my sister. Since that's settled, I want to facilitate the matter between Auntie Ren and my dad.

I finally got a chance to check my texts.

It was& an ad from JD.com. I think I only a bought a mouse from them half a year ago, JD.com has a great memory.

It was advertising a phone for the elderly, something about a gift to show gratitude for your grandparents.

The ad actually gave me a great idea.

Auntie Ren's dad, gramps Ren who taught me Yin Yang Sanshou, gave me his phone number before.

I could always call him if I ran into any problems practicing Yin Yang Sanshou, but now I found another use for it!

It's to tattletale! I could tell gramps Ren that his daughter was pregnant. That the man proposed, but Auntie Ren rejected him and was planning on getting an abortion.

How would gramps Ren react? I know my grandparents pressured my dad to get remarried while waving around a cleaver, so gramps Ren must also want Auntie Ren to find another home.

There was no time to lose. Autnie Ren already went to a gynecologist, so if I don't tell gramps, then my future brother (or sister) will lose their life.

I said something came up and ran out of Xiao Qin's home. Nothing Xiao Qin said to convince me to stay worked. I also told her she couldn't follow me or I would fire her.

I gave gramps Ren a call when I left the neighborhood.

"Who is it?" Gramps Ren answered impatiently, "Who's calling?"

I quickly acted respectfully since I always acted like that in front of gramps Ren since he was an elder.

"Gramps, it's been a while. I'm Xiao Ye Zi, the one who learned Yin Yang Sanshou from you."

"Oh, it's you." Gramps Ren snorted, "I saw the video where you fought with the panty thief. It was quite popular for a period of time."

Huh, gramps saw that video too? What a hip grandpa! Since gramps uses an iPhone and is the current top scorer on Fruit Ninja in our city's martial arts association, then it's not strange for him to watch online videos.

"Gramps, it's& nothing. I was only able to defeat that taekwondo expert with your teachings."

"Of course. If Yin Yang Sanshou can't even beat taekwondo, then it wouldn't be a top martial art. It's a good thing you didn't embarrass me."

That was close. It turns out gramps Ren only cares if I won, but wasn't interested in the fact we were wearing underwear and stockings over our heads.

I got onto the main subject after a few polite words.

"Actually, gramps, I wasn't purposely trying to find out your family name, but I got acquainted with your daughter, Auntie Ren, by chance and also did a dojo challenge with her&"

"Ah, so did you guys win?"

As expected, he only cares if we won and didn't ask how I found out his family name.

"I, I guess we won. The owner didn't personally fight, but Auntie Ren beat one of the masters, and I beat one of the students&"

To be more accurate, it was a female student. She was also the daughter of one of my dad's classmate.

After listening to our fight, although I couldn't see, I could imagine the gramps Ren stroking long eard on the other side of the phone, very proud of his daughter and disciple's (?) victory.

"Xiao Ye Zi, did you call me to report that?"

"No, actually, there's something else. It's about your daughter, but I'm not sure if I should say it as a junior."

"Tell me, what is it. My daughter always makes me worry, what stupid things has she done again?"

I hesitated for a while and said quietly: "Gramps, Auntie Ren& she& she's pregnant."

"What?" Gramps was both surprised and angry, "Who did it?! How do you know?"

"Uh&" I thought about it for a bit and decided to tell the truth, "Actually, the person who impregnated Auntie Ren was my dad&"

Gramps Ren was angry and stayed silent for awhile before he said: "What's your dad's name?"

"My dad is Ye YuanFeng and I'm Ye Lin."

I reported the truth to express my sincerity.

"Okay, okay, okay. You and your father are quite bold, does your mother know?"

I then realized gramps Ren might not know I'm from a single-parent family and might believe my dad and Auntie Ren had an affair.

"Gramps, please calm down, my dad isn't a bad person. He got divorced 14 years ago and after he had the incident with Auntie Ren, he even bought a ring and proposed, but unfortunately he was rejected."

"Eh, so that's what happened. Does that mean your dad brought you up by himself?"

I took the chance to exaggerate my dad's hard work over the years.

After gramps Ren learned my dad used to be a university professor and was currently running a store (online stores are also considered stores), and the reason for Auntie Ren's accidental pregnancy was due to Auntie Ren's drunkenness, gramps Ren gradually became interested, and even laughed from time to time.

"So they lived in the same hotel because of a quarantine? It's preposterous, but it's like a chance bestowed by the heavens. I always said a woman should get married and settle down, then properly fulfill their roles."

I hurried to agree: "That's right. I approve their marriage, but it's a shame&"

"What's a shame?"

"It's a shame Auntie Ren is going to abort her baby. She's already seeing a gynecologist right now."

"An abortion?" Gramps Ren snorted, "Abortions can be damaging, I'm still expecting her to give birth to an even more talented martial artist."

Since Xiao Qin was a martial arts genius, it seems gramps Ren had high expectations of Auntie Ren's progeny. Xiao Qin, who became aware of her female identity and thus stopped practicing martial arts, must have disappointed gramps Ren.

"She can't get an abortion just because she wants to. I have to let her understand that I'm not an incompetent good-for-nothing father."

Gramps Ren vowed before telling me to keep an eye on developments and report back to him, then he hung up.

When I was in grade school, there was a girl in my class who loved to tattletale to the teacher. At the time, I didn't understand her mindset, but I got an indescribable thrill after I tattled to gramps.

I'm not sure if Auntie Ren is going to get a headache over her meddlesome father. I tattled with good intentions, so I don't think I would get punished by the gods.

I suddenly felt I was being followed.

I used my peripheral vision and it wasn't Xiao Qin. The person had a short stature and a childish appearance.

It was getting darker after I ate dinner at Xiao Qin's place. I stopped and looked back at the person. With the assistance of the street lights, I was able to see the person that followed me down the street was a 8 or 9 year old girl with a ponytail.

She began crying when she saw my face, "It's not daddy, it's not daddy~~~"

Of course I'm not your dad, you probably followed the wrong person at the intersection. It looks like your dad is pretty confused if he's not properly looking after his daughter.

I couldn't leave a little girl alone in an era where lolicons are rampant, so I stayed with her top wait for her dad. She kept crying because she was scared by my face, so it inevitably caused passersby to look at us.

I was helpless but I saw a police booth across the street. I held the little girl's hand and crossed the street with her. I opened the door of the police booth and decided to let the officers take care of her.

It was strange because the girl stopped crying once I held her hand, but it seems like it wasn't because she was comforted but rather because she was afraid I would kill her if she kept crying.

After I entered the booth, I saw one old and one young police officer inside. The old police officer was drinking tea and the young police officer looked like a fresh recruit. The young police officer looked at me with vigilance, then he saw me holding hands with a girl too afraid to cry and he immediately asked:

"What are you trying to do? What are your demands?"

Do you think I'm holding her as a hostage? Is it that hard to believe I'm trying to do something good?

The old officer behind him was clearly more experienced and knowledgeable, he understood that a kind face doesn't mean a kind heart and an evil face doesn't mean an evil heart. The old officer took a sip of the warm tea and said in a composed manner:

"The kid is lost, right? Do you know her?"

I said I didn't know her and only bumped into her by chance. Her dad may be nearby and could have a similar body type to me otherwise she wouldn't have mistaken me for her father.

The old officer nodded and recorded everything down. He then took the little girl from me by her hand and comforted her:

"Don't be scared~~ I'm going to help you find your father. Here, come say goodbye to the kind-hearted older brother."

It looks like police officers are great with children. The little girl waved shyly and said, "Bye, big brother."

I turned around coolly and waved goodbye to the officers and the girl. I wanted to leave them with a lasting impression of my back figure.

After walking a while and feeling good about doing a good deed, I bumped into the three triad members after I turned a corner.

I frowned, "What, does Xiao Qin's father want to speak to me again? Can't he finish everything in one conversation?"

Uncle Long adjusted his eye patch and said seriously: "I only came to remind you to not forget the leader's warning."

The fatty to his right said: "That's right, since you're the leader's future son-in-law, then you can only be nice to the the second miss. If you have an ambiguous relationship with other girls, then we might have to teach you a lesson."

The skinny one on the left said: "Why did you help the girl who was lost? It's clear you didn't have good intentions and you probably wanted her to show you her gratitude to you ten years later. Doing this kind of stuff is not allowed in the future."

I was furious to the point I almost died from anger.

I think the scope you guys care about is way too wide. I could still admit it if you called me a lolicon for helping an 8 year old girl, but you're saying I'm going to wait ten years for her gratitude? If that was the case, it would be more reliable for me to help cranes or a frog.

Uncle Long might have thought the skinny guys words were a bit undue. In order to mediate he introduced them to me:

"The fat one's nickname is 'Fat Tiger', you can call him Uncle Hu. The skinny one's nickname is 'Thin Leopard', you can call him Uncle Bao. As for me, the second miss usually calls me Uncle Long&"

I stuck my hands in my pockets and said in a bad mood: "Why are you guys following me instead of protecting Xiao Qin?"

"The second miss told us to not get too close, it would be bad if we were caught by the madam."

The 'madam' he referred to was obviously Auntie Ren.

"The leader told us he could tell your character from your appearance and he knows your going to be a playboy. If we don't watch you, you're going to do something wrong. We were told to keep an eye on you, so you better watch out&"

Uncle Bao reminded me.

Damn, you guys are questioning me for so long after I only sent a little girl to the police. What are you guys going to do if I go the class leader's house for food?

Coincidentally, a taxi drove by from the side. I beckoned the driver to stop and quickly slipped into the car.

"Where to?" The driver asked as he looked at me from the rear view mirror.

"Leave this street first." I yelled, "I'll tell you the way once we leave."

The driver glanced at the three triad members and immediately stepped on the gas. We drove far away before he said:

"Ah, those three looks like criminals, youngster& you&"

He swallowed his words after he got a clear look at my appearance. I suspect he was going to say 'youngster, are you being chased by the triads?'

After I went home, I took out the trash before I went to sleep. I realized Uncle Long didn't follow me, but Uncle Hu and Uncle Bao were creeping about outside of my place.

I felt uncomfortable and was planning to report it to Xiao Qin. But unexpectedly, the private detective Ai ShuQiao hired bumped into Uncle Hu and Uncle Bao because he was also monitoring me, and they gave the private detective a beating.

I guess that counts as doing a good deed for me.

Another unexpected matter was in order to stop Auntie Ren's abortion, gramps Ren actually found the phone number of Auntie Ren's gynecologist friend and pinched his nose and threatened her: If she made Auntie Ren have a miscarriage, then he would kidnap her on her way home and make her wish she was dead.

Those are the actions of a criminal rather than a respected senior! But it was unexpectedly effective because Auntie Ren's ex-husband was a criminal. So the gynecologist classmate who heard about Auntie Ren's ex-husband was afraid of retribution and refused to help Auntie Ren.

Then gramps Ren urged his son, the chairman of Qing Zi Academy, to call his sister home so they could have a long talk. It was probably a chance for them to tell her it was a golden opportunity and she should take it while she was still relatively young.

Auntie Ren didn't know where the information was leaked, but she was still stubborn when faced against her father and brother. Her attitude was that the child was hers and it was her right to choose if it would be born or not.

Gramps Ren knew his daughter was always stubborn. H knew he couldn't convince her, so he thought about the Americans.

He told the director and other staff members of the 'Magic Cauldron' that Auntie Ren was pregnant and she wanted an abortion which caused some unexpected results.

The American director was raised in a Catholic family, so he felt abortions were against God's will. He and Auntie Ren discussed this matter secretly several times, something about how it does not matter if it affects her job and causes delays, but she had to give birth or he would view her as guilty. Then, he said his conscience will not allow him to continue to work with her, and they will have to talk with the investors whether they should change the martial arts director or the director.

Some how, the news also traveled to the male protagonist of the film, Kyle. Kyle, who had always admired Auntie Ren, painfully told her that an abortion is a violation of human rights. He said if she didn't want to raise the child, then she can give it to him to raise. He had many actor friends who adopted Asian orphans, and he felt he wasn't keeping up with the times if he does not follow in suit.

For Auntie Ren, who was extremely dedicated to her work, she would not give up half way because of this.

So the abortion was put temporarily on hold. Auntie Ren used every possible mean so her daughter wouldn't find out while she tried to think of a non-existent perfect plan.

My continued as normal. Other than the extra Uncle Hu and Uncle Bao monitoring me, nothing else changed.

On Monday, the postponed volleyball game finally took place.

The combination of the class leader and Xiong YaoYue was unstoppable and they took down their opponents easily to defend their crown.

I got to see the class leader's shorts as I had hoped, as well as her valiant figure as she darted for the ball.

But I didn't see any boob shakes.

It wasn't a problem with size, but it was like they already agreed to all wear a sports bra beforehand.

Damn the inventor of the sports bra. I hope they always run out of tissue paper when they use the washroom.

After the class leader put the volleyball award for first place on the back wall of the classroom, Loud Mouth proposed that the whole class should go to a buffet in the evening to celebrate the double victories (boys' basketball and girls' volleyball), which was unanimously welcomed by the foodies.

We weighed the pros and cons against the vouchers Loud Mouth had and we finally decided to head to Origus Pizza that was four stops away from our school.

Loud Mouth said the food there was average and she would at most give it a 6 out of 10. But the advantage was the store wouldn't be packed with people and we could combine the tables so everyone could sit together.

If it was only four stops, then we could run over and burn some calories on the way. It's perfect since we would be getting it back at the buffet.

But we had frail girls in our class (like Gong CaiCai) and guys who would rather die than exercise (like Eunuch Cao), so the class leader ordered everyone to ride the route 21 bus. We would assemble together at the bus spot, so it's easier to get a head count.

We were only going four stops, but the class leader acted seriously like she was afraid someone would get lost or get into an accident.

Please, we're not elementary school students.

Our class had 45 people, but if we took away Zhuang Ni who was still on sick leave and a couple of other students who couldn't come because of special circumstances, there were a total of 39 class 2-3 students going to the buffet.

It would have been a nice round figure if there was one more person, the class leader was probably not satisfied about that fact.

There might not be many people who ate at Origus, but at around 6 pm, the route 21 bus was packed with people. It was impossible for everyone to ride together, so we had to separate to three different buses.

"Ye Lin classmate, Ye Lin classmate don't leave me!"

Xiao Qin, who couldn't ride on the same bus as me, desperately reached out from the crowded bus and called to me for help.

"Be careful of the door of the bus."

The class leader, who was sticking close to Xiao Qin, pushed down her hand. Gong CaiCai also weakly urged her from the side, "Four stops will pass quickly, as long as you wait a bit&"

The driver stepped on the gas at the same time and the passengers all leaned back as usual. The class leader grabbed onto a ring to support herself, but Gong CaiCai who couldn't reach the ring, and Xiao Qin who was focused on me, both crashed into the class leader.

The class leader clenched her teeth to bear the pain and realized her breasts acted as a cushion. Xiao Qin benefited from both sides as she was stuck in between Gong CaiCai and the class leader's breasts.

Why are you making such a miserable face at me? If you don't want to ride that bus, then let's switch spots!

After I got onto another bus, I looked around and saw around 10 of my classmates. The nearest one to me was Xiong YaoYue.

I was afraid Xiong YaoYue, who was wearing hot pants and short sleeves, would attract perverts in the crowded bus. In order to avoid arousing suspicion, I purposely pulled away from Xiong YaoYue by at least 5cm.

Even though Xiong YaoYue knew I wasn't homosexual, she still wasn't on guard against me and didn't notice my gentlemanly actions at all. It's possible she doesn't have her guard up against boys at all and it's the reason why they say tomboys have a lot of gay male friends but no boyfriends.

An old grandfather who had a Beijing accent was wearing a straw hat and looked like a tourist. He studied a map of tourist locations in Dong Shan city, then he turned to Xiong YaoYue and asked:

"Excuse me, may I ask if you know if this bus stops at Qing Hai Park?"

Xiong YaoYue, who loved to help people because she thought doing good deeds would improve her character, quickly answered:

"It does! Gramps, just pay attention to where I get off and all you have to do is get off at the stop before mines."

The old man nodded his head in gratitude and kept saying the people of Dong Shan city were simple and honest. Last time he asked for directions in Shanghai, the person asked for money, so it was a world of difference for him.

Wait, before you complement people of Dong Shan city, I think there's a problem with you two's intelligence. Xiong YaoYue told the old man to get off one stop before her& if you already get off then he would have already missed his stop!

Everyone says people from the city has higher IQ. I can't the old man didn't notice Xiong YaoYue's answer was really flawed. The next time you go somewhere to travel, you're going to have to sigh and say: "People from Dong Shan city are simple and honest, but their average IQ is a tad&"

I would rather you call us greedy instead of stupid, it's not like you're any smarter than us.

Thus I said to the old man while trying not to hurt Xiong YaoYue's self-respect:

"From here, the third stop is Qing Hai Park."

It seems the old man wasn't confident about the validity of my words, as he looked to Xiong YaoYue and only felt as ease after he saw her nod. He silently counted the stops and got off at the correct stop.

After we arrived at our destination, the class leader stood in front of the bus stop like she was a kindergarten teacher. She did a head count of everyone from our class, then she brought us into the pizza store.

There was really nothing to say about what happened at the buffet. It was the guys bragging to each other while the girls gossiped and we also joked around with each other.

For example, Eunuch Cao said to Gong CaiCai: "Do you have natural curls because your mom drank hot water while she was pregnant with you?"

Gong CaiCai retorted, "It's not from the hot water, it's natural."

Eunuch Cao snickered: "It's natural because she drank hot water when she was pregnant. If you don't want your kid to have naturally curly hair, then don't drink hot water when you're pregnant, jie jie jie jie jie~~~"

Loud Mouth knocked Eunuch Cao over with her elbow, then she pointed to him as he lay on the ground and said to a server: "There's trash here, can you clean it up please."

Xiao Qin, who had androphobia, didn't have a chance to talk to me due to the crowd. It was only after I ordered some grilled fish from the BBQ station, Xiao Qin ran over three times to ask the the cook:

"Is my boyfriend's fish ready?"

The cook looked at Xiao Qin with disdain as she was so young yet always hung the word 'boyfriend' around her lips.

That's enough, what's the point of showing off your relationship to a stranger!

It was just as Loud Mouth said, the food was average at best, but it was already a improvement for us who had eaten in the school cafeteria for lunch.

The main force of the boys was me, Niu ShiLi and a bunch of boys who love exercise (like the other basketball members), or a bunch who completely don't exercise (fatties like Eunuch Cao).

Among the girls, Loud Mouth and Xiong YaoYue were tied for first. Even though Xiao Qin was also one of the gluttons, the pizza store didn't have any seafood, so her fighting power was greatly reduced. She could only be considered somewhere in the middle among the other girls.

The class leader barely ate, as she used most of her time to maintain order. She advised everyone not to be greed and to not waste food. The class leader got anxious if a student stayed in the washroom for more than fifteen minutes. She would be afraid they got into an accident and have either herself or another classmate to check on them.

She also called home once and told Shu Zhe to put the leftover eggplants he couldn't finish in the fridge so it wouldn't spoil.

Class leader, aren't you tired? Everyone came out together to celebrate, so why can't you have a good time and maybe joke around? It's not like the washroom here is very primitive. If someone is in the washroom for more than 15 minutes, it could be they are constipated or they are playing on their phone, it's nothing to worry about. Class leader, it's like you don't know how to loosen up at all.

Dinner was finally over and after another head count, the class leader told everyone to head home early and don't stay out too late. Everyone saw the class leader's anxious expression and didn't want to worry her by saying they were going to an arcade or a cafe, so they all verbally agreed.

The class leader, who didn't ride her bike today, took a breath of relief after she saw her classmates either walk home or get on the bus, then she also planned to head home.

Because of me, the class leader became Li LaoEr and Guang ZhaoTou's target of revenge, so I felt a bit uneasy letting her go home alone.

But it was embarrassing for me to offer to take her home since we just slept together the other day.

As I was hesitating, Xiao Qin jumped out from the shadows and grabbed my hand, "Ye Lin classmate, can you take me to the subway station. I'm afraid of walking alone at night."

You scared me! Didn't you leave earlier with Little Smart, when did you come back?

Besides, since guns are completely banned in China, it would be very safe for a martial arts genius like you to walk at night. The only person that could beat you would be someone who has a professional boxer's physiques and someone who doesn't get careless when they see you're a girl in middle school.

I looked towards the class leader's lonely back and told Xiao Qin my worries.

Xiao Qin did some quick thinking and said: "I could tell Uncle Long and the others to protect her in secret as long as you come with me to the subway station."

I thought it was a good idea. So after Xiao Qin made the call, I let her grab my arm and I walked her to the entrance of the subway station.

On Tuesday morning, I noticed the class leader, who was on class duty, pick up a short piece of chalk from the floor at the back of the classroom and accurately toss it into the box of chalk on the lectern.

Her throwing level is already Lvl 999, is she still training hard on her throwing weapon skills?

I heard from Loud Mouth later that the class leader was nervous and training hard because she realized she was followed by two people who looked like they were from the triads on Monday night. She wanted to train her throwing weapon abilities to the point where it could be used for self-defense.

Does Uncle Hu and Uncle Bao not understand what protecting in secret means? I told you to protect the class leader, but you ended up scaring her!

But it wasn't a bad thing for the class leader to master more self-defense skills, so I didn't reveal the truth to her.

I didn't feel any regret until I once talked during a study session, and the class leader, who was writing tomorrow's schedule on the blackboard, casually threw the chalk in her hand and hit me square on the forehead.

Wednesday came in the blink of an eye. If I hadn't been reminded, I would have forgot there was still a friendly match between the different grades after the same grade championships.

As a result of the draw, the first match was the class 2-3 girl's volleyball team versus the class 3-3 team, which was the class of the prettiest girl in school. Apparently, all the outstanding volleyball players were in the class and their vicious spikes would make anyone who received the ball cry.

It turns out there wasn't only one great volleyball player in class 3-3, there was a total of three.

I was careless I didn't pay it any special attention.

At middle school and high school level, a students' physical development is measured in hours. The third years might only be one year older than us, but they possess a considerable advantage in both strength and speed.

Xiong YaoYue, who set her sights on first in the school, lined up with the other volleyball members on her team.

Class 3-3 was also the class that had the prettiest girl in school (school beauty). Although we were both the third class in our respective grades, they had no intention of showing us mercy.

The school beauty was a substitute player, but I've never seen her play. She would wear the volleyball uniform and warm up with the team, but then sit on the sidelines from start to end.

Some people say it was because she was awful at volleyball. The only reason she joined the team was for the chance to show her body to all the boys in the school and compete against Shu Sha.

I've already said before that many people think the down-to-earth Shu Sha was more fitting for the school beauty title rather than the current one.

The semester was almost over and the third years are about to graduate. So no matter what, the title of school beauty would have to be passed on.

That's why the school beauty always wanted to compete against Shu Sha, but Shu Sha only cared about her class' honor and there was no chance for conflict.

That's why this friendly match became the only opportunity for the school beauty to get a win over Shu Sha.

Eunuch Cao, who has eyes and ears all over the school (including in the student council), told me the school beauty bribed the three top players with small favors. She was hoping they would brutally 'take care' of Shu Sha and humiliate her in front of the school.

I really don't understand where Shu Sha offended the school beauty, but jealousy between women is frightening.

Before the game started, I told the class leader to be careful not to get hurt. The class leader glanced at me and replied coldly:

"You should be careful not to catch a cold."

She still can't forget about how I hugged her, it wasn't even on purpose!

As a substitute player, the school beauty still stood on the sidelines with a condescending look.

Why are you acting so haughty? Even if you keep changing your posture or rustling your hair, you still get around the same attention as Shu Sha. And your posture is way too unnatural.

I didn't have any more time to think before the opponent had already served an astonishingly powerful ball. It was both fast and traveling at a tricky angle. Xiong YaoYue ignored the risk of scraping her knees, and half knelt down on the floor to barely save the ball and hit it towards the class leader.

"Shit, my hand almost broke!"

Xiong YaoYue, who inadvertently swore, complained while shaking her hands.

The class leader made a few passes, then set up the ball at a suitable position for Xiong YaoYue. Xiong YaoYue lived up to expectations as she leaped up high and sent a deadly smash.

The opponents were too experienced. Three greats players did a triple block and reflected the ball back.

Unfortunately, the ball reflected back and struck the class leader straight on the nose, I even felt her pain. Luckily, some of her teams members supported her from behind or she would have fell straight down.

"Great job." The three students clapped their hands as if they struck the class leader's nose on purpose.

It was good the class leader didn't get a nosebleed. She stressed that she was fine and encouraged everyone to not give up and try their best.

It was 2:2 for the first four sets, and although the points were closely matched due to Xiong YaoYue's numerous heavy spikes, the class leader couldn't hold on anymore at the last set.

The school beauty incited the students to take turns and smash the ball on the class leader, including on her face. The class leader's uniform was covered with dust and even her beautiful hair was disheveled.

"Hey, why do you guys keep hitting our class leader?" Xiong YaoYue yelled at them through the net, "If you have the guts, hit the ball at me and I'll hit it straight back at you!"

Since they didn't violate any rules, the class leader didn't want to argue, she even told Xiong YaoYue to not fight with them.

Right when the class leader was exhausted, there was a commotion on the opponents side: the school beauty who has never played before is going to play.

She gracefully removed her school uniform that was draped over her shoulders and stepped in front of the net like a volleyball player. Her actions triggered a waved of cheers from her supporters.

Did she only want to personally humiliate the class leader once her side had the overwhelming advantage?

As expected, the opponents team members always gave the school beauty easy passes and they let her be the setter. She used unprofessional but light movements as she passed the ball up front and it was up to one of the three athletically gifted students to send the fatal spike towards the class leader.

The class leader was still a skilled player. While the opponent's powerful attacks bruised her wrists, she still clenched her teeth and did her best to hit the ball up and pass it to her team members.

"Xiong YaoYue, did you not eat!" Loud Mouth yelled, "Hurry up and turn Super Saiyan and wipe out the other team or they are going to make the class leader cry!"

Xiong YaoYue responded without looking back, "Call me Winnie."

The class leader gave Loud Mouth a look of resent, "Nonsense, I'm not crying."

But with a faint smile, the school beauty continuously passed the ball to the athletically gifted student with her strange movements.

The three students bombarded the class leader until she couldn't stand it anymore. The class leader knelt down to get one of the balls and couldn't stand back up anymore.

Before the referee could call a timeout, Xiong YaoYue went crazy and was trying to grab the three opposing players through the net.

"Do you guys want to play or fight? I'll keep you company if you want to fight, come one, let's fight!"

If it wasn't for the rest of the team desperately holding Xiong YaoYue back, she would have already started a fight with the other side, and even so, she bared her teeth threateningly like she wanted to take a bite out of them.

As the mastermind, the school beauty hid behind the three students at a safe distance while looking at the class leader and Xiong YaoYue with a smile.

To be honest, her expression really made me want to hit her. Even Niu ShiLi, who was occasionally chatting with me, couldn't keep calm. But men don't hit women, so the two of us couldn't intervene.

A few girls from class 2-3 ran on to the court to check on the class leader. The injuries weren't extremely serious, but both her arms were badly bruised. It was painful for her to even move her arms, so it would definitely hurt if she tried to receive anymore balls.

"Let's change players." Xiong YaoYue said, "Class leader, you go get some rest. Let us take care of these bastards."

The class leader clenched her teeth and wanted to keep going, but Xiong YaoYue sent Loud Mouth a glance and Loud Mouth dragged the class leader off the court by force. But the class leader stubbornly only accepted basic treatment as she still wanted to watch from the sidelines to see who wins.

The player who replaced the class leader was very serious about performing her duties, but unexpectedly, the opponent knocked her to the ground with one fierce spike, and she cried out in pain.

The class leader who was sitting on a chair with ice on her arms stood up in a hurry and requested to play again.

"Class leader, you remain seated." Loud Mouth rolled up her sleeves, "I might be bad at volleyball, but I'm great at whipping people. Let me play and I'll wipe the floor with them."

Xiong YaoYue paused for a bit, then frowned and said: "Loud Mouth, I& I'm afraid you can't play&"

"Why? I thought you didn't need to register players for the friendly match?" To show her determination, Loud Mouth flung a half filled bag of crackers to the ground.

Xiong YaoYue signed, "If you play, you might actually fare better than the other substitutes, but the school rules are all members must wear the volleyball uniform."

"You're too fat, so you won't fit into any of our uniforms."

"&.."

The speechless Loud Mouth picked up the bag of crackers from the ground and continued to eat them with irritation.

I was filled with hate as I looked at the class leader's bruised arms and the school beauty's giddy sneer. I then realized Xiao Qin was standing not far behind Loud Mouth.

I had an idea and brought Xiao Qin behind a crowd and quietly asked:

"Do you know how to play volleyball?"

"Not really~?" Xiao Qin replied happily.

"I'm serious. You don't have to be great, as long as you can receive their spikes."

I emotionally grabbed Xiao Qin's shoulders as I saw the time out was about to end.

Xiao Qin had a slight smile and looked at me slyly, "What benefits would I get if I played?"

"If you win, I'll go a date with you on the weekend, and you can decide the location."

"Really?" Xiao Qin's eyes lit up, "Hmm, although I've always been frail and sickly, I'll reluctantly give it a try for Ye Lin classmate."

I told the class leader to let Xiao Qin play, but she thought there was something wrong with my head.

"Xiao Qin fainted before at the flag raising ceremony, how could she play in such an intense match? And you already saw, they&"

The class leader felt a sudden jolt of pain on her arm and couldn't speak anymore.

I said quietly, "Class leader, don't underestimate Xiao Qin, haven't you personally experienced her strength? I can guarantee that out of all the girls in class 2-3, no one is better suited to play than Xiao Qin."

The class leader was silent for a while, probably remembering the time she was held down by Xiao Qin on the sofa and forced to show her breasts.

"Xiao Qin, can you really do it?" The class leader looked at Xiao Qin with worry.

"Yup!" Xiao Qin was clearly excited because I promised her to go on a date, "Class leader, they made your arms all swollen. I'll help you get revenge."

The class leader talked to the girl who cried after receiving one ball and asked her to give her uniform to Xiao Qin. The two of them actually had very similar figures and her uniform was very fitting.

With my assurance, the class leader went against other people's opinions and let Xiao Qin play. Both Loud Mouth and Little Smart was startled to the point they almost fainted. How could someone who was sickly since birth compete against athletically gifted students?

Xiao Qin had changed into her volleyball uniform and walked onto the court dumbfounded. Xiong YaoYue questioned her:

"Whose awful idea was it? Xiao Qin fainted at the flag raising ceremony after standing for ten minutes, so isn't letting her on court simply a death sentence?"

The class leader pointed to me with her gaze, "It was Ye Lin. He said Xiao Qin was a hidden master, so we might as well give it a try."

Wow, the class leader pushed all the responsibility to me, but it's obvious you were curious about Xiao Qin's true strength. Xiao Qin has shown a strange amount of strength many times and you already judged her to be above Loud Mouth and Xiong YaoYue, so that means you must be looking forward to her performance, right?

"I do remember something now that you mention it." Xiong YaoYue held her chin and said, "I was playing with a ball once and Xiao Qin caught it easily with a single hand when I hit it, so does that mean she's the dark horse of class 2-3?"

"No, I was just lucky." Xiao Qin giggled as she smoothed out the wrinkles on her volleyball shorts, "I don't know how to play volleyball at all, so I hope everyone can take care of me and not blame me if I make mistakes."

Xiong YaoYue, who didn't really believe it would work, still arranged Xiao Qin in the class leader's defense position to give it a try.

"Xiao Qin, you have to make it out alive!" Loud Mouth yelled.

Little Smart didn't shout, but she also worried for Xiao Qin.

It was natural for the girls to begin whispering to each other, but they boys also began secretly discussing about Xiao Qin.

"What's going on, didn't Ren XiaoQin have leukemia? How can she play?"

"It's Zhuang Ni who has leukemia. Ren XiaoQin just has a weak constitution."

"I heard it was Ye Lin who told Xiao Qin to play&"

"Huh, aren't they childhood friends? Ye Lin is so cruel, it's probably another way for him to bully her."

"To be honest, Ren XiaoQin's legs might not be as slender as the class leader's, but hers is also a good. I've actually liked her since the day she transferred here, but too bad she doesn't speak with guys&."

"Shhh! Do you want to die? There's people who has seen Ren XiaoQin linking arms with Ye Lin on the streets. Are you actually going to make a move on Ye Lin's girl?"

"I was just saying&"

When the timeout was over and the whistle blew, Niu ShiLi said to me:

"Ye Lin, what kind of joke are you making by making Xiao Qin play. Her body&"

Before he could even finish his sentence, class 3-3's ruthless server aimed at the new player and sent a ball hurtling towards her.

Even a professional would find it hard to receive a high speed rotating ball. Xiong YaoYue, who was too far and unable to help could only shout: "Careful!"

Xiao Qin stood smiling at the same spot with no intentions of dodging it. Her naturally dumb expression led everyone to believe she would be struck down by the ball and then carried off court.

What was unfathomable was Xiao Qin raised her arms to protect her face in the nick of time. Spectators weren't able to see the intricacies as the volleyball actually changed directions and gently bounced towards Xiong YaoYue. It was as if Xiao Qin had inadvertently given a great pass.

The students on the other team thought Xiao Qin would collapse with one blow and were caught off guard by Xiong YaoYue's spoke, so they lost the right to serve.

A new wave of discussion spread among the spectators:

"That substitute player has amazing luck, I can't believe she was able to pass it in that position."

"And her arms didn't get bruised at all! Class 2-3's class leader only received a couple balls and her arms are all swollen& how did she do that."

Niu ShiLi also had a stunned expression.

But I knew Xiao Qin was using Yin Yang Sanshou. She first removed the force of the ball at a speed that can't be tracked, then she passed it.

In addition, Xiao Qin also made it seem like an accident in front of hundreds of spectators. You could tell how much more skilled Xiao Qin was at Yin Yang Sanshou than me at a glance.

"Don't get careless. This Ren XiaoQin isn't who she appears to be and won't be easy to deal with."

The school beauty shouted unexpectedly to the athletically gifted students.

I then remembered about the time I asked Xiao Qin to help me buy some water. Because there was only one bottle of water left, Xiao Qin had secretly squeezed the school beauty's hand to get the last bottle. It caused the school beauty to always try and avoid Xiao Qin whenever she saw her.

It makes sense the school beauty would be afraid of Xiao Qin with that history behind them.

Thus, class 3-3 began a barrage of attacks towards Xiao Qin.

The speed, power, and angle all got progressive more difficult to handle with each hit.

But Xiao Qin was miraculously able to receive it every time.

Her actions weren't professional, rather they were comical. Every time, she would be flustered and panicked, but there wasn't any danger.

Sometimes she would turn to escape, then hit the ball with her back. Sometimes she would even use her head and face to block the ball.

If a normal person took of those jump serves to the head, they might not get a concussion, but they would at least be in a daze. But Xiao Qin acted as if nothing happened and it was like she absorbed the force of the ball once it came into contact with her body.

It meant Xiao Qin could use the full potential of Yin Yang Sanshou without even using her hands. Her talent in martial arts really puts me to shame and I'm not sure what I have to do to reach her level.

It might have been a coincidence if it only happened once or twice, but the spectators were amazed because it happened every single time. The opponents couldn't take it easy anymore.

"Stop joking, even if it's a friendly match, we can't lose to these younger brats."

The athletically gifted students abandoned the strategy of targeting Xiao Qin to spread out and prioritize winning the game.

But Xiao Qin, who was standing still earlier, began to wander around the court.

No, it wasn't strategical movements, but rather aimless wandering, like she was walking an invisible dog.

The trajectory of the opponents' balls were predicted by Xiao Qin time after time. It looked like she was wandering aimlessly, but she would always 'coincidentally' save the ball and pass it to Xiong YaoYue so she could launch an attack.

Class 2-3, who used to be on the defensive, switched to the offensive.

"Xiao Qin, good job." Xiong YaoYue was overjoyed, "The next time you pass the ball, it can be faster and I'll still be able to get it."

"But I don't know how to pass~~~" Xiao Qin continued to act dumb, "The ball hits me and coincidentally gets sent towards you."

Having send that, her passes became significantly faster, thus Xiong YaoYue's attacks also became faster and caused a great deal of trouble for their opponents.

The class leader, who was sitting on the sidelines, stared straight at Xiao Qin and murmured to the girls around her.

"I can't see Xiao Qin's hands move. If she told me she had superpowers, I might believe her&"

The girl standing next to the class leader was the one who was cried from being hit by the opponent's serve. She was excited to see Xiao Qin, who was wearing her volleyball uniform, showing off her power and she shouted in excitement:

"Anyway, our class is about to win! We can even beat the seniors, we're amazing!"

Due to Xiao Qin and Xiong YaoYue bringing out their best, the unbeatable class 3-3 was pushed back with a score of 14 : 10.

They would win and the game would end if they scored one more time. Xiao Qin, who might have been getting a bit impatient, revealed a more flashy martial arts move to receive a spike. But she became aware of it halfway and purposely fell down to cover up her true skills.

But Niu ShiLi's trembled with fear as cold sweat dripped down his forehead. He stared straight at Xiao Qin as if her movements had triggered a distant memory&

Was it a memory of the time when Xiao Qin gave you a beating at the park? You didn't remember her appearance, but you did remember her fists?

"No, impossible." Niu ShiLi muttered to himself. He probably couldn't believe that androgynous tomboy turned into such a cute girl. Even I had a hard time accepting this fact.

Before Xiao Qin threw herself on the ground, she set up the ball perfectly for Xiong YaoYue to attack. Xiong YaoYue yelled out "good" as she leaped up with all her strength and spiked the ball through the two defenders and towards the school beauty.

If the ball hit the ground, then class 3-3 loses. Even if the school beauty wasn't skilled, she still had to push herself to save the ball.

I'm not sure if it was her bad luck or if Xiong YaoYue wanted revenge, but the ball hit the ground first then bounced back up straight between the school beauty's legs.

The school beauty's face turned pale as she covered her private areas and her legs went limp.

I've heard crotch hits for girls might not be as painful as for guys, but it still hurts.

Cheers of 'we're number one' erupted throughout class 2-3. The school beauty fell into her own trap, she lost to her juniors and also got humiliated in public. I could only say: she deserved it.

The other class that was qualified to participate in the friendly match was the first year class champions, it was Shu Zhe's class 1-4. After they heard we beat the third years, they forfeited and so class 2-3 received the title of first in the school for girl's volleyball.

After the game ended, the class leader went to the infirmary to rest with a happy face. Xiong YaoYue chased Xiao Qin and wanted to learn how she saved the balls, but Xiao Qin used a stomach ache as an excuse and then hid behind me.

"(*^__^*) Hehe& where should we go on Saturday and Sunday?" Xiao Qin said to herself, "It's a rare opportunity to go on a date with Ye Lin classmate, so why don't we go to an amusement park and a zoo?"

"Hey." I reminded her, "I only promised you one date, I never said I would give you the entire weekend. Choose if you want Saturday or Sunday and if you want to go to an amusement park or a zoo."

Xiao Qin twiddled her thumbs, "I want to go to both places, it's hard to choose."

Xiao Qin pondered over whether to have the date on Saturday or Sunday and whether we should go to an amusement park or the zoo. She weighed the pros and cons and I sat next to her everyday watching her bittersweet expression.

On Thursday, after the girl's friendly volleyball match ended, the boys also beat the first grade champions. We didn't want to bully our juniors too much, so I didn't play, but we still won by a large margin.

The next day was the friendly basketball match between class 3-1 and our class. It was captain Guo SongTao's class, so it's not a joke and I have to reserve my strength.

I've already imagined before that if I beat their class, then I would ask the class leader to take a picture with me in her volleyball uniform. But I was too embarrassed to ask for it after I hugged the class leader for an entire night.

June was coming to an end. When I thought about the school beauty almost graduating and her wanting to have a final battle with the class leader, I realized: brother Tao was going to graduate too.

The melancholy enveloped my mind.

I was called on by the language teacher again since I was lost in thought.

"The saying 'shaving to firm your convictions' means to cut off all your hair as a lesson to remember your failures, thus a strong determination to succeed&. Ye Lin, tell me a equivalent expression for 'shaving to firm your convictions'."

I paused for a bit, then answered subconsciously: "Castration to practice the sword".

The whole class laughed while old man Zhang scolded me with a smile: "Seeing as you have the determination to castrate yourself, you may sit down."

Xiao Qin said with discontent: "Ye Lin classmate can't castrate himself. He still has to have a lot of babies with me."

I was still a bit distracted: June 25th ~ 27th was the high school entrance exams, all the third years including brother Tao will graduate& once the summer break is over, we will be the new third years&

Something that seemed to be far away was suddenly right in front of us.

The second half of my second year was the longest half I've experienced and I thought it would never end.

The friendly basketball match with class 3-1 was given other meanings, it might be a farewell game with brother Tao.

Not sure how I should describe the friendly match, but it was an empty game for me.

I didn't have any thoughts of winning or losing. I only checked the score when the whistle blew to signify the end of the match.

60:42, we lost terribly but it was within expectations.

I was simply engrossed in the game and played for pure fun. It was my way of saying farewell.

I noticed Shen ShaoYi watching our game from the sidelines with a complex expression in his eyes.

That day after school, Liu HuaiShui came looking for me. He said brother Tao was about to graduate so the entire basketball team was hosting a farewell ceremony for brother Tao and two other third year students.

"What do you mean by farewell ceremony? You make it sound like it's a funeral, but it's just a farewell dinner party."

"Only for the ones who are graduating, we're not all separating. So are you coming or not?"

Of course I had to go.

Shen ShaoYi was also there, but he was seated far away from me and closer to brother Tao.

The atmosphere was warm at the dinner table, there might have been a bit of sorrow from parting ways, but that's why we had to enjoy our time to the fullest to drown out the sorrow.

Oh, brother Tao also secretly ordered some beer for everyone. 'No wine, no banquet' was already a consensus among men.

When a lot of people started getting tipsy, brother Tao stood up and toasted everyone and thanked us for our support over the years. I couldn't drink a lot and my legs already felt weak, so I toasted him while seated.

"Ye Lin, are you still not joining the basketball team in your third year?"

Brother Tao asked when we were both using the washroom

"No, I'm unorganized and undisciplined, I'm afraid I wouldn't be a good team member. Besides, if you're not going to be the captain anymore&"

"The next captain is Shen ShaoYi."

Brother Tao interrupted me.

I hesitated for a bit, "I think he's probably the best choice."

"Do you support him?" Brother Tao stared into my eyes.

I smiled unnaturally, "I'm not a team member, so he doesn't need my support&"

"What, you're not going to help the team practice anymore after I graduate?"

"Of course not, it's just I'm worried Shen ShaoYi might not want to see me&"

After we left the washroom, Brother Tao patted my shoulder and said in a serious tone.

"Ye Lin, there's an old saying: brothers are like your limbs, while women are like clothes&"

I made a bitter face to Brother Tao, "Didn't Liu Bei say that?Aren't you just trying to persuade me and Shen ShaoYi to reconcile? To be honest, everything that happened between us was a misunderstanding."

Brother Tao was skeptical and said, "I also spoke to Shen ShaoYi: I told him there's plenty of fish in the sea, but unfortunately he's too stubborn and won't listen. You're birthday is earlier than his, so treat him as a younger brother, okay?"

I nodded in agreement, knowing full well that brother Tao was worried Shen ShaoYi and I will continue to clash because of Xiong YaoYue even after he graduates. So, he took used the farewell reception as an excuse to deliberately try and mediate between the two of us.

"I'm tired."

Everyone around us forced Shen ShaoYi and I to drink, so Shen ShaoYi couldn't refuse and drank a glass with me, then we both said the above line simultaneously.

I didn't particularly understand what he meant, but looking at his tired eyes, he was probably feeling that teenage love was torture. Did you just realize? Girls are super troublesome, and trying to date them is about as hard as trying to form a friendship with aliens.

Brother Tao was about to graduate and the relationship between Shen ShaoYi and me was still uncertain. I still felt a bit sad even if I wasn't gay, and I ended up drinking a few more glasses.

Then I got drunk.

I vaguely remember many people offered to take me home, but I was too proud and refused to let anyone take me home, so I said I was fine on my own.

So I staggered and stumbled back home.

It seems that I bumped into someone on the way, but I was drunk and only laughed. I was too tired and just wanted to go home and sleep.

I felt a bit more refreshed when I woke up. I looked up at the stains on the ceiling and wondered if they were the mosquitoes I killed two days ago.

I wanted to get up, but realized my left arm was really heavy, and it was completely numb.

I was shocked: did half my body suddenly become paralyzed at such an young age? I never would have drank if I knew earlier. I'm worried the restaurant sold us fake alcohol yesterday. How about the others, did they all get poisoned? It's a shocking tragedy, the 28 Middle basketball team was completely wiped out.

Upon closer look, I breathed a long sigh of relief. My arm wasn't numb because I was paralyzed, but because there was a girl sleeping on my arm in her underwear.

Scared me to death, I thought I had alcohol poisoning, but it turned out to be just&

Ehhhhhh, the situation is all wrong. I was clearly living home alone these days, so where did the girl come from?

I mustered up my courage and took a look at her face. Wait, isn't this Xiao Qin? Her eyelashes was slightly quivering as she had a sweet expression and was sleeping soundly on my arm.

She was wearing a training bra on the upper half of her body. Her lower half was covered by a blanket, but I assume she was only wearing a pair of underwear.

The first thought that actually came to mind was to lift up the blankets and see what kind of underwear Xiao Qin was wearing. Damn, I'm a pervert, if I spend too much time with perverts, my mind also gets corrupted.

The most important thing was to remember how I get into bed with Xiao Qin.

Was Xiao Qin the one I bumped into last night, but why did I let her in? Why did I let her sleep in the same bed as me? Was Auntie Ren not worried when Xiao Qin didn't ho home? Or did Xiao Qin already tell her mom she wasn't going home for the night?

The sleeping Xiao Qin, was like a small animal that needs to be petted.

Xiao Qin's hair was making me itch but I endured it.

No, I still can't remember what happened last night.

My alcohol tolerance sucks, it's even worse than my dads! I can't even remember what I did after I got drunk!

The good thing is that according to other people, I seem to only laugh when I'm drunk and become a super nice guy, so I don't think I did anything bad to Xiao Qin.

Last night, Xiao Qin who came to see me for some reason, saw me drunk and came up to talk to me. I must have talked to her with a smile and Xiao Qin must have found out I was particularly prone to agree to people's requests when I was drunk, so she refused to let go of this perfect opportunity and asked me to let her spend the night at my house, and I agreed while drunk?

That's the only request Xiao Qin made, right? I don't think I could have violated Xiao Qin while I was drunk, at most, I would have hugged her for an entire night like what I did to the class leader.

Damn it, she took advantage of me while I was drunk! I'm in my underwear, did I take my own clothes off last night or did Xiao Qin do it?

Suddenly, my body stiffened and I was covered in cold sweat.

I found a really scary problem.

My ass hurts.

A lot of people have told jokes about a group of guys drinking then waking up the next day with unbearable pain in their ass.

I was definitely drunk last night and can't remember what happened.

But I slept on he same bed as Xiao Qin! Even if I mistook her for a boy when I was a child, I've already confirmed through various methods Xiao Qin was indeed a girl!

Why does my ass hurt if I slept with a girl?

Can someone please tell me why?

I didn't have any protective feelings for the opposite sex as my butt was in extreme pain. I shoved Xiao Qin to one side and pilled my arm out from under her head.

I then realized Xiao Qin and I were sleeping on the double bed in the large bedroom. It meant that Xiao Qin wasn't the one who sneaked in at night, but she asked me straightforwardly while I was drunk.

Do I actually agree to requests that easily when I get drunk? But what exactly did Xiao Qin ask for last night and why does my butt hurt?

"Ye Lin classmate, since you're drunk let me stick it up your ass."

Was that what Xiao Qin asked last night and did I foolishly agree?

Even if she did make that request, what exactly did she stick up my ass? Did she use her slender fingers or a different weapon?

The root of all evil, the public enemy, the Little Tyrant, gradually began coming back into focus in my mind.

Shit, don't tell me Xiao Qin has gender dysphoria because her body is different than others, basically& she has the outer characteristics of a girl, but she still has a dick like me.

Doesn't that mean I was raped? I had never suffered this much humiliation even at the height of the time when I was being bullied by the Little Tyrant!

I looked at Xiao Qin, who was still asleep and her lower body covered by the sheets. The curve of her waist and hips announced her body was significantly different than that of a mans.

At first glance, she looks like a frail girl, how would guess that she was a boy.

But the annoying burning pain from my ass really made me question Xiao Qin's gender.

In the current situation, the fastest way to find the answer was to lift up the sheets and verify with my own eyes if there was a strange bulge between Xiao Qin's legs.

If there really is an unknown object, it means I was raped by that thing last night. My view of life shattered as my head filled with thoughts of revenge. An eye for an eye, a tooth for a tooth. I have to screw Xiao Qin's ass to vent out my anger, I have to make himher feel my current pain!

But wait, Xiao Qin often changes her clothes for gym class along with Loud Mouth, Little Smart, and the class leader. If she had a bulge under her lower abdomen, she would have already been exposed.

But my ass still hurts.

A Japanese manga mentioned that "some people who know Chinese martial arts can hide their gender inside their bodies". Did Xiao Qin also learn it?Can I not find out the truth without taking off the underwear.

But what if everything was a misunderstanding? Not only will I be removing a girl's underwear, which is already a perverted act, but I would also have to separate her legs and take a good luck. If Xiao Qin woke up in the middle, then I would be ashamed and unable to show my face anymore.

I used my painful asshole as an excuse as I lifted the sheet off Xiao Qin's waist. Her white, jade-like lower half was revealed to me.

Xiao Qin was lying on her side and she was wearing a pair of pure white cotton underwear. Her poor sleeping posture had caused her underwear to slightly shift a bit lower and tightly wrap around her buttocks, carelessly making a sexy pose.

I swallowed my saliva.

There wasn't a strange bulge under the front of her underwear, am I being paranoid?

My body moved against my will and I placed my right hand on Xiao Qin's waist.

It was so soft and smooth that I had the urge to gently pull Xiao Qin into my embrace.

"Hahahaha ahhahaha."

Xiao Qin suddenly burst out laughing, and I immediately retracted my hand.

"I'm ticklish, don't tickle me. If you didn't put your hand on my waist, then you could have done anything to me."

Sure enough, she was already awake when I pushed her aside. She was just pretending to be asleep and observing my actions.

I'm glad I didn't take off her underwear,, then I would have really become the pervert Xiao Qin mentioned before.

Xiao Qin sat up and had no intention of covering herself and proudly showed off her white skin.

On the contrary, my face heated up from being stared at by Xiao Qin while in my boxers. I quickly wore my clothes, then passed a blanket to Xiao Qin so she could cover herself.

"Ye Lin classmate was so gentle last night."

Xiao Qin didn't settle down even when she was only covered by a bed sheet. She hung her feet off the side of the bed and rocked them side to side.

"What did I do last night." I couldn't help but use an inquisitive tone.

Xiao Qin pressed a finger next to her lips and looked to the ceiling in a reminiscent manner.

"Well.. last night, my mom was going to spend the night at a friend's house. I felt bored, so I came to see Ye Lin classmate to discuss where to go on the weekend. I didn't expect Ye Lin classmate would come back drunk. When you saw me standing in front of your house, not only did you not scold me like before, you also invited me in with a smile&"

So I do become generous when I'm drunk? I lead a wolf back into my house!

"Ye Lin classmate sat straight down on the sofa and kept laughing. I discussed the weekend with you, but it's like you didn't hear and kept saying 'okay, okay'. So I tried to ask if I could stay the night and you actually agreed."

You took advantage of me! Then you asked "can I fuck your ass", right?

Out language teacher always taught us to continuously make progress, so I asked if you would sleep with me because I would get nightmares if I sleep alone and you agreed.

What do you mean by continuously make progress? You were clearly stepping all over me and taking advantage of me while I was drunk!

"I know you can't sleep without a hug pillow, so I deliberately hid the pillow, thus you hugged me the entire night. I'm so happy."

Damn it, the class leader was hugged for an entire night because she didn't know about my habit, but you deliberately made me do it!

"I wanted to enhance our relationship even further, but you were too drunk, so I had to forget about it."

"Oh, right." Xiao Qin suddenly remembered something, "Does your ass still hurt?"

So it did have something to with you? I was so angry that I grabbed her shoulders and shook her hard, "What the hell did you do to my ass?"

"Ah, don't be so rough." Xiao Qin giggled and begged for mercy, "Your ass hurts because you ran to the washroom many times throughout the night. You kept complaining to me: someone secretly put a super spicy chicken wing into your bowl, so&"

Ah, I do faintly remember now. At the banquet, Liu HuaiShui played a joke on me when I went to the washroom. He replaced an ordinary BBQ chicken wing from my bowl with a super spicy chicken wing, causing my mouth to burn. Even chugging half a bottle of beer did not help with the heat at all.

So my ass is swollen because I had to use the washroom a lot?

Almost scared me to death, so I didn't get violated by Xiao Qin.

To be honest, I was probably overly suspicious and overthinking it.

Although I don't want to admit it, but with Xiao Qin's skills, if she really wanted to violate me, she could force me without waiting until I was drunk.

It's so embarrassing that I can't even beat my childhood friend! I have to train ten times harder and be able to protect my own chastity from Xiao Qin.

I checked my watch and it was already 7:20. We would be late if we didn't leave for school.

I ordered Xiao Qin to get dressed, and I washed up, then the two of us walked to school together. We bought three crepes at a roadside stall, two for me and one for her, and we slowly walked to school.

On the way to school we agreed I would take Xiao Qin to the zoo for a date on Saturday.

The reason for going to the zoo, in addition to the fact that I like animals, was also because there are many high altitude facilities in an amusement park. I have a fear of heights, and don't want to be laughed at by Xiao Qin.

Xiao Qin accepted since the zoo or the amusement park made no difference to her.

As soon as school ended on Friday, Xiao Qin reminded me that we would meet at the zoo entrance at 9:30 tomorrow, then she went home happily to get ready.

I had nothing to do, so I walked to the nearest bus stop to see which line should I take to the zoo tomorrow.

I didn't expect to meet Gong CaiCai, who was waiting for the bus. There was also a hunchback beggar with a crippled leg bothering her.

This beggar had messy hair, but his clothes weren't too shabby. It looks like his face was smeared with oil rather than it being dirty. He had a rude gaze and didn't feel ashamed in the slightest for begging, but rather deserved to be given hand aways.

"Miss, can you give me five dollars so I can buy some food."

He reached out his hand towards Gong CaiCai.

Gong CaiCai earnestly flipped through her bag, then answered with regret: "Sorry, I don't have any change&"

If the honest Gong CaiCai said she didn't have change, then she really didn't have any change. Even if Gong CaiCai was rich, there's no reason for her to give you a hundred dollar bill. I don't think her parents raised her to be that generous.

However, the beggar didn't believe her. He craned his neck and snorted with an ugly expression: "You think five dollars counts as money?" He instead lectured Gong CaiCai.

Gong CaiCai cowered back and hoped the bus would arrive, so she could get as far as away as possible from this rude beggar.

I couldn't stand it anymore, so I patted the beggar's shoulder from behind and shouted: "The police are coming."

The beggar trembled and immediately straightened his hunchback. His crippled leg was miraculously healed without any medicine and he ran away as swift as the wind.

After scaring away the beggar, right when I wanted to console Gong CaiCai, I was caught off guard and took a punch on the back.

I thought it was the beggar's accomplice looking for trouble, but when I took a look, it was Xiong YaoYue who ran over still carrying her backpack.

"Hey, you beat me to it." Xiong YaoYue laughed and scolded me, "I saw someone bullying Cai Cai, so I wanted to come over and show off."

But Gong CaiCai was wary towards Xiong YaoYue's "good intentions", after all, she had been bullied too much in the past.

"Ye Lin classmate, and Xiao Xiong, thank you&"

Gong CaiCai politely thanked us.

"Call me Winnie." Xiong YaoYue corrected.

"Okay, Winnie the Pooh&" Gong CaiCai was so scared she stuttered.

Bus 19, the one Gong CaiCai was waiting for finally came. She bowed down to thank us again, then she followed the queue and got on the bus.

"The daughter of a rich family has to squeeze on the bus every day." Xiong YaoYue ridiculed as she watched the bus drive away, "What are her parents doing? if I only had one precious daughter, I would want a car to pick up and drop her off every day, plus two beefy bodyguards to accompany her."

Every family has different ways of education. I also heard about a couple who had tens of millions of dollars, but they still rented a place to live in a more rural area in order to create an illusion for their son that their family was poor. The son didn't find out the truth until he went to college, at least Gong CaiCai knows her family isn't poor.

"Plus, there are more and more beggars in Dong Shan city now. In the subways, on pedestrian bridges, and also at the bus stops& and more than 80% are scammers." Xiong YaoYue said indignantly, "They ask for money so they could eat, but they don't come when you offer to take them to a restaurant. And they love to pester single women, the police should really arrest all of them"

It seems that other than Gong CaiCai, there are other girls from class 2-3 who encountered these beggars, so Xiong YaoYue was full of righteous indignation.

I asked Xiong YaoYue what she was doing here instead of going home, and she said that she agreed to go to the zoo to see the pandas tomorrow with Ai Mi, so she came to check which bus to take.

Eh, only the downtown zoo in Dong Shan city has pandas, and they are temporary rentals from Beijing zoo. That means Ai Mi and Xiong YaoYue would be going to the zoo tomorrow at the same time as me and Xiao Qin.

"I took a look at the schedule and there's no direct bus from my house to the zoo." Xiong YaoYue fretted, "It would be the best if I stay overnight at Ai Mi's place, then head to the zoo along with her. But unfortunately my parents aren't easy to deal with&"

"By the way, Ye Lin, do me a favor." Xiong YaoYue massaged my shoulder with her fists, "I'll call my parents and tell them I'm doing homework with a classmate and I'm not going home tonight. Just tell them I'm staying over at your place."

"Hey, if I say that, your parents will come knocking on my door."

"Why?"

"You're still asking me why? I'm a boy, and you're going to stay out all night at a boy's home? Do you want your parents to explode with rage?"

"Ah shoot." Xiong YaoYue clapped her forehead, "I forgot again that you aren't gay. It's all Little Smart's fault because she told me you were weeping at the farewell dinner for captain Guo SongTao and unwilling to part ways, so I got a little confused about your sexual orientation&"

Where did she even get that info, she's spreading false rumors! Who was even crying?

"Then, Ye Lin, can you help me out and ask Xiao Qin to be my proof~" Xiong YaoYue hands together to beg me, "Xiao Qin seems to listen to you, so if you ask her to trick my parents, I'll definitely treat you well in the future."

After thinking about it for a while, I thought it wasn't a big deal, so I called Xiao Qin for Xiong YaoYue, who readily agreed.

But she wanted Xiong YaoYue to speak to her on the phone.

"Winnie, I can definitely help you, and we both had a great time on Wednesday's volleyball game& but can you stop asking me why I was able to get the other team's tricky serves? I said it was just luck~~~~"

"Okay, I won't ask anymore." Xiong YaoYue said quickly, "It's normal for girls to have their own secrets. Anyway, if my parents ask, you have to help me."

After a brief period of "collusion" with Xiao Qin, Xiong YaoYue gave me back my phone.

"I could hear static when I was on the call." Xiong YaoYue pointed out to me.

Indeed, since it had the charging failure, the battery can never be charged to full anymore. Recently there's also been weird static during calls, so I think it's an indication its going to turn into a brick. Domestic counterfeits have really poor quality and stability is its biggest weakness.

The psycho called Fang Xin said the phone would save my life. Now it's almost broken, it can barely save itself. Do I have to spend the rest of my life with a broken phone?

Xiong YaoYue seems to have just remembered the time when she stuffed my phone into her panties in an emergency, then when she got up to answer a question, it shook her to her core.

She couldn't help but blush, wave goodbye to me, then she ran off in the direction of Qing Zi Academy.

To be honest, I also kind of wanted to see Ai Mi. Plus, I was salivating every time I thought of the French chef's cooking.

But fortunately, I didn't go with Xiong YaoYue that day, because something tragic happened in the VIP building.

The two of them cooked together.

Ai Mi and Xiong YaoYue together.

The so-called dark cuisine, is referring to them.

The name of the show "Hell's Kitchen" is like it was made for the two of them.

It began when a talk show in the US, invited who the lolicons consider as Ai Mi's successor, the "Pisces Sisters" as guests. Those evil shows always like to instigate drama, so the host asked the sisters, what do you think of their senior Ai Mi.

They ridiculed Ai Mi's weak constitution and said it was hilarious how she was allergic to everything. They also said it was a waste for such an outstanding French chef to be Ai Mi's personal chef. According to reliable sources, Ai Mi's cooking skills were atrocious and one of Ai ShuQiao's villas was burned down because Ai Mi tried to cook a fried egg.

Ai Mi was very angry after watching the show, and she was particularly concerned about how they criticized her cooking skills.

"The villa only burned down because the gas stove was too primitive. I'm obviously very talented in cooking."

So you really burned down a villa? Although people say no progress can be made without paying the price, but I think that's too big of a price to pay for a fried egg?

Xiong YaoYue, who heard about the incident, immediately sided with Ai Mi and said:

"It must be because they envy you. I remember Loud Mouth also laughed at me for not being able to cook. I even made her fried rice once out of the goodness of my heart, but I accidentally added too much salt. I even gave her water to drink with the rice, but she refused to eat it."

Those two terrible cooks hit it off and planned to cook a sumptuous dinner for the bodyguards and other servants.

Even Peng TouSi, who's went through fire and water, sweated profusely and advised:

"Kitchen work is dirty and tiring, it's better to leave it to the staff.. we can't let the two of you cook for us&"

Obama, on the other hand, was much more honest than Peng TouSi. Once he saw it was Ai Mi and Xiong YaoYue hogging the kitchen, he immediately let out a long howl and went to eat the grass outside the VIP building with a sad and bitter expression.

Ai Mi, who doesn't listen to people's words, was obstinate in her ways. I don't know where she heard that "Only experts can create delicious dishes with the simplest of ingredients", so on a whim, she went to where Obama was eating grass and pulled out a handful of& dogstail grass.

Where in the world is that considered a simple ingredient? She dipped it in flour, fried it in oil and turned it into deep fried dogstail grass.

Ai Mi and Xiong YaoYue didn't eat it themselves, but forced Obama to eat it. Obama would rather die than eat it, so they turned their attention to Peng TouSi.

Peng TouSi forehead was covered in sweat. He clutched his stomach and said, "My acute gastroenteritis is acting up, sp you should let 004 and 005 eat it."

004 and 005 were forced to eat "dogstail grass", and then they also immediately got acute gastroenteritis.

Ai Mi refused to admit her faults, "It's not my cooking skills, it must be because of the serious pollution in China, that's why the dogstail grass is poisonous."

Xiong YaoYue, seeing Peng TouSi's bitter face and him begging her with his eyes, softened slightly and said:

"It's not easy for the bodyguards, if the ingredients are contaminated, let's not make them eat it anymore&"

"That won't work." Ai Mi said angrily, "Next I will use high class ingredients, to make food that would convince everyone that I can cook."

Xiong YaoYue suddenly had a bright idea, "It's not good to let the bodyguards test for poison& no, I mean test the food, I have a better way. There are a ton of fake beggars in Dong Shan city right now. Let's tell Peng TouSi to go out and catch a few of them. The ones who have all their limbs and curse at you when you give them 50 cents are fake beggars. They always say they are too poor to eat, so let's let them have their fill."

Ai Mi immediately looked at Xiong YaoYue with admiration for her great plan.

Peng TouSi and the bodyguards immediately acted when they learned they could catch some scapegoats. They were highly efficient and caught twenty beggars in an hour. The beggars were all people with good physiques and claimed they didn't have enough to eat.

It was unavoidable to be seen in public when they went on the streets to catch people. But not a single person called the police, they only began to discuss among themselves:

"What's going on? Isn't it kind of wasteful to drive such a good car to force these beggars to go to a shelter?"

Coincidentally, when Xiong YaoYue went to "lecture" the group of beggars, then one who harassed Gong CaiCai was also among them.

Xiong YaoYue, who got a pair of sunglasses from Peng TouSi, looked like the leader of the criminal organization. She cleared her throat then said to the frightened beggars:

"Don't be afraid, we're a charity from America. We invited you here today to eat dinner, made with imported ingredients from the US. We have steak, lamb chops, imported lobster, tuna, and crabs. As long as you behave and eat the meal, you will allowed to leave safe and sound."

The problem is that it's impossible to be safe and sound after they eat your cooking.

Ai Mi and Xiong YaoYue were both driven by an impulse and the ingredients they used in they kitchen were all high-class, especially the lobsters and crabs that were far above an average size. It made the beggars suspicious that those were genetically modified organisms and they were caught for human experimentation.

The beggars who couldn't contact with the outside worlds because they had their cell phones temporarily confiscated (There were 15 iPhone 5s among 20 beggars) worried deeply about their fate.

I don't know how they cooked the lobster, but it turned green and emitted a faint fluorescent light.

The crab was clearly boiled in the same pot, but it had turned dark yellow with a suspicious layer of mucous membrane over the surface.

According to the photos Xiong YaoYue brought to me later, my first impression was that the dish should be named "Alien vs Predator" because both ingredients were crustaceans and the horrible color was in line with the aliens.

The beggars, who were forcibly seated at a long table like the "The Last Supper", were dumbfounded when they saw the first dish. It was a green fluorescent lobster along with a slimy yellow crab, they absolutely believe they were genetically modified organisms. Not only were they genetically modified, they were also fed sulfuric acid and melamine, so no one dared to take the first bite.

Don't even mention the "honey braised sea cucumber" that was served next, the so-called "honey sauce" was just soy sauce! They even added needles into the sea cucumber, in addition to the excessive amount of cooking time, the sea cucumber that already had an unappetizing appearance was now an inflated voodoo doll. The beggar who harassed Gong CaiCai at the station fainted when he saw it.

Because of eating the "fried dogstail grass" which caused incessant abdominal pain, 004 and 005, in the spirit of "we're all going to suffer together", splashed cold water on the beggar's face to bring him back from the dead and confront the table of colorful food in front of him.

By this time, more dishes had been served. Most of which were the results of Ai Mi;s bright ideas and Xiong YaoYue's personal efforts. The two could be described as a perfect fit, cooperating seamlessly, as each new recipe was an outstanding contribution to the world of dark cuisine.

"Kobe beef", which is ranked sixth among the "world's top nine ingredients", is normally eaten as steak, teppanyaki, or shabu-shabu hot pot, but Ai Mi and Xiong YaoYue skewered the beef and grilled it over the flame, to the point where it was all burnt.

Ever since the outbreak of mad cow disease in Japan in 2001, China has banned the import of Kobe beef. That means Ai Mi's Kobe beef would have been rerouted from the United States, which strictly speaking, is considered smuggling, The beef traveled miles and miles around half the world just to be burnt by you?

Lobster, crab, sea cucumber, and Kobe beef wasn't even all of the ingredients. The rest of the ingredients were butchered by a knife and burnt in a fire, so you can no longer see their original form, kind of like Picasso's abstract paintings.

So the predictable result was: no one, dared, to, eat, it.

Ai Mi observed the reaction of the beggars through a one way glass and wasn't satisfied, she ordered Peng TouSi.

"Go in and scare them a little with a gun. Winnie and I worked hard to make the food, but they wouldn't even touch it, that's so rude."

Xiong YaoYue, who wiped her oily hands straight onto her apron, said:

"That's right, the color might be a bit special, but the taste should be okay. I deliberately didn't use salt this time, instead, I used soy sauce as a substitute."

How naive! You think it wouldn't be salty if you didn't add salt? Soy sauce is 20% salt, so there's no difference than adding salt and the color will also change.

Peng TouSi first emptied the bullets in his pistol, then aimed the muzzle at the wry-mouthed beggar with the most resistance and said to him gently.

"If you don't want to eat a bullet, then hurry up and eat the food. Damn it, hurry up and eat it."

Peng TouSi wasn't able to keep calm as he was worried if the beggars wouldn't eat it, then the bodyguards would have to finish it.

A voodoo doll sea cucumber was in front of the wry-mouthed mouth beggar. He saw Peng TouSi fiercely pointing a gun at him, and he thought he might die either way, so he made a decision and shouted:

"I'm sacrificing myself for my country."

He picked up a sea cucumber with a fork and stuffed it into his mouth.

"Crap, it's too di&"

As the wry-mouthed beggar was about to shout "too disgusting", Peng TouSi held the trigger and threatened: "Say it's delicious, or I'll kill you."

"Too& too delightfully delicious."

The wry-mouthed beggar wailed out as he was forced to change his words and at some time, two streams of tears flowed down his cheeks.

Inspired by Peng TouSi, the other bodyguards also aimed at the beggar's backs with a gun and asked them to please sample the delicacies in front of them.

So all twenty of them shed tears.

"Ah, I heard that the greatest food can move one to tears." Xiong YaoYue was overjoyed and said, "We did it, we did it!"

Ai Mi, however, didn't look particularly happy.

"Hmph, that's expected. I'm obviously a culinary genius, but the kitchen is greasy and dirty, and I have to take a thorough bath every time I go, so it's too much trouble."

After they "proved" they were good at cooking, Ai Mi completely lost interest in the beggars. He instructed Peng TouSi he could do whatever he wants with them, either release them or bury them.

After being forced to finish most of the questionable food, the beggars were all weeping tragically, their hands and feet twitched, their pupils dilated, and looked like they were about to die.

Peng TouSi made a prompt decision and gave the beggars a large amount of laxatives and emetics. It's good these fake beggars had tough bodies, otherwise they would have already passed away.

After they stabilized, Peng TouSi handed out ¥1000 to each of them while threatening:

"There was poison in the food you ate. If you don't want to die, then report to me every day and I will have an antidote for you. But the antidote has to be taken for forty-nine days to take effect, if any one of you tells anyone about this incident, then the rest of you can forget about getting the antidote."

The beggars were already afraid of Peng TouSi and the others because they have guns, so they only nodded and say they won't tell anyone. In addition, they believed from the bottom of their heart the food was poisoned, otherwise it wouldn't have been so disgusting.

Xiong YaoYue and Ai Mi firmly believed: their cooking skills were at a master level, but it just didn't have a good appearance. Xiong YaoYue even proposed she should invite some friends (such as Loud Mouth and the class leader) to come over and taste her cooking.

The reason she wanted to invite Loud Mouth was to get over her past shameful experience, and she wanted the class leader to come over because she wanted to boast to class 2-3's "food god", right?

Even if the class leader doesn't die from food poisoning, she will die from being pissed at your wasteful behavior.

Anyhow, at 9:30 on Saturday, I met up with Xiao Qin at the downtown zoo.

I saw Ai Mi's car in the parking lot, that means she and Xiong YaoYue arrived a step earlier.

Will we run into each other during the zoo tour?

Located in the center of the city, the Dong Shan city zoo is the largest public zoo in the city. Because the zoo director has a knack for business, he was able to diversify the business and remain profitable even when zoos across the country are currently in a slump. He even has spare resources to rent pandas from Beijing zoo to attract more visitors (especially foreigners like Ai Mi).

I wasn't particularly interested in pandas, my dad already took me to Beijing Zoo when I was in the fourth grade. It was disappointing when I saw the national treasure stick its dirty ass to the tourists while eating bamboo, it never even looked back when called.

In addition, the Dong Shan city zoo charges a separate entrance fee for the panda pavilion. I didn't feel it was worth the extra ¥20, it only cost ¥15 to see all the other animals.

"Do you like pandas?" I tested Xiao Qin when buying tickets at the ticket counter.

Before Xiao Qin could reply, the middle-aged woman ticket seller said with disdain, "You're not even willing to take your girlfriend to the panda exhibit?"

She didn't even ask me before she tried to sell a panda ticket to me as well.

I was disgusted by her forceful sales behavior. Even if you were right, you should still let the customer choose. If I changed my mind in the zoo and wanted to see the pandas, I could still buy tickets in the zoo and it's not necessary to buy it from you.

Or do they get bonuses based on the number of tickets they could sell.

So I waved my hand and told the ticket agent I didn't need a ticket to the Panda exhibit, then I pointed to the sign next to the ticket office that said "¥10 for those under 1.4m", and said to Xiao Qin.

"You should go measure yourself, maybe we can save ¥5&"

"Don't bully me." Xiao Qin huffed and grabbed onto my arm, "I might be shorter than you, but I'm not that short. Nowadays most elementary school students are taller than 1.4m."

That's true, I don't really know many people under 1.4m, Ai Mi would be the only one who fits the criteria. But she doesn't need to save that ¥5 and she would never admit she has a child's body.

After spending ¥30 for both our tickets excluding the panda exhibit, Xiao Qin and I began our date and walked along the river of people into the zoo.

We stopped in front of the sika deer cage for a while, I suddenly spotted the gang members Xiao Qin's father sent, fat tiger and skinny leopard, staring at us.

They didn't have to follow us into the zoo, what could possibly happen inside? But with your nickname& be careful of getting caught by zoo employees and not being let out.

I realized Ai Mi probably had the same feeling when being followed around by 004 and 005 all day.

Xiao Qin seemed to have discovered their presence a long time ago, but didn't reveal it, so I will pretend they don't exist.

Ever since I began Spartan training, the zoo, a place I often visited in childhood, also gradually became an unfamiliar place.I made many new discoveries this time going down memory lane and my mood also got better.

There were a lot of visitors because it was the weekend, and we were able to watch a lot of performances that you usually couldn't see. For example, two monkeys performed a boxing match where the winner gets a bunch of bananas and their performance made everyone laugh. A male elephant performed a spin with its hind feet lifted off the ground rotation, it was a bit clumsy and was more gap moe and still received everyone's fervent applause.

But after watching the elephant spin a few times, Xiao Qin covered her eyes, as if she was embarrassed.

"What's wrong?" I asked curiously.

"It's& the elephant's elephant~~~" Xiao Qin said in an unclear manner.

I turned back to see, and saw when the elephant was spinning, its penis was also spinning with it. It's just like the elephant song (NSFW) sung by crayon shin-chan, which refers to the penis! A real elephant's penis was very exaggerated and over a meter long when in heat.

"Ye Lin classmate is the same as an elephant&"

Stop, if a human had one that was over a meter long, he would be a freak. And if someone had over a meter of erectile tissue, they would definitely be impotent, where would they even get enough blood to pump it?

In order to prevent Xiao Qin from saying anything else, I took her hand and led her away from the elephants and came to the nearby "alpaca" cage.

The "alpaca" was one of the ten mythical creatures also known as the "grass mud horse". Ever since the grass mud horse was popularized on the internet, zoos around the country added alpacas as a way to attract visitors. Dong Shan city zoo in particular, not to be outdone, had no fewer than ten alpacas in captivity.

Since alpacas aren't very threatening, they didn't add a tall railing. But they still hung a wooden sign that says: "Animals currently in heat, cross the railings at your own risk."

I didn't take it seriously and thought it was the same as KFC's "caution: slippery when wet" to clear their responsibilities and they use it all year, but imagine my surprise when I took a look inside.

They really were in heat! A grass mud horse was fucking another grass mud horse! Why couldn't they wait until the park was closed, there were a number of children next tot me asking their parents: "What are they doing?"

"Fighting." This is what parents usually say to fool their children. The children don't realize they were born into the world because their parents were also "fighting".

After retreating from the alpacas, I decided to go see some more ferocious beasts, after all, it would be more in line of the interests of the saber-tooth Xiao Qin.

As it turned out, the tiger was undergoing weird training.

The tiger that was locked behind a cage with tempered glass, had its front paws pressed against the glass, while expressionlessly staring at the people outside.

There was also someone dressed in a tiger costume outside. He didn't show his face, and his whole body was covered with tiger stripes.

However, he didn't seem like a real tiger at all, but more like Tigger from "Winnie the Pooh".

This Tigger sneakily hid behind some tall grass for a while, then he stood up and walked out, looking around as if he just escaped from prison, which drew laughter from the crowd.

At that moment, a gunman wearing a black security uniform ran out and aimed at Tigger. He fired a tranquilizer dart without the needle, Tigger collapsed and was then was carried away on a stretcher.

"I heard my mom say that Japan has done similar drills to teach gorillas not to escape."

Xiao Qin said.

So they were trying to train the tiger? A tiger isn't as intelligent as as a gorilla, so it doesn't understand your "performance". And couldn't you have found a more realistic tiger costume? Other than using the Tigger costume, you even walked on two legs. The tiger might think you failed to escape because you only had two legs to run with.

The spectators also thought that the zoo's behavior was meaningless. At this point, the best part came, Tigger was sent back, and with him came& Wu Song.

Everyone was astonished, only to see Tigger repeat the same trick trying to escape on two legs, when Wu Song jumped out and repeatedly punched Tigger. Tigger dropped down again and was carried away on a stretcher.

Wu Song stared at the real tiger behind the reinforced glass, as if to ask: "Did you understand?"

The spectators naturally laughed their asses off and said that the zoo directors were foolish. They also called and sent texts to their friends and colleagues, so that they could also enjoy the performance.

Later I found out the performance was a marketing ploy created by the zoo director to deliberately attract public attention. To be honest, it worked quite well, several news stations reported about it and even my Dad mentioned it to me on the phone.

After that, I took Xiao Qin to see the white peacocks that refused to open their tails and the monkeys that didn't like peanuts and only ate pistachios.

Xiao Qin was nervous at first because there were a lot of boys our age in the zoo, but she had more and more fun as her attention gradually shifted to the animals. When she was feeding fish to a seal in the oceanarium, she naughtily took advantage of the moment when the seal jumped up to eat the fish to pluck one of the seal's whiskers as a souvenir (so fast). We fed our remaining fish to that seal as compensation.

Xiao Qin also really enjoyed the dolphin performance. We purposely waited for half an hour just to get a front row seat in the next act. We didn't care about being splashed with water when the dolphins hit the ball or jumped through hoops.

I thought I might run into Ai Mi and Xiong YaoYue when I ate at the restaurant in the zoo, but they probably had better food, so they didn't show up.

Instead, when I went to the washroom after the meal, I ran into Tigger in the men's room.

That's right, the one performing for the tiger.

He had his costume draped on his body and it looked like a ridiculous half-man, half-tiger abomination. The guy inisde was actually an acquaintance of mine.

It was Xiao Ding from the pet hospital.

"Damn, why are you here to act as a tiger?" I laughed and asked him.

Xiao Ding shrugged, "Everyone who graduates from the China Agricultural University might end up working at a zoo. I came to meet one of my advisors today, and he asked me if I was interested in earning some extra income& so I acted as a tiger."

After a few jokes, Xiao Ding suddenly asked me: "Who's the girl you were with?"

I immediately had a feeling of guilt: Xiao Ding and Dr. Zhao already acted as the matchmaker for me and Shu Sha multiple times. If I admitted that Xiao Qin was my girlfriend, then I would really be a womanizer.

"You mean the girl the girl who was with me, she's& my sister."

Xiao Ding clearly didn't believe me, "Sister, how come I've never heard you mention a sister before?"

I looked towards the ceiling, "She's a distant cousin, who recently moved nearby for school. It's normal for a brother and sister to stroll around in a zoo."

"Wait a second." Xiao Ding was still skeptical, "When I was acting as the tiger, I saw the girl holding your arm intimately&"

"That's because she's afraid of strangers, especially when she sees a psycho tiger, so she's afraid."

"Eh, I always thought I would only make people laugh, does it actually also scare some people?"

After finally being able to change the topic of conversation, Xiao Ding and I saw a super muscular man walk towards us when we left the washroom.

It was Peng TouSi, which meant Ai Mi and Xiong YaoYue were still in the zoo.

Peng TouSi greeted me affectionately, but he also greeted Xiao Ding before entering the washroom.

I was stunned, "You guys know each other?"

I couldn't help but think towards a bad direction. Peng TouSi was gay and Xiao Ding was nervous in front of girls, did the two of them meet on one of those dating apps?

Seeing my smirk, Xiao Ding said: "What are you thinking, isn't he the owner of the dog called 'Obama'? You and Shu Sha walked the dog back and told me to contact the owner for you, he was the one who came to pick up the dog. He actually speaks really fluent Chinese for a foreigner."

It turned out I was overthinking, I forgot about it because immediately afterwards, the class leader and I got blocked in an alley with no way out.

If Peng TouSi was here, then Ai Mi wouldn't be too far away. Before I could reconvene with Xiao Qin, I saw Ai Mi receiving an ice cream cone that Xiong YaoYue had lined up to buy and was about to taste it with glee.

"Huh, it's the manservant." Ai Mi spotted me while standing at the top of the flight of stairs. She looked down at me with a smug look on her face, "Are you here to secretly protect me? It might be a superfluous action, but I'll take note of your loyalty."

Xiong YaoYue was also surprised to see me. She was responsible for helping Ai Mi buy snacks, and also helping her hold an umbrella to protect her against UV rays, she waved and greeted me, "What a coincidence."

Xiao Ding pulled me aside and asked, "So, who's this blonde loli?"

I blurted out: "She's also my sister&"

"Stop lying, how come you know so many girls?" Xiao Ding said irately, "The previous one was your sister, and this one is also your sister. Who do you think you are?"

I said seriously, "She really is my sister."

"Who would believe you." Xiao Ding adjusted the tiger costume that was draped on his body, "I kind of believed you when you said the previous black-haired girl was your sister, but this blond one is obviously mixed, so if you are her brother, you should also look mixed."

It's ironic, I'm not sure if Xiao Qin will become my sister, but Ai Mi is my actual sister. I was telling the truth, but Xiao Ding took it as a joke.

"The manservant's friends are all weird." Ai Mi didn't lower her voice at all, as if she deliberately wanted Xiao Ding to hear, then she said to Xiong YaoYue, "he's actually walking around the zoo in a fake tiger costume Does he want to be locked in a cage, what a masochist."

Xiao Ding couldn't help but tear up after he heard, then he pulled me further away and said to me with a solemn expression.

"Little Ye, we've known each other for quite some time. Can you do me a favor since you know so many girls?"

"What kind of favor?" I was wary, "I'm not good at introducing girlfriends."

Xiao Ding asked with a bitter face, "Do you remember, I told you before I'll cut all ties with you if you play LOL."

I was shocked, did he find out I secretly played LOL? I only played it occasionally because I was curious about the professional team Ai Mi wanted to make. I was doing push-ups whenever the game was loading.

I never expected Xiao Ding to continue and say: "To be honest, recently the dota faction and the LOL faction started a massive flame war in the Baidu forums&"

I took a sigh of relief, "Don't you guys curse at each other every day?"

"It's different this time. In the past we always talked about how much the other side sucked and how they needed to get more skills. But recently, the LOL faction actually attacked us by saying people who play dota can't find a girlfriend."

"Eh, so that means the ones who play LOL must have girlfriends?"

"Uh&" Xiao Ding hesitated for a moment, "A certain LOL player named 'Unending Flow', uploaded a lot of photos of him with his girlfriend along with a valid university student ID. He wanted to prove it wasn't just elementary school students who played LOL and that many LOL players had girlfriends. After he started posting, both sides began to upload photos, but the LOL faction clearly had more couple photos than the dota faction. Also, some of the photos from the dota faction were revealed to be faked, so we lost more people&"

Don't pretend to have a girlfriend if you don't have one. It's sad for you guys compared to those assholes who obviously have a girlfriend but pretend they don't have one.

"In the midst of the flame war, we found out 'Unending Flow' was also from Dong Shan city. In the spirit of 'Capturing the ringleader first', I provoked him to bring his girlfriend and meet with us. If his girlfriend was also faked, then we will be the winners."

"And what was the result?"

"The result was that he actually agreed very quickly. He told us to send three three active members from each faction that's in Dong Shan city with girlfriends to meet in the cafe. I'm one of those three members from the dota side, I bragged about having a beautiful girlfriend. The meeting is next week and I still haven't found someone who will go with me."

Pretending to have a girlfriend is already playing with fire, and you actually agreed to meet up in person. Let's see how this ends out.

Xiao Ding put his hands together and pleaded: "So, Xiao Ye you have to help me out. Introduce a girl you know to pretend to be my girlfriend and deceive them. If not, then the LOL faction will get carried away and my dota companions will also accuse me of lying and bragging."

I frowned, "What, I'm a middle school student, so the girls I know are mostly all middle school students. You already graduated from university, but you're looking for a girlfriend in middle school, are you a lolicon?"

Xiao Ding made a shush gesture, "I already said it's just pretending to be my girlfriend and eating one meal together. Do you not understand what type of person I am? I will never make a move on them, it's all just to prove the superiority of dota!"

I couldn't really think of any suitable candidate, so I declined.

"Although I know a few girls, but we're not familiar to that extent, I'm afraid I can't help."

Xiao Ding kept persisting and asked, "Don't you have two sisters?"

He was referring to Xiao Qin and Ai Mi, there's no way those two can pretend to be your girlfriend. Xiao Qin has androphobia, and there's no way Ai Mi would do something that condescending..

See me think, Xiao Ding said: "I won't make them come out for nothing, I will pay ¥500& no, ¥1000 as compensation. I'm working hard to act as a tiger to earn money for this. You can't let me get embarrassed in front of my friends and enemies!"

Xiao Ding was quite pitiful, if he was willing to pay someone to play his girlfriend, then Xiong YaoYue may agree, after all, who would refuse money along with a free dinner?

But wait, Xiong YaoYue is too careless, she may reveal everything accidentally with a few words. Plus, she herself is part of the LOL faction, if they an argument over the two games, Xiong YaoYue might involuntarily join in and then Xiao Ding would be disgraced.

"Sorry, I really don't know anyone suitable." I shrugged my shoulders to express regret.

Xiao Ding looked at me as if he was saying "you're really not being a good friend".

"In that case, I might have to tell Shu Sha about you going to the zoo with your two sisters some day&"

"Hey, don't tell her." I couldn't help but panic. Although I told the class class leader that Xiao Qin might become my sister, I still didn't feel a peace at mind.

Seeing my panicked expression, Xiao Ding knew he had caught my weak spot. He snorted twice and threatened:

"Shu Sha comes to the pet hospital almost every day to do volunteer work. Even if I clam up in front of girls, I can still tell Dr. Zhao first, and then let him spill the beans to Shu Sha! When the time comes, you can go and explain to Shu Sha yourself exactly how many sisters you really have."

I really didn't think I would have my weak spot grabbed by an otaku who's only good at dota. I suddenly thought of a more than suitable candidate out of retaliation.

"Okay, I promise you, I'll get it done by next Friday, just wait for the good news."

Xiao Ding was overjoyed when I agreed so quickly. Then, someone came to him to act in the second round of the performance, he told me never to not forget, and went to continue working to earn money.

As I was talking with Xiao Ding, Xiao Qin, who came to look for me after waiting for a long time, ran into Ai Mi and Xiong YaoYue. Peng TouSi also came out of the washroom at the same time.

"I was wondering who it was, isn't this the violent girl?" Ai Mi narrowed her eyes as she looked at Xiao Qin's white dress, "Do you think you're a white swan by wearing a white dress, in my eyes, it's more like the KKK."

"Eh, so the two of you know each other?" Xiong YaoYue was surprised and turned her head to ask Peng TouSi, "What's the KKK, it sounds so familiar."

Peng TouSi's expression briefly turned serious: "It's a group of people who specialize in persecuting us."

Then he immediately smiled again, "But Miss Xiao Qin is definitely not a part of the KKK."

I thought to myself, "It's not the KKK, it's the Triads, which is another illegal organization".

Xiao Qin ignored Ai Mi's mockery and waved her hand at me, "Ye Lin classmate, over here."

Ai Mi crossed her arms in front of her chest and asked with a sneer, "Are you following my manservant? Don't you know that he's here to protect me."

"Hmph, Ye Lin classmate is not here to protect you." Xiao Qin stuck her tongue out at Ai Mi, "We're on a date."

Ah, I was too late to stop it, Xiao Qin said it. Ai Mi had a look of disbelief and she looked at me as if waiting for me to deny it. Xiong YaoYue also opened her mouth wide in surprise, she pointed to Xiao Qin, and then pointed to me, as if she wanted to ask:"You're really dating?"

"Xiao Qin and I& it's because I lost a bet, that's why I came to the zoo with her."

It wasn't technically a lie since I said I would go on a date with her to get Xiao Qin to play volleyball.

"Huh, that's dumb." Xiong YaoYue easily believed me, "What did you bet on?"

"I bet& the math teacher wouldn't collect homework yesterday."

I sent Xiao Qin some glances at the same time to tell her to play along.

Xiao Qin lowered her head dejectedly and pulled on the rim of her sun visor cap, "Ye Lin classmate lost anyway&"

"You miscalculated." Xiong YaoYue laughed, "The math teacher is currently furious because she found her husband was hiding money, so she definitely won't be kind enough to not collect homework."

Ai Mi was very unhappy with the fact that I had accompanied Xiao Qin to the zoo, and she cast me a side glance as if I was also hiding money.

In order to change the topic, I hurriedly asked, "Were the pandas cute?"

Ai Mi raised her spirits a little, "They are, but the zoo won't sell me a panda&"

Of course, it's illegal to privately own a panda in China, and how can a national treasure be sold to a foreigner? Even with Clinton's status as the president of the United States, he was only able to exercise his presidential privileges to take his daughter to see a panda before the zoo opened.

"Hmph, what's the big deal? Next time, I'll make sure my mom gets me a panda. It's fine even if it's from the black market, but something that round and furry should belong to me."

Xiao Qin interjected, "Pandas are actually very dangerous, sister Ai Mi, you shouldn't raise one&"

Ai Mi glared at Xiao Qin, "Who are you calling your sister?"

Xiao Qin smiled wryly, then said, "Anyway, pandas are still bears. When my mother was a martial arts director on a panda show, there was a scene where they used a real panda. The panda attacked my mother two different times, if it was someone who didn't know martial arts, they might have died."

Ai Mi objected, "The panda attacked your mom because she has a bad personality. I heard that the Yellow Emperor raised a panda that was called the 'black and white bear'. It was able to identify loyalty and when placed on the way to the courts, it would eat the traitorous ministers."

Where did you even learn that from? During the time of the Yellow Emperor, they lived in thatched huts, there was no imperial thrones. Also, whether or not a panda eats a minister has nothing to do with loyalty, it only depends on whether they are fed properly.

"Miss, as I've said before, pandas aren't suitable to be raised personally." Peng TouSi spoke up, "Pandas eat bamboo as their staple food because they are too stupid to catch prey, in fact, they are usually very happy to eat rats if they do catch any&"

"I don't care, I want a panda." Ai Mi threw a tantrum at Peng TouSi, "Next time you go back to America, remember to ask mother for a panda or I won't work anymore."

Peng TouSi agreed and exchanged a glance with me. I guess he wasn't even going to bother since Ai Mi had a short attention span and lost her enthusiasm quickly. She will forget all about the pandas after a while.

"By the way, Xiao Qin, thanks for covering for me last night, so I was able to stay at Miss Ai Mi's place."

Xiong YaoYue thanked Xiao Qin. I heard Xiao Qin gave Xiong YaoYue's parents a phone call saying Xiong YaoYue was staying at her house and they believed it. They didn't pursue the matter and they didn't even ask to speak to Xiong YaoYue answer the phone. I guess carelessness can be hereditary.

"Don't mention it, classmates should help each other." Xiao Qin put on a radiant and innocent smile.

Suddenly, a gust of wind came from behind. Ai Mi and Xiong YaYue wore both wearing shorts, only Xiao Qin wore a skirt. Maybe it was because her skirt was made of light materials, but her skirt swayed in the wind and it looked like it was about to rise up and expose her in public.

If I was the only one present, Xiao Qin would have thought of it as a golden opportunity, but she would still feel shame in public. She quickly used her hands to hold down her skirt, but although the danger of being exposed was gone, the sun visor cap on her head was blown away and it floated up the steps.

"My hat!" Xiao Qin looked at me, as if hoping I would help her chase the hat.

With your reaction speed, you could have used a single hand to grab the hat the moment it was blown away. I think you're doing it deliberately. I don't know which shoujo manga you learned it from to let the boyfriend chase the hat and create memories.

What was even more irritating was that Peng TouSi watched the hat fly over his shoulder, he didn't have any intention of stopping it& It would have been as easy as pie for you to grab the hat, and why are you winking at me, do you understand Xiao Qin's shoujo mindset?

I thought it would have been fine to let the hat get blown away, so it would prevent her from doing the same stuff again, but Ai Mi took delight in the disaster and said: "You deserved it for going against me, even God punished you. The manservant won't go after a lousy hat for you."

Seeing as I didn't move, plus her plan failed and she was also ridiculed by Ai Mi, Xiao Qin lowered her head with a pitiful look in her eyes.

I can't help it, I hate that expression. Anyway, running is also a form of exercise, so let me help you get your hat back on the way.

I didn't expect that I was just about to start running, Xiong YaoYue shoved the sun umbrella into my hand and say, "Help me block the sun for Miss Ai Mi." Then she shot out like a rocket to go after Xiao Qin's hat.

Was.. it to show gratitude to Xiao Qin or was she simply warm-hearted? In any case, I stood there at a loss holding up the sun umbrella. Peng TouSi sighed because Xiong YaoYue didn't have the ability to make discerning judgments. Ai Mi said dissatisfied: "Move the umbrella closer this way, the sun's hitting my shoulders. "

Since I began holding the umbrella, Xiao Qin also squeezed under the shade, taking up about half the space.

"Leave." Ai Mi ordered, "This is my shade."

"But Ye Lin classmate is mine." Xiao Qin justified.

"Nonsense." Ai Mi corrected, "The manservant belongs to me in the past, present, and future."

"Ye Lin classmate does indeed like you." Xiao Qin said with a smile, "But his like for you is different from his like for me&"

"Of course it's not the same." Ai Mi didn't understand what Xiao Qin was referring to and interpreted it herself, "The manservant's feelings for me are that of a servant's love for their master. Just like how angels are loyal to God and demons are loyal to Satan."

"If it's just loyalty, don't you already have Peng TouSi." Xiao Qin pointed out.

"That& that's not the same." Amy suddenly stammered. Her snow-white face wasn't exposed to the sun, but it emanated a higher temperature compared to her other areas, "Peng TouSi is old, so he might croak one day. I need a servant who can stay with me for a longer time."

Peng TouSi was only 40. It's sad for you to say that in front of other people, it's a good thing he doesn't take it to heart.

"Ye Lin classmate won't always be with you." Xiao Qin snickered, "He might not even be your manservant anymore in the future&"

"What did you say?" Ai Mi was infuriated, she reached out and ordered Peng TouSi, "Throw the violent girl into the cage and feed her to the pandas."

Peng TouSi didn't move, so Ai Mi turned to me and asked, "Manservant, why aren't you saying anything? Do you agree with what the violent girl said?"

I couldn't help but scratch my head.

Most of what Xiao Qin said was correct. Since my brother-sister relationship with Ai Mi will eventually be revealed, I will no longer have to call myself a manservant, but currently it's better to build our relationship and shouldn't add new conflicts.

So I beat around the bush and at the same time tried to shift their attention to where Xiao YaoYue ran off to get the hat.

We wouldn't have known without looking, but we were shocked when we took a look. Xiao Qin's hat had floated into the kangaroo enclosure! It got suck on a tree branch and Xiong YaoYue was jumping over the railings to get the hat back.

Don't go, don't you see the "animals in heat, it's dangerous to trespass" warning sign? You don't have to act like your life depends on it for Xiao Qin's hat.

I handed the umbrella to Xiao Qin and ran towards the kangaroo area with Peng TouSi, but it was too late.

Xiong YaoYue had easily and cheerfully flipped over the railing and was tiptoeing around trying to take away the hat off the branch. There was a medium-sized kangaroo eating under the tree with its head down, you will definitely be discovered.

As expected, the kangaroo realized there was an intruder behind and immediately stood up in a boxing stance. The kangaroo is a very ferocious boxer, what's incredible about them is that they can use the tail for support, and then use all four of their limbs to attack. At the same weight, the strength of a wild animal was seven times that of an ordinary human, so even if the kangaroo wasn't an adult, it wasn't an opponent Xiong YaoYue can handle.

The spectators around us immediately created a riot, some shouted "come out!" while some people rushed to contact a zookeeper, but many children were began to imitate the kangaroo's boxing posture.

Xiong YaoYue realized the kangaroo wasn't very large and the surrounding kangaroos wasn't going to join in the fight, so she slightly underestimated her opponent and reached out and said.

"Get out of the way, I just want the hat that's behind&"

Before she even finished speaking, the kangaroo hit Xiong YaoYue's shocked face with a left hook.

Of course, Xiong YaoYue couldn't stand it, she even forgot about the hat and began to angrily fight with the kangaroo. The girl vs kangaroo! It was a hundred times better than the fake tiger fight! Many people raised their phones to take pictures and videos, so Xiong YaoYue will definitely be on the local news tonight.

"Hurry and come out, don't fight." A kind-hearted uncle shouted, "You can't beat a kangaroo."

A young man next to him said: "How can you disregard the might of humans, the female student clearly has the upper hand."

Peng TouSi and I wanted to go over the railing to help, but we were stopped by the zookeeper who rushed over.

"Don't go in, or the other kangaroos might get agitated. They are really strong if they swarm you."

The zookeeper looked like he had been beaten by a kangaroo himself and still had lingering fears.

As expected of the boxing champions of the animal world. The kangaroo sent left hooks, right hooks, and upper hooks and it was hard for Xiong YaoYue to deal with.

I don't know if she was influenced by the Tyson vs. Holyfield fight, but Xiong YaoYue's eyes were both red, she went wild and opened her mouth trying to bite the kangaroo's ear.

The kangaroo of course nimbly evaded it.

Xiong YaoYue refused to give up. Since boxing didn't work, she pounced on the kangaroo and locked her hands around its neck.

That would only work when you're fighting against another person! The kangaroo's neck is long, so it wouldn't be easy to choke its trachea, it's not like we were taught a secret method to fight kangaroos in biology class.

As expected, the kangaroo didn't weaken its attack because of Xiong YaoYue's choke. It kept throwing punches at Xiong YaoYue, it even used its tail as support and sent a flying kick.

Fortunately, Xiong YaoYue had a quick reaction and raised her knee to block the attack, but she also grimaced in pain and had to hop on one foot for a while, the kind of scene you would commonly see on "Tom and Jerry".

The zookeeper, or perhaps the kangaroo keeper, called out, "Afu, stop attacking the visitors."

The kangaroo named Afu was obviously in a rebellious period. It would have been better if the zookeeper didn't say anything, as the kangaroo got more into it after he spoke.

I reached out to Xiong YaoYue through the railings, trying to pull her out.

"Stop messing around with the kangaroo. It's animal cruelty if you win, and you're worse than a beast if you lose."

"No way." Xiong YaoYue stubbornly shook her head, "I want to get Xiao Qin's hat back."

"A hat doesn't cost much." I shouted, "Come out and I'll buy another hat for Xiao Qin."

Xiong YaoYue dodged a punch from the kangaroo and remained stubborn, "I hate doing things halfway and I hate losing."

"I'm begging you, please come out."

The zookeeper who had prevented me and Peng TouSi from going over the railings, went in himself to settle the dispute between Xiong YaoYue and the kangaroo.

"Afu, look this way."

The zookeeper pulled out two peanuts from his pocket and tried to attract the kangaroo's attention.

Unexpectedly, the kangaroo was already fed by the visitors, and wasn't interested in food, it was only thinking about beating up the visitor.

Xiong YaoYue looked around the kangaroo enclosure and suddenly had a bright idea. She began running in circles around the kangaroo enclosure.

Afu relentlessly pursued after Xiong YaoYue to finish the match and see who's the victor.

The zookeeper was afraid the kangaroo would hurt someone, so he began to chase the kangaroo from behind. It was Xiong YaoYue at the front, followed by the kangaroo and the zookeeper running circles around the area.

Peng TouSi and I were just about to make our move when things took a new turn.

Xiong YaoYue, who tried to shake off Afu with all her might, ran towards the back of another male kangaroo who was leisurely eating grass. It had attitude that didn't care about the events that were occurring around it.

Xiong YaoYue curled up her index and middle fingers of her right hand and flicked the back of the male kangaroo's head.

Does she want to die? She can't even deal with a kangaroo child and now she's provoking an adult kangaroo?

As it turns out, Xiong YaoYue was the type of person who performs better under stress.

You could say she's quick witted or she acts without thinking, but in any case, after she flicked the adult kangaroo's head, it turned around in anger. Xiong YaoYue had already run five or six steps away, it was the little kangaroo Afu that was the closest.

"You hit your own father?" The adult kangaroo hit Afu down with a smack from its tail.

By the way, I should add that kangaroos don't speak Chinese, I was the one who dubbed in the dialogue above. Actually, I'm not even sure that the adult kangaroo was Afu's dad.

"Da Gang, Afu, don't fight, I'll give these two peanuts to whoever stops first."

The zookeeper's powerless dissuasion couldn't stop the two kangaroos from chipping at each other's heads. Xiong YaoYue took this opportunity to take off Xiao Qin's sun visor from the branch and leapt out of the enclosure quickly, moving nimbly like a panther, causing the onlookers to applaud and cheer.

Xiao Qin and Ai Mi were still arguing with each other, as they walked over together under the umbrella.

Xiong YaoYue didn't really mind the scratch on her face and dirty clothes as she returned the sun visor to Xiao Qin and said:

"The hat didn't even fall on the ground. I'm awesome, right?"

Despite Xiong YaoYue's excellent self-recovery abilities and a body that doesn't leave any scars, I couldn't help but admire her optimism from the bottom of my heart when she was still able to have a simple-minded smile when she was injured.

Xiao Qin was also surprised that Xiong YaoYue did all that for her own hat, so she slightly lowered her head and thought before saying, "Yeah, you're awesome, you were actually able to beat a kangaroo&."

"That's right." Xiong YaoYue flexed her biceps, "From now on you can call me Winnie, the 'Kangaroo Terminator'"

Ai Mi, however, looked angry and shouted at Xiong YaoYue, "Who told you to pick up the violent girl's hat? You belong to me and aren't allowed to privately serve others."

Xiong YaoYue felt a little bit guilty and she scratched the back of her head, "Miss Ai Mi, sorry, I acted on reflexes&"

"How many times do I have to tell you to don't call me Miss." Ai Mi snorted, then grabbed one of Xiong YaoYue's hands and pulled her away.

Ai Mi couldn't drag Xiong YaoYue at all with her strength, but Xiong YaoYue consciously followed her because she was worried about Ai Mi falling down.

"Peng TouSi, you come too." Ai Mi ordered angrily.

"Because Peng TouSi always calls you Miss, I just followed along and it became a habit." Xiong YaoYue tried to justify, "Besides, where are we going?"

"To the hospital for a full body checkup."

"Eh, Ai Mi, are you sick?" This time Xiong YaoYue finally stopped adding "Miss".

"You're the one who's sick." Ai Mi roared as loud as she could, "Didn't you know kangaroos can transmit rabies? Hurry up, we have to head to the biggest hospital or let my medical team give you a rabies shot."

I thought Ai Mi would blame Xiong YaoYue for helping Xiao Qin, but it seems she was more concerned about Xiong YaoYue's health. Although the possibility of kangaroos at a zoo carrying rabies is slim, it was good that my sister to was beginning to care about others.

But I must remind Ai Mi of one important thing.

"Hey, you're going the wrong way. The exit is that way."

Ai Mi blushed and turned in the direction I was pointing while holding Xiong YaoYue's hand.

"Manservant, you talk too much. I was just going to check the road signs."

Ai Mi, who was poor at directions, refused to admit her mistakes.

That day, Ai Mi brought Xiong YaoYue back to the VIP building and did a full examination on her with a variety of high-tech instruments. Of course, she didn't forget to give her a rabies shot. Afterwards, Xiong YaoYue told me, she wore very little clothes while she was being inspected and felt really weird.

Originally, Xiong YaoYue intended to head home, but Ai Mi was worried that Xiong YaoYue would have a rabies attack and die, so she was forced to stay. Xiong YaoYue had to call Xiao Qin and ask her to lie to her parents again, and Xiao Qin did a good job this time too.

As I've said before, room 101 in the VIP building was a luxury residence with two suites. Ai Mi only uses one of them, the other identical room was reserved for guests, and Xiong YaoYue slept there on Friday night.

But Ai Mi became nervous all the time ever since Xiong YaoYue was scratched by a kangaroo and she didn't feel comfortable letting Xiong YaoYue sleep in a room alone. She had to have Xiong YaoYue sleep in the same bed as her, so she would be the first to know if something happened to Xiong YaoYue.

Although Peng TouSi said it was unnecessary, Ai Mi was stubborn and wouldn't listen to anyone, so the two of them slept together in Ai Mi's princess bed.

Afterwards, Xiong YaoYue told me, "Ai Mi had a lot of stuffed bears on her bed, but in the middle of the night, she tossed the one in her arms off the bed and hugged me instead, as if I was her hug pillow."

Apparently we both like to hug other people in our sleep? Fortunately, Ai Mi and Xiong YaoYue were both girls, so it wasn't as awkward like it was between me and the class leader.

"By the way, Ai Mi also talked in her sleep when she hugged me, she said 'don't die' or something&"

Ai Mi is indeed very insecure, because both her grandfather and the sniper Vasya died. She felt that people close to her will die, so hugging Xiong YaoYue in her sleep was one of the ways for her to show concern.

When Xiong YaoYue told me about it on Monday, the scratches on her face had completely healed without leaving even a faint scar. It's clear now that Ai Mi was worried over nothing.

"Haha, you're cousin gets very touchy when she's asleep." Xiong YaoYue lowered her voice and said to me, "Not only did she sleep with her arms around me, but she also touched my breasts."

She said to me while sticking out her chest as if I didn't know what she was talking about.

"I thought I would be the only one losing out if I let her touch me, so I touched Ai Mi's butt. To be honest, it was smooth and it felt great"

Xiong YaoYue snorted hot air from her nostrils, as she made gripping actions with her hands with a face of excitement.

Don't talk about Ai Mi's butt in front of me! You two are obviously the same sex, but why was it way more flirtatious than when I slept with the class leader? For us, it was only me who touched the class leader, but you guys touched each other.

With a strange feeling, I called Shu Zhe out from class 1-4 and told him I had another job for him.

"Blowing balloons again?" Shu Zhe looked disinterested, he always felt he earned too little from blowing balloons.

Hmph, I still haven't made you blow condoms which will give you even more money, but I was going to give you a much more difficult than the previous ones. I want you to dress as a girl and pretend to be someone else's girlfriend.

"What, you want me to wear women's clothing in public?" Shu Zhe shrieked, "You're crazy, no way."

I objected, "Why not, didn't you already wear women's clothing in public before? You even went to the women's washroom& did you forget?"

"That& that was after dark, and I was alone. I'll get exposed if I pretend to be someone's girlfriend and have a meal with them. I'll be embarrassed if I was revealed in public."

"It's just having a meal with a group of geeks, how can they expose you? You've been practicing your fake girl voice by chatting with 'Cilantro Buns' online, plus you don't really have a visible Adam's apple. As for the chest, you could just buy some fake breasts. As long as you don't take off your pants, no one could tell you're a man dressed as a woman."

Shu Zhe hesitated for a moment, "Even if I can do it, what would I get?"

"You can get a free meal." I said.

"Hmph, then I really would be an idiot if I agreed just for a free meal."

Shu Zhe tossed a piece of gum into his mouth and said while chewing, "Since you agreed to help someone by acting as a pimp, you must be getting money."

Who's acting as a pimping? I don't care about people spreading rumors about me committing homicide and arson or selling ecstasy, but I don't want to be accused of being a pimp! At most it would be equivalent to the Japanese "rental girlfriend" business. I really wanted to help out those dota friends, so I made this plan.

After I sternly corrected Shu Zhe's wrong statement, I told him: "There's money to make, Xiao Ding especially wanted to really stand out in front of the LOL faction. As long as you pretend to be his girlfriend, he'll give you the ¥1000 he earned from his part-time job."

Shu Zhe's eyes lit up when he heard the substantial pay and then said, "Xiao Li has recently taken a fancy to a set of imported cosmetics, and I'm a bit tight on money right now&"

"But when you said Xiao Ding, is he the one who works at the hospital that my sister visits and blushes every time he sees a girl?"

I nodded my head.

"That doesn't work." Shu Zhe panicked, "I've been to the pet hospital several times to find my sister and Xiao Ding has seen me. I'll be screwed if he told my sister that I was dressed as a woman."

"You're still an immature kid." I sneered, "Did you think I haven't considered it? My life would also be in danger if your sister found out. Xiao Ding is the type of friend where we could eat from the same bowl of cup noodles at a net cafe, so he will never reveal it, I guarantee there will be no consequences."

Actually, Xiao Ding doesn't know the "temporary girlfriend" that I was going to send him is a trap, but I think Xiao Ding isn't a particularly demanding person. As long as I could meet his requirement of showing off in front of others, who cares if it's a man or a woman.

Shu Zhe asked me the specific time, and then murmured: "I could give it a try if I could make some money. I already practiced my fake voice for so long, it would be a shame if I only used it in voice chats with Cilantro Buns&"

"That's right." I agreed, "You can take whatever women's clothing you need from my family store."

Shu Zhe clicked his tongue and waved his hand as if to say 'no need'.

"Bro Ye Lin, the women's clothing from your store is either leopard print or silk, most of which can't be worn outside. I happen to have a set of clothes I was planning to give to Xiao Li, so I'll wear that set."

Eh, are you going to wear your girlfriend's clothes once before you give it to her, that sounds so strange.

"However, you have to buy all the other necessary equipment I need to prevent me from being found out."

"Other equipment? What other equipment, don't you already have clothes and wigs?"

Shu Zhe blushed slightly, "You just said it yourself, so why are you feigning ignorance? I'm talking about the breast pads! I won't buy any substandard goods for anything that touches my skin, so you will have to reimburse me."

Actually, I don't think that's even necessary. Since you're so skinny, no one would be suspicious if you had a flat chest. Or is it because Shu Zhe loves to look good in front of others, so he wants to be the prettiest among the other girlfriends even when he's cross-dressing?

I think you're being competitive in a strange place. I don't see you train harder even when you're second last in the 800 meter race.

"Ye Lin classmate, what did you do Sunday?"

Xiao Qin asked me when we had some free time in language class.

My schedule on Sunday was much busier than what a normal middle school student should have.

Apart from managing the online store, I was discussing with director Cao about the upcoming filming schedule for "Bloody Battle of Jin Ling".

The second episode with me in it has already been broadcasted on the Internet. Although viewers complained about how the heroine wasn't raped by Jin Ling Young Thug, it was still more popular than the first episode.

I really admire the make-up artist's skill, because of their godly skills, the audience didn't even realize the actor for Jin Ling Young Thug changed in the middle of the second episode. I was also saved from bringing trouble to myself because of this production.

Director Cao wanted to make a last minute change to the script for the third episode to make it more eye catching. He arranged a scene where Jin Ling Young Thug and the male protagonist would fight naked in a stream and he asked me if I agreed.

I might consider it if I was fighting naked with the female protagonist, but with the male protagonist? Are you trying to please the fujoshi viewers?

In the end, we each took a step back and decided to change the scene to where we were only naked on the top half of our bodies.

"There are so many thieves in Dong Shan city these days."Director Cao complained to me after we finished discussing the film schedule, "The iphone 5s was stolen before I could even break it in."

"That's what happens when you buy the newest trend." I touched the counterfeit phone in my pocket with a sense of superiority, "No one will steal it if you buy a domestic phone like me."

Director Cao rolled his eyes, "If you don't use a foreign brand phone as the director, then the actresses will think you're a fake director. But that thief shouldn't be too pleased, because I used the iphone 5s fingerprint function and they won't be able to use my phone for a while."

"I heard fingerprint locks are quite easy to crack." I said, "Apparently foreign children can use gummy bears to ge the fingerprints off the screen, so I'm afraid your phone&"

Director Cao waved his hand and said proudly, "A high-end person like me wouldn't be able to stand out if I used my fingerprint, so I used my nipple print! The thief is out of luck, he's going to put in a lot of work for nothing."

That was the only interesting thing that happened Sunday, but I don't think it was appropriate talking about "nipples" with Xiao Qin, so I told her I was at home sleeping.

"What a coincidence, I stayed home all day on Sunday too." I drew a manga about our trip to the zoo on Saturday, do you want to take a look?"

She said as she handed over the manga.

What should I say about it? If it wasn't for Ai Mi's umbrella, I wouldn't even be able to tell who was an person and who was an animal.

"Is this a gorilla." I pointed to a black ball and asked, "I don't think there were any gorillas in the zoo."

"Oh, that's Peng TouSi." Xiao Qin replied happily, "It's pretty close, right?"

Well, it actually looks kind of like gorilla. Based on Xiao Qin's drawing skills, it was already remarkable progress.

"Ye Lin, stand up and answer the question." The language teacher called me up again, he just didn't like me.

"Page 57." Xiao Qin reminded me.

I turned to page 57 and waited for old man Zhang to ask a question. Instead, he put the book down on the podium and asked:

"Let's review what we learned before. If you hit your family's dog and it wailed, is it an interjection or an adverb?"

My brain immediately shut down and I hesitantly said: "Teacher, I don't think we've learned this before?"

Old man Zhang snorted, "If I said I've taught it, then I've taught it. Let's change the question, if a beggar saw a dog barking at himself, would that be a linguistic description, or a psychological description."

Huh, what's up with old man Zhang and dogs today? Wouldn't it be humiliating if I can't even answer a single question, the class leader is still looking at me.

I thought for a bit and answered: "For the dog, it's a linguistic description. For the beggar, it's a psychological description."

Old man Zhang sneered: "I'm asking about you, are you in favor of the dog or the beggar, which do you want to be?"

Wow, way to insult me! Is it just because on the last essay with the "contradiction" topic, I used a ultra-modern writing style and wrote, "I looked at my eyes, licked my tongue, and walked to the edge of a round table, and said 'good morning, good night' to the long-haired bald teacher.

It's not like old man Zhang was the only bald teacher. There's no need to get revenge on me in class.

"They say 'It's better to be a dog in a peaceful time than be a man in a chaotic period', there are many times when people are worse than dogs, sigh"

Old man Zhang turned around to face the blackboard as he muttered those words.

"Ouch!" Someone threw a piece of chalk at the back of old man Zhang's head and the classroom quickly turned silent.

The class leader might be skilled in throwing, but there's no way she would be so rebellious and go against the rules.

Xiao Qin pretended it had nothing to do with her and smiled as she wiped away the chalk dust from her fingers with a tissue.

"Ye Lin classmate, why do you keep staring at me? If you keep looking at me like that, I'm going to blush."

You should blush for throwing chalk at old man Zhang. We were only bickering, you didn't need to intervene.

Old man Zhang was naturally furious, but he wasn't able to find out who threw the chalk, so the entire class was forced to write a reflection essay.

Xiao Qin, who was happily writing her reflection essay in the self study period, was suddenly called into the hallway by the class leader.

I am afraid Xiao Qin couldn't escape the class leader's eyes. The class leader might not have pointed out Xiao Qin was the real culprit in front of everyone, but she still had to scold her afterwards, so she would remember not to do it again.

After the study session was lunch break, but the class leader and Xiao Qin still hadn't returned. I assumed the two of them probably went to lunch together, which meant the conversation was quite peaceful.

But I was stunned when I saw the class leader face down on the ground in a curved alley behind the food stall street, while Xiao Qin was holding a wooden stick in her hand.

"What have you done!" I yelled at Xiao Qin, "You made the entire class write a self reflection and the class leader already helped you out by not exposing you in front of everyone. Can you not even take a little criticism? In the end, you still only resort to violence?"

Although the incident of throwing chalk at the teacher's head began with me, you should direct your grievances at me, there's no need to take out your anger on the class leader. Compared to Xiao Qin, the class leader's combat ability was at kindergarten level, she could easily oppress her and there was no need to use a wooden stick as a weapon.

It was Eunuch Cao who passed by this alley on his way home during lunch break. He saw the class leader lying in front of Xiao Qin, while Xiao Qin was holding a murder weapon with a dreadful look in her eyes. Eunuch Cao immediately scrambled out of there and reported it to me when he saw me on the food stall street.

"Master, something bad happened! Your wife went on a killing spree and she took out the class leader!"

I angrily rebuked Eunuch Cao for his nonsense, but he pointed at the alley while cowering and said:

"Master, there's no way I would lie about that. If you move fast, the class leader's body will still be warm, but it will turn cold if you're late. Anyway, this is your family business, so I'll get out of your way. Master, please take care."

As I watched Eunuch Cao's fat body disappear from my field of view, I was unsure and went to the place he pointed at to take a look and surprisingly, I really saw the scene he described.

Xiao Qin's expression was as if she was recovering from a burst of violent anger and a gray ember was still lit in her eyes.

The wooden stick in her hand looked like a sawed-off wooden teacher's pointer stick. A weapon often used by hooligans as a substitute for a softball bat. The advantage was that it didn't cost anything, all you had to do was steal it from the school and wrap some bandages around the bottom for a better grip.

Did Xiao Qin pick up the weapon in the alley? As far as I know, some hooligans think they are clever by hiding weapons by walls. In case they meet their enemies, they can run towards the alley they are familiar with and look for the weapons while they run. Xiao Qin used to be the leader of the Rose Group, so she must have known about it. She could have easily guessed where a weapon was hidden with experience and taken it out to deal with the class leader.

But Xiao Qin didn't need a stick to beat the class leader. Did she use a weapon to not leave behind any fingerprints?

"No, no." Xiao Qin gradually calmed down from and explained to me in a trembling voice, "Ye Lin classmate, it's not what you think. It was an accident, no one was supposed to get hurt."

"An accident?" I said coldly, "Then what's with the stick in your hand?"

Xiao Qin hesitantly twirled the stick, "This is&"

I was startled to see bloodstains on the tip of the stick.

Not only the stick, the stone floor was covered with tiny blood spatters. I didn't notice it earlier because the sun was too bright.

"Did& did you have to be so vicious." I felt like I was going to erupt with anger, "Are you going to kill the class leader? Since you have connections to the underworld, you can simply let your people deal with the corpse and you can rest easy."

Xiao Qin's slender arms trembled along with the stick in her hands.

"I& I've never thought that way." The voice of the agitated Xiao Qin became sharper, "Why don't you have any trust for me, sob sob&."

Tears are useless, this isn't something that could be forgive by crying.

I dropped down and carefully checked the class leader's injuries.

Her head didn't have any obvious signs of bleeding, but it could have been covered by her hair.

I checked the class leader's breath. Although it was slow and soft, it was relatively stable.

Then I put my hands on the class leader's soft neck and felt her pulse. Her pulse was strong and it didn't seem like her life was in danger.

I breathed out a sigh of relief and looked up to see Xiao Qin looking at me with teary eyes. I asked in a bad mood:

"Why are you still here? Do you want to finsih the job after you realized the class leader hadn't died yet?"

After being repeatedly questioned, it finally exceeded the limit of her patience and she threw the stick to the ground and said exasperatedly:

"It's not my fault, the class leader did more than what was necessary& she brought it on herself."

She then turned around and ran away crying, but I didn't chase after her. Attempted murder shouldn't be encouraged and the class leader needed someone to take care of her.

I knew a bit of first aid, so I didn't want to rashly move the class leader because I was afraid it would aggravate her injuries. There might be no obvious wounds, but we can't rule out the possibility of a concussion.

Finally I decided to give a call to the school doctor, Chen YingRan. She might be a pervert, but her medical skills are excellent, and the class leader will not be taken advantage of by her since she was a girl.

Chen YingRan arrived quickly at the scene of the incident, much faster than I expected. It must have been tough running over in high heels.

Seeing the class leader lying motionlessly on the ground, Chen YingRan raised an eyebrow and asked directly: "Did you do it?"

"It wasn't me!" I yelled at her, but saving the class leader was top priority. I let Chen YingRan to first check the class leader's injuries.

Chen YingRan opened the class leader's eyelids to check her eyes, then she felt her pulse and sighed, "It's a shame&"

What, is it impossible to save her? No way, the class president is supposed to become a righteous police officer, how could she die before she even graduates? If that's the case, isn't Xiao Qin now a murderer? Who would have thought that this would be the result of writing a simple self reflection essay. What a screwed up butterfly effect.

Chen YingRan admired the look of horror on my face for a while before saying slowly: "It's a shame there's nothing wrong with her. It's been too boring lately and I was hoping I would run into something exciting."

Damn it, you scared me! If you want something exciting, my home has a lot of products that you can buy. I'm still worried about how the European and American models aren't selling well.

Under Chen YingRan's guidance, I carried the class leader back to the infirmary on my back. Inevitably, there were passersby, but luckily the majority of them recognized the school doctor and could guess what happened. None of them suspected I had bad intentions and was carrying the class leader to a bad place.

In my opinion, the infirmary where Chen YingRan molested countless shotas was a bad enough place.

It seems like you want to ask if I took advantage of the class leader when I had the chance?

There's no way a man like me would take advantage of someone when they're down. At most, I felt the class leader's legs, but it was necessary contact for me to carry her back.

After I arrived at the infirmary and put the class leader on a bed, the first thing I did plug up my nosebleed with some medical cotton swabs. It had nothing to do with me taking advantage of the class leader, it's simply because it was too hot outside!

Chen YingRan told me to leave just as I sat down beside the bed.

"Stop watching, go back to class and help your class leader request a leave of absence. Don't let anyone come visit her, she needs to get some rest, got it?"

"I& I want to wait for her to wake up before I leave."

Chen YingRan frowned and crossed her arms on her waist, "What, you don't trust my medical skills, or you waiting for the good show?"

I didn't understand, "What good show?"

Chen YingRan laughed and pointed to the class leader, "I'll have to undo her bra to make her breathing more relaxed. Do you want to stand by and watch?"

I blushed and got up to take my leave, "Then I'm going back to class, give me a call if the class leader wakes up."

"Got it, got it." Chen YingRan shooed me away, then murmured, "Her breasts have developed, but she refuses to get a new bra. Wearing a smaller bra is likely to lead to oxygen deprivation."

Huh, so was that one of the reasons why the class leader fainted? She refuses to throw away bras that have become too small because she's frugal& Xiao Qin would defintely cry when she hears her worries.

Speaking of Xiao Qin, she was the main culprit and I'm not sure how she will act in class.

When I returned to class, Gong CaiCai was cleaning the blackboards. I asked her to tell the teacher that the class leader had taken a fall and was recovering in the infirmary and might be absent from the next class. Gong CaiCai was extremely worried for the class leader and wanted to go see her, but I stopped her because she needed sufficient rest.

When I returned to my seat, I discovered Xiao Qin's seat was empty. I shouldn't say I was surprised, she didn't want to face me after what she had done.

My anger still hadn't completely subsided, so I didn't put much thought into where Xiao Qin went nor did I give her a call.

Xiao Qin had skipped an entire class. The teacher asked about it, but no one knew where she had gone.

Hmph, let her do a bit of self reflection. The class leader treated her as a friend, but she hurt her. It's nasty behavior and even repenting in front of a wall for a month isn't enough.

As soon as the bell rang, Xiong Yaoyue, who had learned in class that the class president had been injured, rushed to the infirmary impatiently. I couldn't call her back, so I followed behind her.

In the end, Chen YingRan never let us in. She said that the class president was no longer unconscious, but she was still in a deep sleep and shouldn't be disturbed. Xiong YaoYue and I reluctantly returned to the classroom. Gong CaiCai, Loud Mouth, and the others who followed behind us were also driven back together.

The second class was politics, I suddenly received a text message from Chen YingRan: "She's awake, do you want to come over?"

I looked at Xiao Qin's seat that was still empty. In order to clear up some suspicions, I had to talk to the class leader, so I raised my hand and said, "Teacher, I want to go to the washroom."

The political science teacher was surprised and fearfully allowed it.

After leaving the classroom, I walked straight to the infirmary.

Chen YingRan wasn't there when I walked into the infirmary. The class leader was sitting upright on the bed holding a cup of coffee with both her hands. She was staring forwards with a vacant look in her eyes.

The class leader probably heard from Chen YingRan that I carried her back to school on my back, so she blushed slightly when I came in, but it was well hidden by the steam of the coffee.

"I didn't realize Xiao Qin was so incredible&" she muttered to herself.

That means the class leader has gotten a glimpse of Xiao Qin's true identity as a martial artist. I can't believe a martial arts genius had to use a wooden stick to beat her opponent.

"Why were you guys fighting?"

Since the class leader and Xiao Qin ate together on food stall street, it meant they initially had a peaceful conversation at first, so what did they say that caused the conflict.

"We didn't get into a fight?" the class leader said surprised, "Xiao Qin promised she wouldn't throw chalk at the teacher's head anymore, and I made an exception to cover for her this one time& oh right, is Xiao Qin okay?"

Huh, why are you asking if she's okay after she hit you? Did she damage your brain?

"Did Xiao Qin get hurt?" The class leader asked again in a more urgent tone.

"She has Super Saiyan blood, so how could she be injured?" I shrugged, "She just didn't have the face to see me, so she ran home by herself."

The class leader got serious, "Why would Xiao Qin not have the face to see you. Even if I found out she's actually super strong, it has nothing to do with you, right?"

Huh, is this a repercussion from the concussion? Why are you sticking up for her even after she knocked you down? The Justice Devil has turned into a saint!

The class leader placed the cup of coffee on the bedside table and sighed.

"Because Xiao Qin's mother is an MMA champion, so after the volleyball incident, I suspected Xiao Qin was also a martial arts master. I witnessed it with my own eyes today& unfortunately, I was a hindrance&"

"Wait wait wait, don't sigh." I furrowed my brows, "Class leader, you're confusing me. What happend between you and Xiao Qin today, wasn't she the one who knocked you out?"

"Xiao Qin, knocked me out?" The class leader likewise furrowed her brows, "Why would you think that? Xiao Qin was protecting me."

It was then when I noticed Chen YingRan didn't wrap any bandages around the class leader's head, which meant there was no blood. So the blood on the wooden stick that Xiao Qin was holding didn't belong to the class leader.

I realized that I have wronged accused Xiao Qin after I listened to the class leader's story.

The class leader and Xiao Qin had lunch together and was planning to head back to school. That's when a junior student ran over and told the class leader that someone hung a wild cat by a wire in the alley because it had stolen some fish and no one was helping.

As a member of the cat-loving faction, the class leader didn't determine the authenticity of his words and immediately followed the boy to the alley to find the "dying cat", but was unexpectedly surrounded by hooligans wearing bizarre clothes.

They claimed to be Zhao GuangTou's underlings and wanted to avenge their boss. The first-year boy had no other choice because he was bullied by them.

"You're Shu Sha?" The leader had a countryside style scene fashion, he kept fiddling with the sawed off teacher's pointer in his hand, flaunting his authority.

"I heard you look innocent, but actually loves to seduce men. Even Ye Lin and the that fool, Li CunZhuang, are willing to act as your hired thugs. Let's see what you can do today when you're alone, if you're afraid, then kneel down and beg us."

These four unlucky bastards, completely ignored Xiao Qin and thought she had her head lowered because she was scared silly.

While the class leader was thinking about how to break out from the unfavorable situation and maybe ask Xiao Qin to run out for help, Xiao Qin's face changed.

After being surrounded by four men of similar age who was bad-mouthing them, Xiao Qin's androphobia instantly shot up through the roof and her self-defense mechanism triggered.

She moved as fast as lighting and sent the leader flying with a kick and then grabbed the teacher's pointer from his hand. As everyone was turned pale with fright, a second punk got hit with a sweeping kick and fell flat on his face.

The class leader originally had her hand in her skirt pocket and secretly clasped a coin. She was intending to throw it at the enemy so she could take advantage of the chaos to escape, but she was confused by the sudden change and didn't know where to use the coin.

Xiao Qin was also wearing the school skirt like the class leader so she didn't transform as much, definitely not as much as the time when she gave a beating to the Five Tiger Punishment Squad. Perhaps it was because she was subconsciously afraid of exposing herself.

It was lucky for the class leader because she would have been wiped out too if Xiao Qin had transformed completely.

The hooligans only reacted after two of their companions had fallen. The two remaining punks split up and one attacked from the front while one attacked from behind.

The class leader was unsteady after she saw Xiao Qin knock down two people. The enemy was closing in from two directions, so she didn't have time to think and threw the coin. It good she was practicing lately as the coin hit the target's eye.

"Ah!" The punk, who wasn't a threat to Xiao Qin, was hit by the class leader's coin and then received a strike from Xiao Qin's stick and collapsed.

However, the class leader was only concerned about the safety of Xiao Qin, that she herself was punched in the back of the head and then she fainted.

What happened afterwards wasn't witnessed by the class leader, but it wasn't hard to guess.

The class leader got injured trying to protect Xiao Qin which further enraged the transformed Xiao Qin. She went on a rampage and taught her enemies a lesson so brutal that the tips of the wooden sticks was stained with their blood.

The punks who had never seen such a scene before, were so frightened that they helped each other up and fled in fear. Xiao Qin held the bloody wooden stick as she tried to regain her composure while guarding in case they returned.

Similar to my "berserker" state, Xiao Qin's darkened state also takes time to calm down. It just so happens that I received a report from Eunuch Cao at this time and entered the alley to see this scene, so that's why I misunderstood Xiao Qin.

When Xiao Qin said "it was her own fault", she was referring to the fact that it was completely unnecessary for the class leader to help.

I& I'm such an idiot, how could I suspect Xiao Qin before I got the facts straight? The class leader was saved from the hooligans because Xiao Qin was there. Where was she now, did she go home?

"Class leader, since you look okay help me tell the teacher I will be taking a sick leave in the afternoon. I have something I have to do."

"What are you going to do?"

I didn't answer the class leader's question and briskly walked out of the infirmary.

No one picked up when I called Xiao Qin's phone which meant it was already turned off.

No one answered at Xiao Qin's home either.

I called Auntie Ren, but she couldn't hear me clearly due to the noisy set, but I could tell that Xiao Qin hadn't gone looking for her mother.

The question now is where did Xiao Qin go?

I thought I knew enough about Xiao Qin, but today I was wrong. Not only did she not hurt the class leader, instead, she saved the class leader.

To deduce where Xiao Qin went, I have to use my knowledge of Xiao Qin to analyze her way of thinking.

Xiao Qin is not the type of person to suffer in silence, unless the person who bullied her is me& I feel ashamed at that thought.

If she was wrongly accused, she would need to release her grievances, so where would she release it?

Those four punks were the cause of everything!

First, because of them, her martial arts was exposed in front of the class leader. Then she owes the class leader for being helped and she was misunderstood by me& this triple whammy isn't something that could simply be solved by giving them a beating.

She has to get her revenge! Since they introduced themselves as Zhao GuangTou's men, then Xiao Qin will certainly find Zhao GuangTou's base and turn it upside down.

Did Xiao Qin go by herself? Xiao Qin isn't following common sense and is someone who clings to her own ways.

I felt my heart tightening.

Zhao GuangTou was sent to the hospital last time by Li CunZhuang, Tang Jiang, and the class leader. I'm not sure if he was discharged, but he has a lot of henchmen. And the younger they are, the more they rely on the "Minors Protection Act", to commit ruthless crimes.

Even if Xiao Qin's combat power is off the charts, it's still dangerous going against a crowd.

No, even if the chance of her being there is slim, I have to go to Zhao GuangTou's base to check it out. If Xiao Qin really went there, then I have to make sure she comes back safely no matter what.

After making up my mind, I took a cab to the "Tu Qiao" bus station near the outskirts of Dong Shan City.

It was the place where Gong CaiCai got lost. Thanks to that incident, 28 Middle students could now use cell phones.

It was a dangerous are to be in.

A large area of dilapidated houses and shanty towns waiting to be renovated has become a paradise for outlaws. The Tu Qiao Casino was an open secret in Dong Shan city which was still operational even after repeated prohibitions. It's even said there were drug deals happening.

Zhao GuangTou's base was also nearby.

In an old and dilapidated enclosed courtyard, Zhao GuangTou often shared the spoils with a dozen of his men, played cards, and sometimes used the courtyard as a place to carry out lynchings.

The courtyard was considered superior when compared with the surrounding collapsed and crumbling walls. The courtyard was also filled with stolen furniture and it was like a gathering hall.

It was about 4 in the afternoon. The sun was shining intensely and the dry wind made the area feel desolate and gave you a feeling of isolation.

"Surround her and get rid of her." A hoarse voice was carried through the wind, "What will happen to our reputation if it gets out we were badly beat by a girl!"

My heart thumped: it's fortunate I came, it looks like I still understand Xiao Qin. I don't know how she found the location of Zhao GuangTou's base, in any case, it seems she did come to go on a killing spree.

It seems Xiao Qin had the upper hand based on the sound of people falling down in the courtyard. My help might not be necessary, but since I came, there's no reason to let Xiao Qin fight alone.

The two of us, hand in hand, will destroy Zhao GuangTou's gang without leaving anything behind.

I saw a familiar figure in the collapsing courtyard when I stepped into Zhao GuangTou's base.

Is it Xiao Qin, or a memory that exists in my mind which I can't forget.

For a moment, I thought I saw the Little Tyrant from many years ago.

I don't know where she changed, but she replaced her school uniform skirt with some casual pants. She had bandages wrapped around both her wrists and had the professional look of a martial arts master.

The figure of her trampling the enemy under her feet was so familiar.

Of course, my point of view wasn't the same as before, but it still made me feel nostalgic.

Five punks fell left and right in a circle around Xiao Qin, the other side only had two people left standing. If I had arrived a little later, the battle would have had nothing to do with me.

"This woman's a monster." One of the guys said.

"Who are you calling a monster?" I took large strides forward, "Even if she was a monster, it's not up to you to say."

It was at this point Xiao Qin came to her senses because of my voice. She looked at me with a puzzled look as if she had just woken up from a dream.

In order to deal with her androphobia, Xiao Qin had to black out in order to fight the punks. It was very similar to the time with the Five Tiger Punishment squad where Xiao Qin woke up as soon as I spoke.

"Ye Lin classmate."

Xiao Qin was shocked when she first saw me, then her lips trembled and she unclenched her fists. She disregarded her opponents and began running towards me with a face full of tears.

"Sob, sob. You finally came. I'm so happy& that Ye Lin classmate could guess that I would be here."

She pointing while crying, "Ye Lin classmate, they bullied me, you have to avenge me."

The face of the two people who were still looked unwell. One second, it was like Xiao Qin was possessed by the god of war, the next second she flung herself into my arms like a little girl. It made the two people scared out of their wit's and made them suspect they weren't on earth.

Since it was already two against two, unless they had a gun, it was impossible for them to turn the tide. So I first comforted Xiao Qin and even said cringey lines like "good girl, don't cry".

The two people actually showed us respect (or they were scared silly), and they forget to take advantage of the opportunity to escape.

"Aren't Uncle Tiger and Uncle Leopard secretly protecting you?" I asked, "Since it's an underground feud, why not use the real triads to deal with them?"

Xiao Qin said while wiping tears: "Since they followed us to the zoo and didn't give us any privacy, I told them not to follow so closely every day or I would call the police."

Call the police, are you going to punish your own family? It really sucks Uncle Tiger and Uncle Leopard took on the task of protecting Xiao Qin.

But this also explained why Uncle Tiger and Uncle Leopard didn't show up at noon when Xiao Qin and the class leader was in a dangerous situation.

To be honest, it wasn't even a dangerous situation for Xiao Qin. If the class leader knew Xiao Qin was so strong beforehand, she wouldn't have made the extra effort to rescue Xiao Qin and then be knocked down herself.

I gently pushed Xiao Qin away before my chest was completely soaked with her tears. Then I turned to the two trembling guys and beckoned to them saying:

"You two can come at me together."

The two men shook their heads continuously. As Zhao GuangTou's men, they had probably met me before and knew of my notorious reputation, but I didn't remember them.

Xiao Qin consciously stepped back and cheered me on, "Be careful, Ye Lin classmate, if you fail, there will be no one to protect me."

It's the other side that needed protection, right? I untimely sympathized with the enemy.

At that moment, Zhao GuangTou calmly led a thin student wearing a middle school uniform inside.

The wall next to the back door had already collapsed and it had a big hole in it, but he still had to put on airs and walk through the back door.

So he was already released from the hospital, but it was too arrogant to only bring one person as support.

And the student behind him didn't look like he could fight. He wasn't wearing a 28 Middle uniform, but it was a common blue and white stripes style. Because he was quite thin, the sleeves of his uniform swayed along with him.

But after getting closer, I noticed the student had a scar that extended from the corner of his forehead to his jaw.

Zhao GuangTou was slightly surprised to see me, but didn't stop in his tracks.

"I heard there was a crazy chick causing a disturbance beating everyone up, so it turns out that she's your girl. You guys are really like a pair of mad dogs."

Xiao Qin suddenly blushed, she took a embarrassed pose and whispered behind me.

"Ye Lin classmate, I think we misunderstood. Mr. Zhao seems like a good person."

He's insulting us! Don't say he's a good person just because he called us a "pair".

"It's none of your business what our relationship is." I cracked my fingers, "Anyway, you've repeatedly caused trouble for the people around me, it's time to settle this. All four of you can come together and I'll teach you a lesson."

To my surprise, Zhao GuangTou let out a sinister laugh.

"Heh heh heh heh&Ye Lin, like I said before, you're not invincible, there's always someone stronger. Today, I'll let you meet your match."

Then he waved and beckoned the middle school student, "Go, show him your strength."

I already judged the middle school student to be abnormal, but I didn't expect Zhao GuangTou to be confident enough to let him fight me alone. I immediately took a defensive posture and made my preparations.

I didn't expect the middle school student to turn a deaf ear to Zhao GuangTou's orders. He squatted down on the ground and began playing with an Ultraman model with a scary look in his eyes.

Zhao GuangTou was so angry, but he was afraid of him and couldn't act violently, so he had to persuade him with gentle words.

"Di Yun, I already bought you a full set of Ultraman models, you should at least help your big brother out."

The other two punks had complicated expressions, and one of them said to Zhao GuangTou.

"Big bro, is there something wrong with this guy who claims to be from 'the Tiga Ultraman Nebula' and we don't even know his real name. He doesn't seem right in the head."

"That's right." The second punk stared at the appalling scars on Di Yun's face and added, "I heard that when he was a kid someone grabbed his Ultraman toys, and he ended up tearing and biting up his rival who was ten years older."

Zhao GuangTou glared at the two useless men and reprimanded: "You know what, Deng Xiaoping once said, it doesn't matter what color the cat is, it's a good cat if it can catch the rat. Regardless of whether Di Yun has brain problems or not, it's fine as long as he can fight."

Next, he bent down and said to Di Yun:

"Di Yun, you can just stand by and watch, the tall one standing over there intends to steal your Ultraman toys."

Hearing these words, Di Yun abruptly snapped around. His eyes emitting killing intent, as if he wasn't an existence from this world, he trembled violently.

"Are& you the one who wants to steal my Ultraman&?"

"Pfffftt" Xiao Qin couldn't help but laugh.

What are you laughing at? Did he remind you of my relationship with brother Optimus Prime? I'm not the same as him, I'm already 14 and stopped playing with robots, but he's still obsessed with Ultraman toys and thinks he's an alien from the M78 nebula!

As if the calm before the storm, Di Yun looked at the red Ultraman model in his hand. The punk next to him hurriedly said, "I'll take care of it for you."

Di Yun glared at him, then carefully placed the Ultraman model at the foot of the wall like it was a living object, and bowed to it.

"If someone wants to hurt you, please transform."

Holy shit, he's really sick. As I looked at Zhao GuangTou's smug expression, I wondered if he was playing mind games with me? Was Di Yun simply mentally ill and he wanted me to hurt him then get sued?

I knew I was wrong when Di Yun took his first step towards me.

Even Xiao Qin let out an astonished gasp.

What is this speed? It's completely unlike any martial arts, it was a posture defied the mechanics of the human body. How can he be so fast, the karate chop he sent towards my eyes was so fierce it looked like a attacking cobra.

I used my all to dodge the blow and I was covered in cold sweat.

Zhao GuangTou laughed from the rear and said, "Ye Lin, you're going to suffer. Half of our brothers got sent to the hospital before we were able to subdue Di Yun."

That explains why there were fewer than ten people when Xiao Qin stormed his base. But Di Yun's strength obviously greatly exceeded my expectations, I might be defeated if I just relax slightly.

He attacked while hollering: "Ultimate Shining Blast, Final Cross Shield."

It seems like it was all Ultraman moves and I've seen it on TV as a child. It feels really embarrassing fighting this guy.

I retreated under his continuous attacks and didn't even have the opportunity to use Yin Yang Sanshou.

I'm not sure if Di Yun trained day and night with becoming larger and stronger like ultraman as his goal, but he has a surprising amount of endurance and power contained within his skinny frame.

These kinds of people have a screw loose, but have an unusual talent in a certain area, the so-called "rain man".

Suddenly, it occurred to me that I had fought hundreds of fights ever since I set out to be a Spartan, but this was the only fight for Xiao Qin. She was neither an opponent nor an unrelated party, she was right behind me cheering me on with her eyes wide open.

I had sworn I wouldn't lose to anyone my age other than the Little Tyrant, so how could I lose to Di Yun while Xiao Qin was watching? Plus, as far as I could see, Di Yun seemed to be a year younger than me.

So I concentrated, I dodged Di Yun's rabid dog attacks while thinking of a good way to break through.

Seeing that I was only defending but not attacking, Zhao GuangTou thought his plan had succeeded and he burst into laughter "What, are you scared? It's not hard to find a hired thug like you who doesn't care about their life as long as you are willing to spend some time to search."

Then he tapped his head with his finger and said, "In today's society, the most important thing is politics. Someone like you who could only risk their lives will live the rest of their lives working for people like us."

I saw his two rows of white teeth glistening in the sun and said sarcastically: "Zhao, does it hurt getting porcelain teeth? Would you get half off the next time you get a full set of porcelain teeth?"

The last time he blocked me and the class leader in the alley, I heard one of Zhao GuangTou's colleagues had injured brother Gang's hands, so I went berserk and knocked out all of Zhao GuangTou's teeth with a steel pipe. None of his current teeth are genuine goods.

But it is a lot whiter than before and definitely improved his appalling appearance a bit, so it could be considered a good deed.

Zhao GuangTou subconsciously touched his cheek, as if he still had lingering fears at the dentist.

"Di Yun, beat him to death!" Zhao GuangTou said angrily, "As long as you defeat Ye Lin, I'll buy you a full set of Ultraman models imported from Japan."

Di Yun's martial arts was really hard to deal with. I should be able to win if I used berserker mode, but I never use it in front of allies, because it's too humiliating.

If I screamed out chunni lines like "ashes to ashes, dust to dust; to the end of the world." in front of Xiao Qin, she would laugh at me.

Di Yun, who was constantly yelling out Ultraman moves, was a real portrayal of me in the berserker state. I really feel ashamed for him, and I really feel ashamed for myself.

"Ye Lin classmate, do you need my help?"

Xiao Qin watched our battle and became more interested. She also unconsciously imitated some of Di Yun's attack movements, did she already reach a new realm of martial arts? But I don't think his movements are suitable for a girl to learn and use.

"No need, I'll deal with him alone."

I might have been trying to act brave, but the main factor was that Di Yun wasn't a part of Zhao GuangTou's gang, but just a "Rain Man" who was bribed with Ultraman models.

I didn't want to hurt Di Yun from the bottom of my heart. His love for Ultraman models was no different than my former love for brother Optimus Prime (of course, I don't like playing with toy robots anymore, really).

"Di Yun, I'm not going to take Ultraman away from you." I tried to convince him, "Stop, don't you know that Zhao GuanTou is just using you?"

"No one can take away my Ultraman, no one,." Di Yun teeth clenched, completely unable to listen to my words, and attacked more frequently.

I'll be damned, he lifted his body up with two hands and performed a chain of kicks and he nearly kicked my jaw. It was street dance moves but with 120% power. His attack were too creative and too unexpected.

No, if my opponent was too flexible and I wasn't going to go all out, then my only choice was a tackle.

I was still larger and stronger, so as long as I hold on tightly he will have to give up his creative moves. Two men hugging together looks a bit unattractive, but it's fine as long as it works since Spartans don't care about being a little unsightly.

After making up my mind, I tried to jump in several times and grab Di Yun around the waist, but he reacted quickly and dodged within a hair's breadth every time. He was also able to take advantage of the opportunity to counterattack.

When would this fight come to an end? As I was troubled, I realized Zhao GuangTou quietly whispered with his men and they quietly began to retreat.

It was because he heard from his men that Xiao Qin had strength at least on par to mines. They had high hopes in Di Yun, but he was only able to fight on par with me. After carefully weighing the situation, they realized they were disadvantaged, so they decided to let Di Yun stall for time while they retreated.

It was spineless. I didn't think the mindset of "let the leader go first" existed in hooligan circles too.

"Don't let them get away!" I subconsciously shouted to Xiao Qin, only to remember she had androphobia and would only fight them in her darkened state. Xiao Qin certainly didn't want to use her darkened state in front of me like how I don't want to enter berserker mode in front of her.

However, Xiao Qin moved quickly at my shout.

Zhao GuangTou, like a startled, transitioned from a slow retreat to a full on sprint.

But Xiao Qin's first target wasn't Zhao GuangTou. In a couple of steps, she flew by the wall and picked up the Ultraman model that Di Yun had placed there.

"(^__^) Hehehe&" Xiao Qin looked at Di Yun's back with malicious intentions. I suddenly felt sick, like the day when Optimus Prime was snatched away from me.

I thought Xiao Qin would choke the Ultraman model and say to Di Yun, "Stop or I'll choke him to death."

But Xiao Qin didn't do that. She took the Ultraman model, and while Di Yun was distracted, she flew after Zhao GuangTou, who was running the slowest because he had just been discharged from the hospital. She then shoved the Ultraman model violently into Zhao GuangTou's pocket.

Then she cupped her hands around her mouth to act as an amplifier and shouted: "Not good, Ultraman was caught by the bad guys, can anyone save him!"

Di Yun's face immediately turned blue, he used his peripheral vision to glance towards the wall and the Ultraman model was no longer there.

"Ahhh& ahhhhhhhhhhhhhhhhhhhhhhhhhhhhhhhhhhhhhhhh.."

Di Yun's roar was somewhere in between one of a gorilla and an alien. He snapped his head back and saw part of Ultraman sticking out from Zhao GuangTou's pocket. You could actually only see its two feet, which meant Xiao Qin really did stick it in there with a lot of force.

"Ultraman, give me back Ultraman, otherwise, I, will, be, angry&."

Di Yun declared, then he left me alone and turned around to chase after Zhao GuangTou and the others as he vowed to get Ultraman back.

Zhao GuangTou could see Di Yun's distorted face as he got closer and he couldn't pull the Ultraman model out in a moment of desperation. His anxious face was completely red and he could only say:

"Di Yun, calm down. I'll put Ultraman down, just don't come after me."

But Di Yun looked like a mad dog who had his bone snatched away by Zhao GuangTou and he couldn't be reasoned with.

In a panic, Zhao GuangTou exerted all his strength and gave the Ultraman model a hard tug and it finally came out.

Unfortunately, only half out, Lord Ultraman was split in half. Was it because Zhao GuangTou got greedy and bought cheap goods, or was it because Xiao Qin tampered with it? Based on how Xiao Qin covered her mouth and snickered, the possibility of the latter was greater.

Zhao GuangTou's lips turned purple with fright when he saw Di Yun's precious Ultraman broken in two halves. He quickly said:

"Don't get mad, I'll buy you a new one. I'll buy you a better one."

Di Yun's eyes were bloodshot. He bit his lips to the point it almost bled and said hatefully:

"Can a life be bought back with money? My comrade-in-arms was killed by you and I have to avenge him."

"Taste my beam. I'll use all my energy and not leave any material behind. Die, die, die, die&."

"My brother-in-arms, don't be afraid. I'll freeze your body and bring you back to the Land of Light."

"The spirit of Ultraman lives forever in your heart and all enemies fly into oblivion."

Driven by rage, Di Yun caught up with Zhao GuangTou from behind and used all the Ultraman moves he could remember on Zhao GuangTou.

I could only say the scene was too tragic. Di Yun hit Zhao GuangTou while sitting on top of his stomach. Zhao GuangTou initially struggled a bit then he completely stopped moving.

After this battle, not sure if it was because Zhao GuangTou was bald and didn't have any cushioning, but he got a concussion and developed transient global amnesia. From then on, he could no longer play with "politics", sometimes he would even forget on the way to the washroom and only remembered when he pissed his pants. I guess what goes around comes around.

As for Di Yun, although he was prosecuted for assault, but was evaluated to be mentally ill and he was a minor, so he was not punished by law.

But the reason he was involved in the lawsuit was because Xiao Qin broke his Ultraman. I later found out Di Yun's real name and home address out of guilt and sent him an identical Ultraman based on memories with a message: "Don't be sad, I've been resurrected."

Apparently, Di Yun cried tears of joy after he received the model. His mental state was really at a child's level.

After accidentally finishing off one of the evil forces, Zhao GuangTou, Xiao Qin looked happy because she was able to vent her anger and she didn't fuss about my misunderstanding of her.

There happened to be a physical education class the next day. When Xiao Qin once again said she didn't want to participate because she was frail, the class leader, who knew the truth, stood right next to her and simply listened as Xiong YaoYue's agreed to Xiao Qin's request.

"Did you say anything to the class leader?" I asked Xiao Qin, who was fiddling with cross-stitching.

"Nothing much." Xiao Qin shrugged as she compared her cross stitch to the example illustration, "I told the class leader I have a severe case of androphobia. If I get threatened by boys, I won't be able to stop myself from going crazy and beating them up, and that's why I don't attend gym class with boys. Otherwise, what would happen if I black out and go berserk when I'm hit by basketball they threw. It would be embarrassing for me and it would be awful for class spirit."

There were truths mixed with her lies, so there was no reason for the class leader to not believe her. But actually Xiao Qin's androphobia isn't that severe and there's no way she would go crazy from only being hit by a ball. Just yesterday, didn't she stuff an Ultraman model into Zhao GuangTou's pocket?

Although Xiao Qin once again enjoyed some beneficial treatments, but after knowing the truth, the class leader no longer treated her as a spoiled younger sister.

On rare occasions, the class leader would ask Xiao Qin to go with her to the offices to grab tools. When she was too busy, she would also ask Xiao Qin to run some errands, kind of treating Xiao Qin as the second Xiong YaoYue.

"Class leader, I can go and buy ice cream for the entire class, there's no need to let Xiao Qin go."

Loud Mouth objected to the class leader's order, while Xiao Qin hid behind Loud Mouth.

The class leader smiled and said, "You walk slow, if I left it to you, the ice cream will melt halfway, plus you have a habit of eating while you walk&"

"But Xiao Qin is frail and sickly." Loud Mouth insisted.

The class leader glanced at Xiao Qin as if she was asking with her eyes "is that so?". Xiao Qin, who felt guilty, could only go and run the errand.

"After the supporting character caught onto my weakness, she's ordering me around every day." Xiao Qin complained to me after she bought the ice cream, "She's awful."

Although that's what she said, it doesn't seem like she's harboring any resentment towards the class leader. It could be because the class leader chose to save Xiao Qin rather than protect herself, so now Xiao Qin feels like she owes the class leader.

But in fact, it was Xiao Qin who protected the class leader from those four hooligans, but Xiao Qin didn't have any intention of taking the credit. Perhaps it came naturally to her and Xiao Qin never even thought of leaving the class leader behind.

It seems Xiao Qin's bad intentions are only up to the level of "mischievous pranks". At least for those who we study and interact with every day, she won't abandon them when they are in danger.

I felt gratified since I was used to always seeing people fight. A pure friendship is a better way to heal people's hearts.

The class leader had put a lot of thought into it, and the other reason she asked Xiao Qin to run errands was the same as why she made Gong CaiCai to be a class committee member.

It's a rare opportunity for a transfer student to gain popularity by buying ice cream for the class on a hot day. The class leader wanted Xiao Qin to slowly integrate into the class and eventually she wouldn't be afraid of boys anymore.

It's just that Xiao Qin won't understand the class leader's painstaking efforts.

The fact that Xiao Qin knew martial arts was a secret between the three of us. As for when the class leader and Xiao Qin would communicate with each other with their eyes at certain times, everyone had their own interpretations.

Some people said Xiao Qin stole the class leader's limelight in the volleyball match, so the class leader was getting revenge, but these people clearly don't really understand the class leader.

Some people said that Xiao Qin's body wasn't weak, but in order to continue to skip physical education classes, she made a deal to always listen to the class leader's orders. This statement was closer to the truth.

The most outrageous explanation, surprisingly, was uttered by the timid Gong CaiCai.

Once, when we were cleaning the class, I was assigned task of fetching the water for the girls to clean the windows. While I was carrying a bucket of water back, Gong CaiCai carefully asked:

"Ye, Ye Lin classmate, did& did the class leader give you up to Xiao Qin?"

I was shocked, looked around to see if anyone was around me and asked in a hurry, "Why would you say that?"

Gong CaiCai lowered her head and stammered:

"Because& Winnie told me you went to the zoo with Xiao Qin on the weekend, and Xiao Qin has always been ordered around by the class leader recently& so I could only guess if the two of them reached an agreement in private&"

They did have an agreement, but it had nothing to do with me! I think you watched way too many Korean dramas, all you saw was me kissing the class leader, then kissing Xiao Qin. You don't have to keep adding on different layers with your imagination, Loud Mouth and Little Smart must be a bad influence on you, that's why you're so nosy now.

Friday came in a flash. Xiao Ding called and nervously asked if I was able to find a temporary girlfriend for him.

"Don't worry, I've already made arrangements."

I responded with a very "dependable" voice.

"Ah, then I'm very thankful." Xiao Ding expressed his thanks. He was never that polite before, but I guess the fight between LOL and dota was that important to him.

"But there's something I must tell you in advance. The girls in our class are all a bit shy and none of them is willing to pretend to be your girlfriend. But it wasn't really a huge problem, I made a snap decision and found you a man&"

Xiao Ding immediately choked on his words.

"Wha-, what did you say? I trusted you and you found me a man? The LOL faction already ridiculed us dota faction members for having no girlfriends, only gay friends. Wouldn't this only validate their words?"

"Calm down for a bit." I let Xiao Ding calm down, "I might have found you a man, but he's not a man like you and me. He's a cross dresser, you've probably heard of them before. As long as they look good and can bring you into the spotlight, who cares if they are a man or a woman."

Xiao Ding said skeptically, "You better not be making it sound good, but actually deliver a trash product. If it was someone like Ru Hua, I might as well bring a real man. You better not con me, if the cross dresser isn't up to par, I.. I might as well bring you with me&"

"Don't worry, he's definitely up to par." I lowered my voice, "You've met our class leader, Shu Sha, before right?"

"I know her." Xiao Ding was overjoyed, "Did you convince Shu Sha to be my temporary girlfriend?"

Then he said, "But I don't really have the guts to talk to Shu Sha, so wouldn't it get exposed?"

"It's not Shu Sha." I gasped, "I just not told you, it's a cross dresser, which means a man. The class leader isn't a man, but I'm letting you borrow her brother."

"Her brother." Xiao Ding hesitantly said, "I think I met him once. He's a boy who doesn't really like animals&"

"Yeah, he doesn't like animals, but he likes money. Recently, he's getting more and more into cross dressing& as long as you pay him, he will gladly go with you to the offline meetup."

"Wait, Shu Sha's brother actually has that kind of hobby?" Xiao Ding's reaction was as I expected.

"Who cares about other people's hobbies? If you guys are allowed to like dota or LOL, then why can't others like women's clothing? Anyway, it was the only temporary girlfriend I could find and I guarantee it won't get exposed.He looks very similar to his sister and can even pass off as her twin sister. "

Perhaps my last sentence struck a chord with Xiao Ding, he hesitantly said, "Then bring him over Saturday afternoon and let me take a look, then I will decide whether to take him or not&"

"Then it's settled." I said, "But you have to remember, whether you agree to take him or not, you can't say a word about it to Shu Sha. If his sister found out, we will all be in trouble."

Xiao Ding laughed bitterly: "Of course, it's already humiliating enough to need a temporary girlfriend. If people found out it was a cross dresser, then I wouldn't even be able to leave my house anymore. Besides, I couldn't really talk to Shu Sha in the first place&

On Saturday afternoon, Shu Zhe lied to his sister. He came to my house under the pretext of using my home gym equipment.

After he freeloaded a takeout meal at my place, he ran proudly to the large bedroom to change. He even warned me not to peek. Who would even want to see your naked body, maybe I would if it was your sister.

After nearly an hour of dressing up, I almost didn't recognize Shu Zhe when he came out of the room.

The "girl" standing in front of me was wearing a denim skirt with a small denim jacket. The jacket was open and revealed a white shirt adorned with silver flowers. There were also suspicious bulges under the shirt (should be breast pads).

Below the denim skirt and on top of the black stockings was a snow white absolute territory which can definitely become the focus of attention of passing men.

He had a pair of white canvas shoes, the kind with leather tassels with a cute style. I felt pain thinking about the fact that I would have to bear the cost of these shoes.

As for his appearance, he really does look like the class leader's twin sister. Although he used bangs and medium length hair, he also doesn't have the class leader's domineering aura, but if he was seen by acquaintances they will still suspect he was related to the class leader.

To further increase the difference, I asked Shu Zhe to wear the colored contacts he used before when he took those rope model pictures, which made him seem more multiracial.

"Hey, I'm only doing it for money. Can you stop staring at me, it's embarrassing."

He may have said that but he already admired himself multiple times in the mirror. And every time he turned around, he would subconsciously twirl his skirt.

At 4 in the afternoon, I brought the cross dressing Shu Zhe out to meet up with Xiao Ding.

Since he now has experience from walking at night in women's clothing and I was by his side, Shu Zhe was much more fearless than usual. Perhaps talking to Cilantro Buns through video chat has also increased his confidence.

He walked next to me while being slightly behind me. The passing men and women cast thirsty or envious looks and it made Shu Zhe elated.

The most unbearable part was that many men also sent me looks of admiration, they must think that I'm Shu Zhe's boyfriend.

Shu Zhe took in all of those looks and became even more proud and arrogant.

What is there to be proud of? Your breasts are fake! Dressing in women's clothing attract more attention and it's a great way for a super vain like yourself to inflate your self worth.

In order to avoid anyone recognizing me or causing unnecessary trouble, I put on a pair of sunglasses before I left. So the passing men are just jealous that I have a beautiful girlfriend and didn't really give looks like they just saw beauty and the beast.

Shu Zhe originally carried a more neutral satchel to put his daily supplies, but when we passed a bag store, he suddenly said he wanted to buy a more appropriate satchel for his current look, and he walked into the store without saying another word.

After entering the store, Shu Zhe had a natural and smooth conversation with the female sales associate. He left me standing foolishly to the side waiting to pay the bill as if I was actually his real boyfriend.

After spending more than ¥400 on a bag, Shu Zhe transferred his stuff over and happily put on his new bag. He then gave me the old bag to be put away.

"You're taking advantage of the situation." I said angrily after we left the store "I only promised to reimburse you for your outfit. I never said I would buy you a bag again."

Shu Zhe gently lifted up a lock of his long hair and said with disdain: "A bag is part of a girl's outfit."

Of course, Shu Zhe's spoke with his "fake girl voice". Ever since he started speaking with the sales associate, he has been using a gentle feminine voice to speak. He didn't arouse any suspicions, even when I knew the truth, I can't help but admit Shu Zhe was nearly unparalleled in pretending to be a girl.

"Anyway, there's no such thing as a good business. Since you were the one who introduced me to Xiao Ding as a temporary girlfriend, you must have gotten a lot of benefits too."

Shu Zhe conjectured while full of malice.

"I never got anything." I denied, "Why can't you believe that there are 'friends' who don't only try and see what benefits they can get from the relationship."

"Because I don't have that kind of friend." Shu Zhe replied bluntly, "Some of them are my 'friends' because I'm generous or that I have a beautiful sister. The ones who used to be jealous of me and bad-mouthed me behind my back came begging like dogs for me to be their friend after they heard you were protecting me. Although I despise them, I still allow them to be my friends. There's no harm in it and friends are meant to be used anyway, who knows when they will come in handy one day."

Hmph, he might look like a sweet girl on the outside, but he's still as selfish as ever on the inside.

We met Xiao Ding in front of Xinhua bookstore and he was stunned once he saw Shu Zhe.

"Uh& Xiao Ye, you better not be playing with me." Xiao Ding pulled me over and whispered into my ear, "She's clearly a beautiful girl, why are you saying she's a man?"

"Okay." I nodded, "It's fine if you want to treat him as a girl, does he meet your requirements?"

"His appearance is first-class, but her voice&"

After careful consideration, Xiao Ding felt there was no reason for me to bring a girl then insist she a boy, but he was still a bit concerned about the voice.

Shu Zhe looked at the slightly chubby Xiao Ding with contempt, he crossed his arms in front of his chest and spoke:

"Cut the crap, give me my money first. Who knows if you'll stiff me like brother Ye Lin."

The "fake girl voice" made Xiao Ding faint a bit when he heard, it was clear he thought it was really cute. He pulled out his wallet without saying a word, then gave all the extra money he earned pretending to be a tiger to Shu Zhe.

Shu Zhe took the money and checked the watermark against sun out of habit, then carefully placed it inside his new bag.

The people who came in and out of Xinhua bookstore were suspicious when they saw two men making a payment to a woman in the streets. Some people whispered and suspected we were carrying out an illegal transaction.

To be honest, I really did look like a pimp standing in the middle of the transaction while wearing sunglasses. Fortunately, we didn't run into the police or tomorrows headline in the newspapers would be "Middle school student prostitutes cross dresser".

"Say, are you really Shu Sha's brother, Shu Zhe?"

Xiao Ding asked an unbelievable question.

A disgusted expression instantly appeared on Shu Zhe's face when he heard his name.

"Don't call me by my real name, what if we get found out? From now on, call me by my pseudonym, Xiao Hong."

So he was still using the name that was derived from Southland Red Berries? I guess he was accustomed to it after constantly being called that by Cilantro Buns on video chats.

"When does the otaku gathering end?"

Shu Zhe played the role of a barbaric girlfriend in front of Xiao Ding.

"About 8 o'clock, I think&" Xiao Ding wasn't short, but when he talked with "Xiao Hong", he would always lower his head and blush, appearing much weaker.

But it's already considered good compared to his usual. When Xiao Ding saw a beautiful girls, he couldn't even say a word, so a cross dresser was the best option for a temporary girlfriend.

"Then, brother Ye Lin, come here at 7:40 to pick me up. Don't be late, got it?"

Eh, it looks like Shu Zhe really plucked up some courage to speak to me like that.

"Brother Ye Lin, can you not put on a scowl?"

"I have to leave my outfit and my new bag at your place before I can go home, otherwise my sister might find out and then you& and you&."

He pointed at me and Xiao Ding, "You would both be out of luck."

I have to admit Shu Zhe had a point. Plus, Xiao Ding, who was going to receive Shu Zhe's help, could only nod and didn't dare disobey.

The Xinhua Bookstore was only two stops away from the cafe. Xiao Ding suggested to walk over so they could get their stories straight and not get exposed at dinner.

Shu Zhe, however, complained that his feet hurt from walking in new shoes and asked Xiao Ding to take a cab. Xiao Ding hesitated for a second, so Shu Zhe wrapped one of his arms around one of Xiao Ding's arms and pouted.

"I want to take a cab~~~"

Xiao Ding's face suddenly turned red and steam erupted from his head like he was drunk. He beckoned a cab while staggering and then the two of them rode it away together.

Before entering the cab, Shu Zhe gestured me with his eyes as if to say, "Look how stupid men are, all I have to do is use a little charm and they are at my beck and call."

Remember that you're also a man before you say such things.

I watched the cab drive away, then I returned home bored. Other than running the online store, I was still a little worried that Shu Zhe and Xiao Ding would mess things up.

I went to Xinhua bookstore at 8pm to pick him up (I deliberately didn't t go at 7:40). He arrived nearly half an hour late and looked completely out of it. I asked him what happened, but he would not say.

After changing, he reluctantly left his women's clothes behind at my house and went back home.

It was strange, usually he would ask me money for a cab home. Plus, I only paid for the new bag, he still hasn't asked for reimbursements for the rest of the outfit which wasn't like him.

Is it possible Xiao Ding couldn't control his lust and raped him? But Xiao Din wasn't that kind of person and Shu Zhe's clothes weren't damaged, so what was going on?

I called Xiao Ding several times that night, but he didn't answer. Fortunately, he was there when I went to look for him at the pet hospital the next day. He said he would treat me to a meal while telling me what happened last night.

I noticed that the corners of Xiao Ding's eyes were bruised. He also had cuts over his arms like he was beaten.

Did he meet violent resistance when he tried to lay his hands on Shu Zhe? If that was the case, Shu Zhe would have asked for a psychological damage fee, why was he silent?

Xiao Ding ate the shredded potatoes with rolled spring pancakes while looking out the window, then he sighed and said:

"Actually, last night, I got into a fight with the leader of the LOL faction, the guy whose id is 'Unending Flow'."

Ah, so it went from an online flame war to an offline PK battle.

As far as I know, this is what usually happens in their online flame wars:

First, the Dota veterans comment: "LOL players are dogs." Then LOL guys reply: "If you dare come play a game with us, we'll wipe the floor with you." The dota players gets angry: "LOL is a retarded game only elementary school students play, real men play Dota."

After the end of their usual arguments, they will enter the next stage where they go back and forth three hundred rounds, which looks like the below:

Dota faction: "You're dumb." LOL faction: "You're dumb." Dota faction: "You're dumb." LOL faction: "You're dumb."

After three hours both sides would be exhausted and there would be no winner. They would each retreat back to their own sides.

I didn't think two sides who could only curse at each other online actually had the courage to do a real life PK battle. Was this the sign of an all-out war?

I asked Xiao Ding how they got into a fight. Xiao Ding took a bite of his pancake and said:

"It all started with Unending Flow. He introduced himself as Fan Chuan or 'Xiao Chuan'. He was indeed a university student and his girlfriend was a classmate and I couldn't hind any holes in his story&"

Huh, the name Fan Chuan sounds familiar.

Speaking of Fan Chuan, wasn't he the one who in love at first sight when he saw Shu Zhe and said it didn't matter that he was a trap? He even said he would break up with his girlfriend.

So he was the leader of the LOL faction in Dong Shan city. It looks like he didn't break up with his girlfriend and even flaunted his girlfriend in front of the dota faction.

I can't really remember what Fan Chuan's girlfriend looks like, but I remember she was wearing high heels and looked like a pretty serious type of girl. It must have been hard for her to attend a video game meeting full of otakus with her boyfriend.

It was supposed to be 6 couples meeting at the cafe, but in the end, only 2 pairs of couples came from each side. It seems like there were braggarts in both sides.

As for Shu Zhe, he still attracted everyone's attention as expected. Everyone in the cafe used going to the washroom as an excuse to deliberately walk past him and sneak a few more glances.

Xiao Ding was naturally pleased that his "girlfriend" was far more beautiful than the others. He crossed his legs and and began to yak about the superiority of dota, as if it was all thanks to dota that he was able to get a girlfriend.

But Shu Zhe was more nervous.

It's not that he lost confidence in cross dressing abilities, but it's because he recognized Fan Chuan and was afraid of being exposed.

But Fan Chuan didn't do that, instead he stared devotedly at Shu Zhe and even wasn't focused on the conversation on which side was superior, which made his companion very dissatisfied.

The offline meetup ended early with a weird atmosphere and Shu Zhe took a long breath in relief. As he was about to put on a pretense and walk out a bit with Xiao Ding, he realized Fan Chuan was following him.

"Xiao Hong, are you really Xiao Hong?"

Fan Chuan called out to the two from behind in an eager tone.

"Go out with me. It's fate that I was able to meet you a second time!"

Shu Zhe was scared to the bone and Xiao Ding was even more astonished. Then a wave of anger surged through his body and shot straight to his head.

He blocked himself in front of Shu Zhe and said to Fan Chuan: "What the hell are you talking about, don't you have a girlfriend? Why are you hitting on my girlfriend, do you want a real life PK?"

Fan Chuan adjusted his collar and sneered: "In order to find my true love, I just officially broke up with my girlfriend. She wants to study for graduate exams and I want to play LOL, so we don't have the same goals in life anyway."

She broke up with you that easily? It looks like she can't tolerate you anymore, I sincerely hope she can find a more reliable person.

Xiao Ding said angrily: "It doesn't mean you can hit on Xiao Hong just because you broke up with your girlfriend, just leave."

"Xiao Hong, tell me the truth, you're not actually this fatty's girlfriend, right?" Fan Chuan ignored Xiao Ding and shouted directly at Shu Zhe, "The relationship between the two of you doesn't look right. Come with me and I promise you won't regret it."

Shu Zhe couldn't speak because he felt guilty and Xiao Ding and Fan Chuan argued some more. Fan Chuan finally couldn't help but reveal the truth.

"Damn fatty, Xiao Hong is cross dresser, not a real girl. Are you still going to fight me?"

Xiao Ding retorted, "I'm not fat, I'm just big-boned& huh, how did you know Xiao Hong was a cross dresser?"

Fan Chuan acted smug, "I just know. I already knew I liked cross dressers the first time I met him. Do you also feel the same way? If you don't, then let go and let the cross dresser run to a happier future."

Xiao Ding looked at Shu Zhe, who looked more awkward than usual, and a sudden heroic spirit rose from within and he shouted:

"Don't look down on other people, so what if he's a cross dresser, I feel the same way as you. I will never hand Xiao Hong over to you."

Xiao Ding seems to have completely forgotten that Shu Zhe was only a temporary girlfriend for that night.

Fan Chuan provoked, "If you're not willing to let go, then then let's have a duel between men. Whoever wins gets Xiao Hong, okay?"

"Then let's duel. We might have to 1v5 towards the end game for dota, but you would only 1v3 in LOL, so you're not my opponent."

Xiao Ding didn't forget to state the superiority of his game even when he was about to fight, he really is qualified to be a member of the dota faction.

It was a large street fight between Xiao Ding and Fan Chuan, and it attracted the a large group of spectators. The two otakus had limited fighting power and there was a low chance of them giving each other serious injuries. Xiao Ding's black eye was the most serious injury obtained in the fight.

"What are these two people who look like university students doing?" The spectators began to discuss among themselves.

"What do you think? There's a beautiful girl standing near them, so they must be fighting over a girl."

"Say, their girlfriend looks a bit young, is she a middle school student? She really doesn't know how to cherish herself, she's so young but already seducing all kinds of men&"

"Strange, why does that girl look familiar."

I'm not sure if that person has seen Shu Sha somewhere before, or has seen my the rope model photos from the online store, but the fact people began to question his identity gave Shu Zhe quite the scare.

Shu Zhe, who was already feeling uneasy because of the fight between Xiao Ding and Fan Chuan, was now in danger of having his identity exposed. Plus, being in women's clothing and all those psychological blows caused him to begin crying in public.

"So cute&"

Fan Chuan, who had a few scrapes on his face, suddenly said.

"What?" Xiao Ding didn't understand.

"I mean, the crying Xiao Hong is also cute. Cute enough that I want to raise her, I want to comfort her with my embrace, get out of the way."

"No." Xiao Ding defended his dignity as a man, "If you want to touch Xiao Hong, you have to step over my dead body."

"This little vixen really knows how to seduce men&" a middle-aged woman who was jealous of Shu Zhe's beauty said in a very loud voice.

"What did you say?" Fan Chuan immediately gave up on Xiao Ding and ran to to question the middle-aged woman, "How dare you call my girlfriend a vixen? You better apologize to my girlfriend or I won't let you go easily."

Xiao Ding, who had no experience with girls, also aimed his attacks at the middle-aged woman when he saw Fan Chuan change his target, "You're not allowed to say any words that hurt Xiao Hong, apologize."

The middle-aged woman was probably a tiger mom at home. She spat on the ground and said: "A slutty vixen is a slutty vixen. I'm not going to apologize, what are you going to do, hit me?"

Xiao Ding was hesitating, but Fan Chuan was eager to outperform in front of Shu Zhe and he slapped the middle-aged woman on her face. The middle-aged woman immediately cried out: "He hit me! He's going to kill me!" Then she and Fan Chuan tore into each other.

Xiao Ding saw the situation getting more and more chaotic and it wasn't a good place to stay or they may get taken away by the police for questioning, so he took Shu Zhe's hand and called a cab to send him back.

Shu Zhe looked outside the car window and saw Fan Chuan fighting the middle-aged woman because of him and felt a bit bad.

As a male, he has never enjoyed such care and attention, especially in front of me, because I often hit him on the head.

I don't know what he was thinking, in any case, Shu Zhe didn't let Xiao Ding accompany him and left in the cab by himself.

Afterwards, Fan Chuan was locked up for a few days because for hitting the middle-aged woman, but he said he had no regrets, because "it was all for the sake of love".

Xiao Ding, who was chatting with me, had bewildered eyes.

"Xiao Ye, do you think there's something wrong with me? Xiao Hong is very beautiful, but he's a cross dresser, I originally didn't really think of him that way& but Fan Chuan knows he's a cross dresser and broke up with his long term girlfriend to pursue him& I now feel like the times have changed and there's nothing wrong with getting a cross dresser as a girlfriend&"

Of course there's soothing wrong! Don't get influenced by that pervert Fan Chuan. If you go after Shu Sha's brother as one of my buddies, then sooner or later the truth will be exposed. If there's a billion to one possibility that you do become a couple with Shu Zhe, then Shu Sha will rip me into parts since I was the one who introduced you to him.

"What does Xiao Hong like?"

It was like Xiao Ding was looking through rose-tinted glasses.

"He likes money." I replied in a bad mood, "If you want to chase him, then earn 5 million first."

"5 million? Even if I win the lottery, it's not enough after paying tax&"

Xiao Ding said to himself in a daze.

I really want to throw myself at a wall.

I loaned him Shu Zhe out of the goodness of my heart, but didn't expect him to fall to a cross dresser's charm.

That means there's now three men pursuing Shu Zhe. It includes Tang Jiang, who doesn't know his identity as a cross, dresser and Fan Chuan and Xiao Ding, who do know.

As a male but having three male suitors will piss off those girls who no one wants.

But what was going on with Shu Zhe last night?

As a male, he said he had no sincere friends, but as a female, he was enthusiastically pursued by two people last night. One of them was even detained for him. Did this kind of devotion touch some inner part of Shu Zhe's heart?

Shu Zhe, who always acts weak in front of strong people, will be the type who wants to be pampered and conquered. He took the initiative to be my little brother, so he could get benefits at school, but I refused to step up my game to protect him.

I guess he realized a lot of people were willing to risk their lives to protect him when he wore female clothing?

That means it's true being a cross dresser will turn people bad. Those people online were right, the sense of being pampered will turn a person into a complete degenerate. I feel that the Shu Zhe's motive for cross dressing is becoming less pure. He clearly loves the female version of himself and even his thinking is turning more feminine.

After parting with Xiao Ding, I subconsciously avoided high-rise buildings because I always felt that there might be a sniper with long, flowing hair nested above.

If Shu Zhe changed his sexual orientation, then I will be blamed as the initiator. The day Shu Zhe goes to the Netherlands to marry a man is the day the class leader uses me as a blood sacrifice.

In a blink of eye, there were only two more weeks until summer break.

In other words, there was the same amount of time left before the finals.

Other than the politics exam on July 5 which was an open-book exam, I have to make sure to not get careless on the other exams. My dad didn't really have any requirements for my grades, but I always felt I should at least reach the minimum standards.

The only exception was English where my scores were usually in the single digits. I wouldn't be able to create a miracle no matter how hard I tried hard.

The students also communicated less as we entered the cramming period for the finals, but since 28 Middle was chosen as the examination site for the high school entry exams, we were able to get a rare break during that time.

Although the high school entry exams meant the basketball team's captain Guo SongTao will graduate, but on the bright side, we were given three days of vacation from June 25 to June 27.

But although we can be rest for three days from June 25 ~ June 27, we have two attend two days of classes on the weekend on the 29th and 30th. It's still not that bad since some schools will have classes on two consecutive weekends, which meant that you actually had to attend an extra day even after given a three day break.

By the way, I just learned that Gong CaiCai's birthday is on June 26th.

That day is also the International Day Against Drug Abuse and Illicit Trafficking, International Charter Day, and the International Day in Support of Victims of Torture. I always felt that God let Gong CaiCai be born on this day because there's some kind of hidden meaning of protecting the weak.

On Monday, June 24, Gong CaiCai sheepishly invited the class leader to attend her small-scale birthday party the day after tomorrow.

"Because, because my parents left for Hainan for business matters, I was given permission to invite some of my classmates to come and spend my birthday with me, but I can only invite a maximum of five people& class leader, can you come?"

"Of course I'll go." Although it was close to the finals, the class leader still agreed, and she looked very excited, "I still haven't felt the white rabbit enough the the last time I went to your house."

"The rabbit&" Gong CaiCai apologized and lowered her head at the class president, "My parents didn't let me keep it, so I've already passed it on to my aunt to take care of it, I'm sorry to disappoint you&"

Are they talking about the rabbit they got on the pedestrian bridge? If it was touched by the class leader, it must have been shivering with fear. It might still have nightmares of the class leader's hunter aura while living at Gong CaiCai's aunt's place.

Since Gong CaiCai's parent set a limit of five people and Gong Cai Cai was very obedient, choosing five became a very difficult task. After careful considerations, she invited the class leader, Loud Mouth, Little Smart, Xiong YaoYue, and another unknown person.

Originally, Gong CaiCai only planned to invite the class leader, Loud Mouth, and Little Smart, because those three were the ones who bullied her the least in class 2-3. The other girls either cause trouble for her because of jealousy (like Xiao Qin) or take advantage of her because she's a weakling. As for inviting a boy, she never even considered it.

Even though Gong CaiCai instructed them to keep it a secret, Xiong YaoYue still heard about it from Loud Mouth. She immediately went to Gong CaiCai and questioned why she wasn't invited to the birthday party.

"Is it because I eat too much? Loud Mouth eats way more than me. Invite me, I'll bring a cake."

Loud Mouth came up from behind, "You always bully Cai Cai, so it's normal for her to not invite you."

Xiong YaoYue got anxious, "I& it's because Cai Cai is too cute, I can't help but bully her. I still consider Cai Cai as a good friend, if she doesn't invite me, my heart will break. From then on I'll become an emotionless zombie running continuously around the track.

A zombie who really likes exercise?

Gong CaiCai loosened up a bit after Xiong YaoYue begged her.

"If you stop bullying me until the final exam, I& I'll let you attend my party&"

"Hip hip hooray." Xiong YaoYue jumped three feet in the air to celebrate, she landed then suddenly asked mysteriously.

"Cai Cai, I heard that you can invite a total of 5 people, did you pick someone for the last spot?"

"No& I can't think of anyone else, it will just be the four& "

The class leader glanced at Xiao Qin's empty seat like she wanted to invite Xiao Qin, but it was Gong CaiCai's birthday, so she shouldn't overstep her bounds. They can't just invite another person to participate simply to fill the quota of 5 people. Plus, Xiao Qin took off early in the morning because of menstrual cramps, so she might not even get better before the day after tomorrow.

Xiong YaoYue, however, didn't have as many inhibitions as the class leader and she cheerfully suggested.

"I have a new good friend I made, can I bring them along to Cai Cai's birthday? I really hope you guys get to know each other ah, because you're both cute.."

Gong CaiCai asked awkwardly, "Is& she also a girl?"

"Yeah." Xiong YaoYue two eyes flashed with anticipation, "I won't bring any boys to Cai Cai's to cause trouble, I'm bringing a cute girl."

"Then, in that case, you can bring her&" Gong CaiCai feebly agreed.

"Thank you, you won't be disappointed.." Xiong YaoYue once again made a celebratory "hooray" gesture.

"Wait." The class leader stopped them, "Cai Cai is the host, so what if you brought someone who doesn't match her personality. Your birthday only comes once a year, but if it becomes unpleasant&"

Before the class leader finished speak, Xiong YaoYue whispered something into her ear. The class leader blushed a little then quickly changed her stance:

"Another person is fine, the more the merrier. Maybe we can even become good friends hahaha&"

What a suspicious laugh, who's the person Xiong YaoYue wants to bring that made the class leader instantly change her opinion? She blushed in the same manner as when she sees a cute animal.

I don't care, it has nothing to do with me anyway. Gong CaiCai definitely doesn't have the guts to invite boys to her house and now the quota of 5 people is already full. I'll just leisurely enjoy my three day vacation.

On the afternoon of the 26th, I received a message from Ai Mi saying she was going to attend a 'civilian event' and asked me to accompany her. Peng TouSi was the one who drove her outside my home.

I sat in the back with her full of doubts.

"Manservant, when we get there you can't speak out of place, look at me before acting, understand?"

Ai Mi crossed her legs, her rainbow socks looked like it came out of a fairy tale world. The bowknot used to her double ponytails was also extremely cute.

"What exactly is the civilian event?" I questioned, "Some sort of community warmth event?"

"It's not a big deal." Ai Mi squinted one eye, yawned, and pretended to be disinterested and said, "I was invited by Winnie to go to a commoner's birthday party people. I was bored today anyway&"

Huh, isn't that Gong CaiCai's birthday party? So the "good friend" Xiong YaoYue was going to bring is you! The class leader treated you like a cute animal the last time she saw you at Henderson Mall and kept on trying to pet you. So that's why the class leader changed her mind, it's because she really wants to pat your golden hair.

Then wouldn't I be the sixth person? I'm also a boy, so Gong CaiCai will be worried about being scolded by her parents, even though one more person isn't a big deal&

"Why should I accompany you?" I suddenly felt it would be a bit awkward if I was the only boy with six other girls.

"It's because I need to have a bodyguard." Ai Mi said in a serious tone, "Winnie can't even beat a kangaroo, so her fighting ability still needs to be improved before she could be considered a competent bodyguard. If I don't take you with me, then I have to take Peng TouSi."

Then you would rather take me. Peng TouSi, who looks like King Kong, would look even more out of place among middle school girls.

In addition, if the qualification test to become Ai Mi's bodyguard was to beat a kangaroo with bare hands, then I'm afraid not many people would be able to pass. If you're that focused on a kangaroo, why not just hire a kangaroo as a bodyguard?

I suddenly remembered I still don't know my sister's birthday.

"By the way, Ai Mi, when's your birthday? Winnie and I will come to celebrate when the time comes."

Ai Mi shivered for some reason, then spoke while looking out the window, "I don't like celebrating birthdays, it's noisy. Only commoners celebrate their birthdays like a holiday."

No way. If you're dressed so beautifully, it means you definitely value the birthday party. Or are you extremely excited and curious because you've never been invited to a commoner's birthday party?

Peng TouSi, who was driving silently, said with a laugh, "The Miss isn't too fond of her birthday because it's the anniversary of Leslie Cheung's death, it's a bit unlucky&."

I'm not surprised a gay person like Peng TouSi knows Leslie Cheung, but I don't think Ai Mi would know Leslie Cheung. But the day Leslie Cheung jumped off a building was April 1 or April Fool's Day. That means Ai Mi's birthday happens to be the same day as April Fool's Day, what a tragedy. Even if she sincerely invited others to attend her birthday party, they will probably take it as a lie.

"Peng TouSi, shut up, do you want to die."

Ai Mi viciously stopped all conversation about her birthday.

After driving in the fast lane for a while, the car stopped in front of a ten-story apartment building. When you looked up, the dark blue glass walls reflected the sun's rays, so people couldn't look straight at it. Gong CaiCai really does live in a very luxurious place.

Before I could open the car door, Xiong YaoYue ran out to welcome us, but she was obviously stunned when she saw me.

"Eh, you're here too?" Xiong YaoYue scratched her head and frowned, "I told Cai Cai that I would only bring one friend over and didn't count you, so wouldn't that be one more person?"

Ai Mi said with some dissatisfaction, "The manservant is my bodyguard, so he doesn't count as a person."

"Oh, that's right." Xiong YaoYue easily accepted it, "Then let's hurry up, the class leader has already started to prepare dinner. As the two 'food gods' we can't miss the opportunity to show off our skills."

Hey, you should at least hesitate a little bit, why do I not count as a person? This is discrimination against bodyguards!

And please, you two should have some self-awareness. If we let you prepare dinner, then everyone will get poisoned and bleed to death.

We left Peng TouSi to wait in the car as me, Ai Mi, and Xiong YaoYue rode the elevator to the eight floor and rang the doorbell to Gong CaiCai's home.

After hearing a pleasant ring, Gong CaiCai personally came over to open the door.

"Sorry for the long wait&"

Halfway through her sentence, Gong CaiCai saw the doll-like Ai Mi and the conspicuous me behind Ai Mi and she froze for a moment.

Xiong YaoYue introduced her to Gong CaiCai: "This is my new good friend, isn't she even cuter than you thought? I've wished you guys could meet for a while now."

Ai Mi's expression was cold as she tilted her head and casually swept a glance towards the interior.

"Ha, is this a commoner's birthday party, it's an unexpectedly shabby place."

How is it shabby? It's a 280m2 (approx 3000 sq ft) duplex condo with top grade decorations. The living room alone was 60m2 with a dazzling chandelier in the middle.

Are you using alien standards to judge this place as shabby? It's really rude to say such harsh words to the birthday girl, so I have to find a way to apologize to Gong CaiCai.

I didn't expect Gong CaiCai to apologize instead.

"I'm sorry, we could only do some simple decorations&"

Ai Mi gesture at me with her finger then pointed to Gong CaiCai. I didn't understand what she meant and raised one eyebrow waiting for her to explain.

"How stupid, I wanted you to give out her birthday present. Otherwise, what's the point of bringing a manservant."

I then suddenly realized the bag Ai Mi asked me to bring out from the car was Gong CaiCai's birthday present. Despite all the verbal nitpicking, Ai Mi still knew the basic etiquette for attending a birthday party. It might have been her first time meeting Gong CaiCai, but because she was Xiong YaoYue's friend, she also had to carefully prepare a gift.

There was a rectangular crimson box. My first guess was it was some sort of jewelry.

When I took the box out and gave it to Gong CaiCai, she received it timidly and was embarrassed to say even the usual polite words. Xiong YaoYue stuck next to Gong CaiCai and whispered in her ear: Miss Ai Mi is Ye Lin's distant cousin and her family doesn't want her out alone, so they sent Ye Lin with her, I hope you don't mind."

Gong CaiCai nodded with an unknown meaning, then she expressed her gratitude to Ai Mi for the gift and invited her inside to rest on the sofa.

"Hey, you big breasted cow, do you not like my gift?"

Ai Mi crossed her arms in front of her chest and was very dissatisfied.

"B-big breasted cow&" Although people often called Gong CaiCai that behind her back, she didn't know how to react when someone said it straight to her face.

Xiong YaoYue once again whispered in Gong CaiCai's ear, "Miss Ai Mi is an American, and it's an American custom to open a gift on the spot when you receive it then complement them. It would be even better if you say you really like the gift."

"Thank you, thank you for, tis, this gift&" Gong CaiCai clumsily opened the gift and was a bit tognue-tied when she expressed her thanks.

"Don't be afraid." Xiong YaoYue encouraged Gong CaiCai, "Miss Ai Mi might seem mean, but she's a very affectionate person. She was very worried about me after I was attacked by a kangaroo."

"Who was worried about you?" Amy turned her face away to one side, "I just thought it would trouble me if you died of rabies."

Gong CaiCai had opened the gift box, on the metal-trimmed black velvet pad, laid a magnificent rose gold watch.

The Omega logo was bery conspicuous and each hour on the watch had a diamond embedded on it. The face of the watch also had snowflake diamonds on it almost as if diamonds didn't cost anything. The diamonds and the 18K rose gold made the watch shine.

Ever since Director Cao got a watch merchant as an investor, he often brings international watch promotional pamphlets to school, I also took a few as to use as pads& I think I saw this brand of women's Omega watches before. I don't know the exact model, but the cheapest in the series costs ¥47,000 and the most expensive one is ¥600,000. The rich really lives in a different world than us.

"Hey, it's a nice watch. Cai Cai, try it on and see if it fits."

Xiong YaoYue, who didn't understand its worth, suggested.

Gong CaiCai, however, trembled, she might have seen her parents' friends wearing thses expensive watches, and hastily declined, saying.

"It's such an expensive gift, I& I can't accept it, I appreciate your kindness&"

Ai Mi's sapphire blue eyes immediately filled with killing intent.

"What, you actually don't like it?"

"No&" Gong CaiCai felt pressured by Ai Mi despite being two years older, "It's just that this gift is too expensive and I really can't&"

"Don't worry about if it's expensive or not ,just say if you 'like it' or not."

Being forced to choose one of two options, Gong CaiCai could only reply, "I like it&."

"Hm, since you like it, show me your appreciation."

"Thank you for the gift, I like it very much&" Gong Cai Cai parroted as if she was being trained by a beast tamer.

Ai Mi waved her hands to tell Gong CaiCai to move to the side and she strided into the living room that was filled with ribbons and balloons.

"What should I do about this?" Gong CaiCai held up the expensive watch like it was a headache and didn't know what to do with it.

"Anyway, put it away first." Xiong YaoYue, who still didn't know the real value of the watch, didn't think the same way as Gong CaiCai.

Gong CaiCai's living room was covered with light brown carpet, so it seems they were the same as Xiao Qin's family and didn't wear slippers. Ai Mi's complexion changed right when her rainbow socks touched the carpet and she said in alarm: "There's killing intent."

Before she could evade, she was picked up from behind by the class leader who had just taken off her apron and rushed out of the kitchen. The class leader acted excited like she just saw the world's cutest animal.

"Let me pat your head, just once. Just once is enough."

Ai Mi shouted at me to help after she was captured by the hunter, but it was a rare oppotunity to see the class leader's infatuated expression. Ai Mi, please sacrifice yourself a bit for your brother.

"Why is Katyusha here?" Ai Mi yelled furiously at Xiong YaoYue, "Why didn't you tell me beforehand?"

"Huh, is this Ye Lin's distant cousin that Winnie talked about?"

Loud Mouth and Little Smart also came out of the kitchen one after another. The formed a circle with the class leader and surrounded Ai Mi.

"What a cute mixed child. She looks nothing like Ye Lin, exactly how 'distant' are they?"

"Who's related to the manservant." Ai Mi was hugged by the class leader and forcibly had her face rubbed without being able to escape, "The manservant is my subordinate, I picked him up off the streets. Commoners like you are not allowed to touch me, manservant, get rid of them."

I shrugged my shoulders and spread my hands to use a common American gesture to show that my hands were tied.

It's wasn't easy to have an opportunity to mingle with ordinary girls, so I should my sister get familiar with normal human interaction.

As this point, it was like the class leader just realized I was also a guest at Gong CaiCai's birthday party.

She gave me a look as if to warn me not to interfere with the happy interaction between her and Ai Mi.

How is Ai Mi happy, the only one happy is yourself! Now that I think about it, cats who are caught by cat lovers and petted all over may not feel happy either. Ai Mi had the same expression a cat would make in the same situation.

And Ai Mi was unable to resist at all. Ai Mi only had 0.5 times of Gong CaiCai power, but the class president had 3.5 times Gong CaiCai's power, which meant she was a whole 7 times stronger than Ai Mi.

Little Smart, who had been silent for a long time, suddenly looked at Ai Mi and said, "I had a blonde Barbie doll when I was a child and it really looked quite similar to her&"

The class leader's eyes suddenly dazzled, "Didn't we just see a lot of Cai Cai's childhood clothes when we were in her room that were all well-preserved, why don't we&"

When she set her gaze back on Ai Mi, Ai Mi had a look of despair like she was a deer caught in a hunter's trap.

Loud Mouth suddenly understood and clapped her hands, "class leader, all girls dreamed of dressing a real doll as a child. Today, we have a chance to make it a reality&"

"NO~~~~~~~~~~"

They ignored Ai Mi's cry and led by the class leader, the three girls dragged Ai Mi into Gong CaiCai's room and locked the door.

Before the door was closed, Ai Mi stared at me with frightened eyes, as if asking why I didn't save her& but it wasn't good to disturb the class leader who rarely acts wild. And Ai Mi has always been too arrogant, so occasionally being "bullied" would be beneficial to her growth, right?

Then I could hear the cheerful discussion of the girls coming from inside the room.

"This pair of denim overalls is also cute&"

"Then lets try this white princess dress, but her rainbow socks are a bit out of place. Class leader, you hold her down from behind, and let's take off the rainbow socks first&"

"Stop, stop, you barbarians, who said you were allowed to take off my clothes? I'm already an adult, I'm not wearing children's clothes. I'm not going to wear children's clothes, do you hear me?"

"What does it matter, we're all girls. But your underwear is so mature, the class leader doesn't even wear this mature underwear&"

"Bastards, how dare you humiliate me. Just you wait, I'm going to have Peng TouSi kill you all, and kill the manservant who neglected his duties. Winnie, Winnie, hurry up and save me!"

"Ah, the door's locked, I can't get in." Xiong YaoYue pretended to knock on the door, then looked back at me with a smile and whispered, "Actually, I want to go in and have some fun too. Even the class leader is having so much fun, I'm also itching to have some fun."

Ai Mi was extremely unhappy after being forced to wear different outfits even after she changed back to her own clothes. She threatened multiple times she would call Peng TouSi and tell him to kill us all with submachine gun. She calmed down reluctantly after Xiong YaoYue did her utmost to apologize on behalf of the class leader.

It was a weird situation because it was usually Xiong YaoYue who caused trouble and the class leader dealing with the aftermath, but it was reversed today.

Ai Mi puckered her lips as she sat on the sofa and sulked. She scared Gong CaiCai who came to pour drinks, it was like Ai Mi the was the interviewer for a job and Gong CaiCai was the interviewee.

The class leader treated Ai Mi like a small animal, after she had her fun, she went back to the kitchen to prepare tonight's banquet. Gong CaiCai's aunt originally wanted to order from a restaurant, but the girls led by the class clear, decided to cook their own meal. They could also improve their relationships through cooking and the aunt thought it was interesting, so she agreed.

"Youngsters have their own way of having fun, so I won't stay here to spoil the fun." After telling everyone to be safe, Gong CaiCai's aunt made sure there was enough food and left.

"You didn't even hire a chef for a birthday dinner?" Ai Mi mocked while eating the pistachios Xiong YaoYue peeled for her, "If Katyusha kneels down and begs me, I can lend my chef to you guys."

Loud Mouth was cutting onions loudly on the chopping board, and Ai Mi's voice was completely smothered.

"My eyes hurt." Loud Mouth couldn't stand it after a few chops, "I'll be washing my face with my tears if I keep on cutting. I'll have to rest a while first."

"I'll cut it." Gong CaiCai felt apologetic about being excluded from the kitchen, so she enthusiastically asked to help Loud Mouth.

"No, it's okay." Loud Mouth waved her hand in a hurry, "The birthday girl herself doesn't need to do any work, and there aren't many plates left&"

Everyone knew Gong CaiCai was clumsy and would often trip and fall for no reason at school, but it was the first time I've heard about her destructive power in the kitchen.

She was weak and had poor balance, plus the fact that her ample breasts may have partially obscured her view, it caused her to frequently break dishes.

Especially the large plates that were used to hold the food, they are all bound to break as soon as they pass through Gong CaiCai's hands.

After Gong CaiCai broke seven plates, the class leader realized that she can't let Gong CaiCai enter the kitchen anymore. If she kept on breaking plates, other than the fact they wouldn't have enough plates for dinner, the class leader's heart wouldn't be able to handle it anymore either.

"In the future, Cai Cai has to marry a rich man." Loud Mouth teased, "Otherwise, just the money he has to spend on plates will make him bankrupt."

"I, I don't break this much every day&" Gong Cai Cai blushed, "I'm just a bit more nervous today&"

In addition, Ai Mi gave Gong CaiCai her birthday gift right when she entered and broke the usual routine of giving birthday gifts after blowing out the candles. So Xiong YaoYue suggested everyone should give their gifts to Gong CaiCai in advance.

The class leader gave a very beautiful DIY gift. You might not believe it, but it was a lampshade made with a few hundred cola can pull tabs plus old lighting to make a lamp. Even Ai Mi was impressed with the class leader.

Loud Mouth gave a crystal ball bedside ornament, with the sleeping beauty inside it; Little Smart gave a peace bracelet, but no matter what it looked like prayer beads to me.

Xiong YaoYue prepared a pair of jeans for Gong CaiCai.

"I've never seen Cai Cai wear jeans, so I bought her a pair. What do you think, the material is very strong and wouldn't get damaged even if you craw or roll."

I think that's your own standard, Gong CaiCai doesn't need that strong jeans, it's not like she's going to participate in a triathlon. Gong CaiCai's life would already be in danger before the jeans gets damaged.

"Thanks, thanks&" For some reason, Gong CaiCai face turned red, "I love everyone's gifts, but there's a reason why I don't wear jeans&"

"Is it because you're afraid of your curves being seen by boys?" Xiong YaoYue blurted out, making me, the only boy present, very embarrassed.

"What's there to be afraid of?" Ai Mi interjected, "Being watched means you're attractive, although they do get annoying&"

After Ai Mi found a bottle of cola in the fridge and half a bag of chips, she sat on the sofa lazily enjoying it and no longer said she wanted to leave.

Gong CaiCai's face reddened even more and said hesitantly, "Its, actually not just jeans, I have difficulty wearing any clothing that requires a belt because it's hard to see the holes and takes a lot of effort to put on&"

"How?" Xiong YaoYue patted her own belt, "I could wear my belt in less than ten seconds every morning, Cai Cai you just need to get used to it."

Ai Mi had a chip between her fingers as she stared at Xiong YaoYue's chest for a moment, then stared at Gong CaiCai's chest for a moment, and suddenly realized:

"It's because her chest is too big. Her line of sight is blocked by her chest, that's why it's inconvenient when putting on a belt, no wonder she's a dairy cow."

Gong CaiCai was so ashamed she wanted to crawl somewhere and hide. Xiong YaoYue and class leader couldn't really think of any words to comfort Gong CaiCai.

It reminds me of that joke: men with big beer bellies can't see their penis. It turns out that women with too large breasts also have a lot of unspoken troubles.

"Eh, Ye Lin, what gifts did you bring?"

Xiong YaoYue just had to bring it up. I was suddenly called out by Ai Mi to act as a bodyguard, so I didn't even know I was going to Gong CaiCai's birthday party, otherwise I definitely would have prepared one beforehand. That's not good, I was the only who didn't bring a gift, it's so embarrassing. Gong CaiCai if you found a place to hide, we could go in together.

"I brought the manservant, so he's like my carry-on luggage. Have you ever seen luggage give people gifts?"

Ai Mi defended me.

Although it was true, it would be even more perfect if the luggage didn't need to eat.

"Ye, Ye Lin classmate actually already gave me a gift&" Gong CaiCai whispered as she twiddled her thumbs, "The little rabbit is living very well at my aunt's house, I still go visit it often&"

"What, the rabbit was a gift from Ye Lin?"

The class leader, who hadn't spoken, was surprised and she frowned slightly as if she wanted to ask when I was on gift giving terms with Gong CaiCai, but swallowed her words after thinking carefully.

"Let's go and cut onions." The class leader said to Loud Mouth, "It won't irritate your eyes if you freeze the onion in the freezer for a while."

"It's true." After trying it, Loud Mouth admired the class leader's housewife experience.

The common saying was "three women are enough for a drama". Now that there were six girls in the room, including the two gossip masters Loud Mouth and Little Smart, it was incessant chatting and I wasn't interested in any of the topics.

Clothes, beauty, dieting& relationships, enemies, who got married, who got divorced& even Ai Mi perked her ears up and would say a few lines once in a while about how even American gossip is better than China's.

I was bored, so I strolled to the study and found a book to read. I put a copy of the Classical Chinese Tales of the Supernatural on the ground to read while doing push ups.

"101, 102 &&" right when I was reading the shower scene, I suddenly had a tingly feeling on my scalp like someone was watching me.

I looked up at the window, but there was nothing there. However, it felt like I saw a black shadow disappear from my peripherals.

I went to the window and looked outside carefully, but I couldn't find any clues. Ai Mi called me loudly at the same time, so I returned to the living room.

It turns out that Xiong YaoYue, under Ai Mi's orders, managed to mess up the sweet and sour fish dish the class leader had almost finished cooking (does anyone even want to eat spicy and salty sweet and sour fish). The class leader chased those two food destroyers out of the kitchen. They couldn't stay, but they found a violin in Gong CaiCai's bedroom.

"Eh, Cai Cai, do you play the violin?" Xiong YaoYue's eyes widened, "How come I've never heard you mention it before? If I knew, I would have let you perform on stage at last year's New Year's party."

Ai Mi muttered on the side, "I hate the violin&" Ai Mi, who was forced to practice various instruments as a child, had a good reason to not like instruments.

"I, I don't play it well&" Gong CaiCai squirmed and tugged at her skirt, "I can't perform in front of people at all&"

"What are you afraid of?" Xiong YaoYue stuffed the violin into Gong CaiCai's hands, "Play a song for us. Ai Mi is an expert and she can give you some guidance."

"Really, can I really play it? My skills really aren't up to par&"

The more modest Gong CaiCai was, the more curious Xiong YaoYue got. Loud Mouth and Little Smart also came over to join in on the fun, finally allowing Gong CaiCai to pluck up the courage to pick up the violin and start playing.

She had a serene expression with a slight smile. She had elegant movements and it was clear Gong CaiCai has worked hard on this aspect of the violin. She probably hired a tutor and she really likes this instrument.

But& liking is not the same as being good at it. What is this terrible sound? It sounds like a cat beating up a baby.

Xiong YaoYue was shocked and Loud Mouth and Little Smart were both petrified. Ai Mi covered her ears in horror and even the class leader who was busy in the kitchen, had flames erupt from her frying pan.

The most frightening part was that Gong CaiCai wasn't aware of it at all. She was still intoxicated in playing the dream violin melody that existed only in her own mind.

A bang was accompanied with the 'homicide serenade' and a short-haired girl fell through the balcony window and laid on the balcony without moving.

"Damn, is the underwear thief back?"

Xiong YaoYue rushed to the balcony to see what was going on. Gong CaiCai's also stopped playing the violin for the time being, so everyone breathed a sigh of relief.

The young girl who fell onto the balcony was clearly not the underwear thief. She was wearing finger gloves for better grip and she was also wearing a pair of warm socks.

Xiao Qin always made sure her lower extremities was warm when she had menstrual pains, plus she had a history of climbing buildings, so the one who was shot down by the terrifying violin sounds was without a doubt Xiao Qin.

Damn it, didn't I tell you not to do anything dangerous. What would you have done if your hands slipped?

Xiong YaoYue turned Xiao Qin over and was shocked when she got a closer look at her face.

"Xiao Qin, why did you come in through the window?" Xiong YaoYue shook Xiao Qin, who was stunned by the horrible violin sounds, "I already noticed you were different during the volleyball game, could it be& your real identity is Spider-Man?"

Xiao Qin blinked after she became more clear-headed. She looked at Ai Mi who was sitting next to me and played dumb.

"Sorry, I got lost and accidentally stumbled in here. I had absolutely no intention of spying on Ye Lin classmate or anyone else&"

Would an ordinary person get lost and end up on the 8th floor? It's obvious you came to spy on me and based on your expression I could tell you still have menstrual pain. That's quite the dedication to follow me while bearing the pain.

Before I could speak, Ai Mi suddenly jumped up from the sofa. She ran a few steps and kicked towards Xiao Qin's waist as hard as she could.

Of course, she didn't hit because Xiao Qin nimbly avoided it and naturally used the momentum to stand up. Only after seeing everyone's flabbergasted looks, she covered her forehead like she was exhausted.

After Ai Mi missed the blow, she stood opposite to Xiao Qin and said angrily: "Stop using getting lost as an excuse& my men have been lost many times, but none of them have ended up in front of the windows of a high-rise building. It's so obvious you came to spy on the manservant, plus you weren't even invited to the dairy cow's birthday, so even if you are lost, you can leave now."

I don't think you received a direct invitation from Gong CaiCai anyway. Plus I don't think it's right constantly calling the host a dairy cow.

Xiao Qin was left speechless after being reprimanded by Ai Mi. She looked at Gong CaiCai with a pitiful expression.

Gong CaiCai, who was often bullied by Xiao Qin, couldn't stop shaking as she wasn't sure what Xiao Qin was going to do.

"Sob sob sob, I want to participate in Cai Cai's birthday party too."

Xiao Qin suddenly sat down and tears poured out as she rubbed her hands around her eyes.

"I also want to eat birthday cake, why didn't you invite me~~~ aren't we good friends~~~ I'm so sad."

Whose your good friend? Are you the kind of good friend that threatens to flip up their skirt if they don't let you copy their homework?

Gong CaiCai, who's usually always crying, also can't stand seeing others cry. After Xiao Qin cried for over ten seconds, Gong CaiCai mumbled:

"I& I originally intended on inviting more people, but my parents only let me invite a maximum of five people. Since we're already over the limit, you can join in too& the more the merrier&"

"Thank you so much." Xiao Qin immediately stopped crying and jumped up from the ground. She then looked at the vacant position beside me after Ai Mi left and headed over to sit down.

"Keep dreaming." Ai Mi, who had seen through Xiao Qin, also ran back and tried to get back to her seat first.

Xiao Qin didn't try her best since there were a lot of people around, which resulted in Ai Mi sitting on the sofa first. As if to declare ownership, she grabbed my left arm, just before she finished her sentence: "The manservant is my&"

She was sent flying by Xiao Qin's butt.

I hurriedly wrapped my arms around Ai Mi's slender waist to prevent her from falling down on the carpet. Ai Mi, who lost her spot, turned around and glared at Xiao Qin. She let out a low growl from her throat similar to that of an angry baby lion.

"How did you get in here?"

Loud Mouth and Little Smart were still confused as to how Xiao Qin had suddenly appeared outside the window.

"I said I was lost~" Xiao Qin said perfunctorily, and after a while she changed her tune, "Perhaps it was sleepwalking. A lot of people have abilities they don't normally have when sleepwalking and it turns out I'm so powerful when I'm asleep, hahahahaha&"

"Nonsense." Loud Mouth said, "I could only open the refrigerator to eat when I sleepwalk."

At this time, the class leader came out of the kitchen and she asked Loud Mouth to keep an eye on the stove.

"Do I have to stir fry the food every couple of minutes?" Loud Mouth asked.

"No." The class leader said, "It's already cooking on low heat, you just have to block the entrance to prevent Winnie from going in and messing with it."

The class leader glanced at Xiao Qin who was sitting beside me and she had a slight smirk. The class leader must have knew Xiao Qin used her martial arts skills to get outside the window.

"Don't do this again." The class leader said to Xiao Qin in a serious tone.

"Okay." Xiao Qin raised one hand and promised, "I won't sleepwalk anymore, I'll make sure to tie myself up before I go to sleep. Of course, it would be even better if Ye Lin classmate ties me up&"

Xiong YaoYue ran over to the balcony and looked around like she was checking to see if Xiao Qin used any tools.

"Is it possible a window cleaner just passed by?" Xiong YaoYue asked herself.

"You're hiding something from us." Little Smart patted Xiao Qin's shoulder with a serious expression, and then glanced at the violin that Gong CaiCai put back in the bedroom, "But good job, your appearance saved everyone."

Ai Mi, who was robbed of her seat by Xiao Qin and was unwilling to sit anywhere else, suddenly had a strange idea to sit on my lap.

"What are you doing?" I exclaimed. Although my sister was as light as a feather, the intimate physical contact wasn't something I was prepared for.

I could feel Ai Mi's curves through her thin skirt and it felt criminal.

However, Ai Mi was unaware of my thoughts and treated my body as a "throne" to declare victory. She had a smug posture and looked down at Xiao Qin and said:

"When I need it, the manservant will act as my chair. You will always just have to be content sitting next to the manservant."

I thought it was inappropriate, so I put my hands under Ai Mi's armpits and tried to lift her off, but she turned around and glared at me fiercely. Xiao Qin also had an expression of "I'll sit there as soon as she leaves," so I gave up on my plan.

"That's a goog relationship between cousins." Little Smart said in admiration.

Ai Mi snorted, she didn't bother correcting them anymore.

"They are not cousins&" Xiao Qin muttered quietly to herself as if she was also reminding me of my relationship with Ai Mi.

I understand without you needing to remind me. The evidence is that I didn't pitch a tent even when her clothing is so thin. Especially when Ai Mi kept shifting around and grinding on top of my lap.

After 5 minutes of suffering, I felt like I was reaching my limits, so I hurriedly excused myself to the bathroom and let Ai Mi sit in my spot on the couch.

Gong CaiCai's bathroom was large. The transparent glass surrounding the bathtub and sauna room all looked high, the tub at Xiao Qin's place feels narrow in comparison.

Right after I walked out of the bathroom, Ai Mi was waiting for me outside.

She looked at me with a frustrated look and asked, "Are you not feeling well lately."

I had a bad cold after the basketball tournament and later got drunk once, but overall I'm still quite healthy, why do you ask?

Ai Mi crossed her arms in front of her chest, "It's so rude to have a cute girl sit on your lap and not react at all."

Why would that be rude? Would it be polite if I pitched a tent, where did you even learn your manners?

"When I sat in Santa Claus' lap at the mall when I was a kid, his stood up straight and saluted me. You're a mere manservant, do you think you're better than Santa Claus?"

Where did that pedophile Santa Claus come from? If I met him, I'll make sure he couldn't stand up again. I used a great deal of effort to suppress my reaction, but in the end was accused of having "no manners". Ai Mi's outlook on life has been corrupted, if I don't correct it she would be hopeless.

When Xiao Qin was using the bathroom, the class leader and told everyone that Xiao Qin "suffers from severe androphobia. Although her body was fine, she occasionally loses control, so she can't perform strenuous exercise", which slightly reduced everyone's doubts.

"That's what I said. Xiao Qin's mother is an MMA champion, how could she not inherit some martial arts skill."

"Huh, I have a doubt." Xiong YaoYue suddenly said, "If Xiao Qin has androphobia, why isn't she afraid of Ye Lin?"

The class leader explained, "Because Xiao Qin and Ye Lin are childhood friends, so they're used to it."

"If you're used to your childhood friends, there's no reason to be afraid of other boys, right?" Little Smart pointed out.

The class leader frowned and coughed before saying, "It's probably& probably because Ye Lin looked like a girl when he was a child, and Xiao Qin didn't& realize."

It was the complete opposite! The class leader completely sold me out in order to cover for Xiao Qin! Look at everyone's expressions, even Gong CaiCai was curiously staring at my face wondering how I looked like a girl.

"It's true." The class leader emphasized, "I've seen the photos of Ye Lin when he was a child and he's much better looking than now. He even& looked like a cross dresser."

The girls laughed even harder.

Who's a cross dresser? Your brother is going on dates dressed in women's clothing, so you're not qualified to say that about me!

Xiong YaoYue asked a serious question:

"Eh, then if Xiao Qin's androphobia is that serious, then wouldn't she only be able to marry Ye Lin?"

"What are you guys talking about?" Ai Mi, who found another bottle of Coke from the refrigerator, interjected, "The manservant will never marry the violent girl. He's only temporarily acting as her girlfriend to play with her feelings."

Everyone was shocked by her statement, excluding Xiao Qin who still hasn't returned from the bathroom. The class leader, Xiong YaoYue, Loud Mouth, Little Smart, and Gong Cai Cai, all looked at me like I was trash.

Of course, the subtext in everyone's gaze was different based on their personalities.

The class leader's eyes said: didn't you say she will be your stepsister in the future? What kind of trash plays with the feelings of their stepsister?

Xiong YaoYue's eyes said: I thought only pretty boys can play with girls' feelings, can Ye Lin even be a playboy with his appearance?

Loud Mouth and Little Smart: found trash&.

Gong CaiCai: Ye Lin classmate told me before he was scum and likes to womanize, so it was true&

"Hey, you guys misunderstood, it's all a child's nonsense." I hurriedly defended myself and kept sending glances at Ai Mi. Ai Mi clicked her tongue, then she turned her head to ignore me and focused on drinking her cola.

At this time, Xiao Qin returned to the living room and everyone tactfully ended the discussion.

"It's my first time helping a classmate celebrate their birthday, I'm a bit nervous&"

Xiao Qin spoke to Gong CaiCai as friendly as possible which only made Gong CaiCai more uncomfortable and she couldn't help but shiver.

"Speaking of which, apart from Cai Cai, when is everyone else's birthday? How about we all spend it together in the future?"

Xiao Qin continued to ask with a smile on her face.

"My birthday passed in May." Xiong YaoYue said grumpily, "At that time the Wasteland Wolf team celebrated my birthday at a internet cafe and the team captain personally played support for me. In the end, we were unlucky and lost seven times consecutively. I get mad just thinking about it&"

"Mine and Little Smart's birthday are during winter break." Loud Mouth said with a bit of regret, "We always celebrate it with family every time, so we don't really have a chance to invite classmates, what a pity."

Ai Mi, whose birthday was on April Fool's, silently went to the balcony to look at the scenery, but soon came back because of her fear of heights.

"(^__^) Hehehe& since everyone finished, my birthday is on July 28. I really hope to receive a gift from Ye Lin classmate."

Hey hey, the class leader and I still didn't say our birthdays. Even if you know my birthday, you shouldn't skip over the class leader. Do you not want me to know the class leader's birthday that badly?

The date July 28 also sounds familiar. Didn't we learn in history class that World War I started on the same day? So Xiao Qin was born on the outbreak of World War I, no wonder she's always surrounded by carnage.

"I remember the class leader was born on New Year's Eve, right?" Sure enough, someone brought up the class leader's birthday. Loud Mouth laughed and said, "It's because the class leader was in a rush to leave the womb, so she's the only dragon in our class and all the other students are snakes."

"I can't control when I'm born&" the class leader wasn't proud even though there was a saying that dragons rule snakes. It's probably because the obsessive compulsive class leader wants to be a snake like everyone else.

As for me, I was born only a few hours later than the class leader, so I was born on the first day of the year of the snake. I lost the majestic "dragon" title, and I was younger than the class leader by a year based on the lunar calendar even though the difference is only a day.

Ai Mi suddenly asked, "Violent girl, what gift did you bring?"

Ai Mi used the question I was troubled with earlier to stump Xiao Qin. The two of them were always causing trouble for each other.

Gong CaiCai hastily came out to resolve the dispute, she waved her hand and said, "No need for gifts, I'm happy that everyone is here&"

"I'm sorry." Xiao Qin sincerely bowed at Gong CaiCai, "I came out in a hurry and didn't bring any gifts, I'm so sorry."

"To show my apologies, I'll perform a magic trick."

Huh, I knew Xiao Qin knows martial arts, but I never heard she knows magic. Is she going to use her super fast hands to perform a slight of hand? I have to keep my eyes open to see if I can catch the trick.

"What magic trick are you going to perform?" The class leader was also curious.

"Hmph, at most she's going to make some cutlery appear." Ai Mi didn't think much of Xiao Qin's performance.

"I& I'm going to transform a person."

Xiao Qin shouted confidently.

"Disappearing act." Xiong YaoYue said excitedly, "That's quite a difficult magic trick. Xiao Qin you can perform it without being on stage? I want to see it, I want to see it."

"Uh huh~" Xiao Qin coughed, "I need a volunteer to participate&"

"Pick me, pick me." Xiong YaoYue raised her right hand in excitement.

"Sorry, I'm not that skilled at this trick, so the volunteer must be Ye Lin classmate."

Xiao Qin said and took a step closer to me, while Ai Mi made the threatening expression of a fierce dog protecting its food.

I'll volunteer. I'd like to see Xiao Qin's skills, and what she could do to make me disappear.

"In addition to Ye Lin classmate, I also need some other props." Xiao Qin continued, "Cai Cai, do you have a blanket I can borrow."

"A blanket?" Gong CaiCai was surprised, "Don't they usually use red cloth?"

"Haha, my school is more traditional, we're used to using blankets."

How much arm strength would a magician need to use a blanket to make a person disappear? Is it actually tearing the blanket apart and stuffing the person inside? Please don't destroy Gong CaiCai's property and please don't destroy the reputation of magicians!

After Xiong YaoYue enthusiastically carried over a blanket, Xiao Qin didn't take it, but instead told Xiong YaoYue to spread it out in the middle of the living room.

It's not the typical routine I'm familiar with.

Xiao Qin laid her hands out flat with her palms down, then mumbled a bunch of gibberish. If you listen carefully, you can hear her say something about the skies and the spirits.

I thought it was time for the volunteer to take the stage, but I didn't expect Xiao Qin to take a step forward and naturally lie down on her back on top of the blanket.

Her eyes were closed and her hands were clasped together in front of her chest, both like a prayer and the posture of a mummy.

Everyone was baffled and held their breath, not knowing how Xiao Qin was going to perform her trick.

"Ye Lin classmate." Xiao Qin called my name with her eyes closed.

"It's your turn."

"Eh, what should I do?" I walked next to the blanket and looked at Xiao Qin who was lying flat on her back.

"Just pounce."

"What?"

"Just throw yourself on top of me." Xiao Qin's tone suddenly turned coy, she rubbed her two well-proportioned legs against each other, "Pounce on me like you wanted to do before. Hold me down under you and do what you love, then after ten months my magic trick&"

Magic trick my ass. First, there's no way you can get pregnant while your on your menstrual period and there's no way I would mate with you in front of others.

Xiao Qin closed her eyes and called out, "Come Ye Lin classmate, I can't perform the trick without you&"

I hit Xiao Qin's head with a knuckle and brought tears of pain to her eyes.

"Ah, Ye Lin classmate is bullying me, he said he would be a volunteer."

I'm a magic volunteer, not a sperm donor volunteer, give me something a little more normal.

"Hahahahaha,." Xiong YaoYue suddenly covered her stomach and laughed, she pointed at Xiao Qin and said, "This is too interesting, it's not magic but a comedic skit. I have to write it down, it may come in handy later. Class leader, let's let Xiao Qin perform this at the next New Years party.

"So it's a skit." Loud Mouth breathed a long sigh of relief, "I thought Xiao Qin was serious when I saw her expression earlier. You shouldn't make these kinds of jokes even if you are childhood friends."

No, Xiao Qin was serious. If I didn't set the line right now, then Xiao Qin would have actually performed a real life AV video in front of everyone. She was using the gift as an excuse to show off her dominance to the class leader and Ai Mi.

"I'll go check on the food." The class leader's words caused the conversation to turn in a normal direction. After Xiong YaoYue put away the blanket, everyone agreed the blanket event was now over.

As the girls resumed their conversation about cooking, I noticed the class leader hiding in the kitchen, trying desperately to wipe a plate.

Why wasn't she using water, was she trying to be frugal? I went over to say something, but when I got closer, I noticed that she was wiping the plate with a piece of sandpaper and the plate she was holding was missing a piece.

"What are you doing class leader?" I was very puzzled, and the class leader was embarrassed she got caught.

"Nothing, just& recycling it&"

I suddenly realized: was class leader going to sand the plate smaller so the hole would disappear? I think that would be as difficult as grinding an iron pipe into a needle. It might appear to be frugal, but it's incredibly stupid.

"Don't bother." I grabbed the plate and threw it into the trash, "No matter how many plates Gong CaiCai breaks in the future, someone will always buy them for her, so what are you doing?"

The class leader glared at me with discontent. At this moment, Xiao Qin walked in happily and took a deep breath.

"It smells delicious. Class leader, teach me how to cook."

Of the 6 girls not including the class leader, Xiong YaoYue and Ai Mi were cooking disasters, Loud Mouth only knows hot to eat, and Little Smart was more inclined towards vegetarianism, so none of them had good cooking skills. If we remove Gong CaiCai who always destroys plates and ingredients, then Xiao Qin will be the second best option.

"Just in time, you can help me out. Since you still have menstrual pains, I'll wash the vegetables, okay?"

"Alright." Xiao Qin nodded at the class leader and put on the kitchen slippers.

"By the way, help me block the kitchen door." The class leader laughed lightly and said, "Don't let Winnie and Ai Mi come in, or our dinner will be ruined."

Although I was no longer worried Xiao Qin would secretly attack the class leader, I was still a little worried Xiao Qin would commit mischief (such as deliberately making the class leader's cooking awful, so that she would be embarrassed in front of the others) but it turned out that my worries were unnecessary. Xiao Qin was very serious about learning cooking with the class leader, and seemed to have made up her mind to learn from her enemy.

The average person might think that spending a birthday with so many girls is great, but in fact it's quite the opposite.

If it was a boy's birthday and there was only one girl attending, then she would be treated like a star.

The reverse is not true. In this birthday party, as the only boy among 7 girls, I became the target of bullying and teasing.

"Ye Lin, I heard you were working as a substitute actor inside that show "Bloody Battle of Jin Ling", is that true?"

Loud Mouth was the first to launch an attack.

"Occasionally, a few scenes here and there&" I replied sheepishly.

"So will you be an actor in the future?"

"No way&" I laughed to cover it up the past. It would be nice if I can act as a hero like Bruce Lee or Jet Li, but if I always have to play the villain&

"What about kiss scenes? Have you ever done a kiss scene as a substitute actor, it must be very exciting."

"Loud Mouth, do you get dumber when you're hungry? Why would you need a substitute actor for a kiss scene? Unless the female lead is too ugly, it would always be the male lead acting in the kiss scene."

"That's boring. That means you're only responsible for the somersaults, jumping around, and getting beat up?"

It's not wrong to say that, but it sounds a bit embarrassing&

"Who says you don't need a substitute for kiss scenes?" Ai Mi suddenly spoke, "I always have a substitute shoot my kiss scenes."

Kiss& kiss scene? Did Ai Mi already progress to kiss scenes? With who, that bastard Kyle?

Everyone's heard about Ai Mi's "singer-actor"reputation, but Ai Mi's hasn't really talked much about it so everyone thought she was only a regular child actor. But the class leader was very interested in Ai Mi's performance, so she asked Xiong YaoYue to give her some records and some recordings of Ai Mi's performances to her.

"I always use a substitute for my kiss scenes." Ai Mi said like she was an industry expert, "Rather than a substitute, it's more accurate to say doll. In "Life of Pi", whenever the male lead interacts with the tiger, the tiger is just a doll. That means all film and television are all tricks, fortunately there are still brain dead people who are willing to watch it."

Ai Mi suddenly stared straight at Gong CaiCai as if she had discovered something new about her.

"Hey, dairy cow, do you want to be on TV? If you're willing to take off, I'll can offer you a bath scene in our show."

Gong CaiCai was terrified, "No, please forgive me, showing my body in front of a camera, I& I will faint."

"What does it matter, everything below your shoulders will be under water&. but forget it if you don't like it, how boring."

The topic soon turned into the hard and interesting parts of working at Film City. Ai Mi, spoke about mostly hard work, while Xiao Qin, a bystander, spoke about a lot of interesting things.

"The day before yesterday the crew hired two elephants from the circus for filming. Who would have expected the elephants to steal beer, they ended up destroying several studios and they incurred heavy losses."

"Hmph, what's so funny, only people who knows martial arts like the violent girl and her mom could look at it as a joke. Ordinary people like us were in danger at the time, but thanks to the elephants, I could rest for two days&"

I finally had a use at dinner time as I helped serve the dishes. The result of the class leader and Xiao Qin's efforts was a table of sumptuous food.

Pineapple sweet and sour pork, fresh salad, sweet and sour fish (remade after being trashed by Xiong YaoYue), stirfry eggplants, candied sweet potatoes&

The meat and veggies were well-matched and seasoned with care. I haven't eaten her cooking ever since I hugged her and now I feel so nostalgic.

Actually a birthday banquet wasn't much different from an ordinary dinner party, but on top of the eating and drinking, there were also blessings made to the birthday girl.

"May Cai Cai grow more and more beautiful." That was an blessing made by ordinary girls like the class leader, Loud Mouth, and Xiao Qin.

"May Cai Cai's life be more diverse." That was a blessing made by literary girls like Little Smart.

"May Cai Cai's breasts get bigger and bigger." That was a blessing made by stupid girls like Xiong YaoYue.

"The last one, doesn't count." Gong CaiCai quickly denied it, as if there was a fairy who could make the blessings come true listening in, "I would sometimes use my stockings to wrap up my chest when I sleep hoping it would get smaller&"

Ai Mi and I were the only ones left who didn't say a blessing. After Ai Mi finished her cola, she hung one arm on the table with boredom.

After listening to the previous conversations, Ai Mi said in a strange tone, "So, would you be happy if I wished your breasts to get smaller?"

"Yeah." Gong CaiCai agreed quickly, "I am working towards that goal, thank you."

I carelessly noticed Xiao Qin who was sitting on my left secretly clench her fist. She must have thought that Gong CaiCai's trouble was detestable. But it's her birthday, so I won't ignore it if you cause a scene.

I breathed a sigh of relief after Xiao Qin worked hard to suppress her jealousy. I raised my glass that was filled with fruit juice and wished Gong CaiCai to get better grades. It was probably the best blessing for a student and Gong CaiCai was also satisfied.

After the blessing, it was time to blow out the candles and cut the cake. When the lights were turned off, I suddenly found a small, tender hand on my thigh.

I don't even need to say that it must be Xiao Qin's hand. You actually have the nerve to sexually harass me in front of so many people?

I acted without thinking and hit towards her hand. But before I hit her, Ai Mi had noticed Xiao Qin was assaulting her manservant, so she reached over and tried to swat Xiao Qin's hand away.

As a result, I struck the back of Xiao Qin's and Ai Mi's hands simultaneously. The two of them both shrieked simultaneously, which made the class leader towards us suspiciously.

Don't misunderstand, they did scream because of me, but it wasn't because I took advantage of the darkness to touch them. It's more correct to say they were the ones who touched me, of course, the credibility of the statement was low& but at least believe me that I won't molest my own sister.

"Ye Lin classmate is so rough&" Xiao Qin murmured.

"The manservant actually hit the master? I guess you don't want to get your monthly wages anymore."

Hey, I don't even get paid or are you talking about that unlimited American Express card? That card was wasted a long time ago, your information is too delayed. I'm basically working for free as your brother, so you should at least be a bit grateful.

Gong CaiCai puffed up her cheeks and blew out 14 candles in one breath, then closed her eyes and made a wish.

Loud Mouth meddled and asked, "What did you wish for, was it to find a good husband?"

"Ignore Geng YuHong." The class leader said, "The wish won't come true if you tell us."

"There's nothing to hide&" Gong CaiCai said shyly, "My wish is world peace. It's what I wish for every birthday&"

"Why is it world peace?" Loud Mouth questioned, "World peace isn't even something the UN can control and your wish doesn't really benefit yourself either."

"Well& it's actually good for me." Gong CaiCai explained, "My elementary school teacher once taught us the saying 'It's better to be a dog in a peaceful time than be a man in a chaotic period', if a war started&"

"I see." Xiong YaoYue suddenly realized, "Cai Cai is really far-sighted. If there's a third world war, I, the class leader, Xiao Qin and Ye Lin can join the army to serve the country. Loud Mouth and Little Smart can go work in the propaganda department. Only Cai Cai can't work or cook, so when the time comes, she may be forced to become a comfort woman& sob sob& what a sad fate."

As a result, the class leader grabbed her ears and taught her a lesson. After Xiong YaoYue came to her senses, she repeatedly apologized to Gong CaiCai. It's not always good to be straightforward.

"It's true I would be useless in a war." Gong CaiCai admitted, "But I pray for world peace mainly for the weak animals to survive. Otherwise, when even humans can't survive, the animals will suffer even more&"

Perhaps Gong CaiCai was really an animal protectionist, she did eat very little meat which was a stark contrast to me who only ate meat dishes.

I thought the day would end on a peaceful note, but then I suddenly received an anonymous text message.

"Ye YuanFeng has been arrested for carrying a large amount of drugs. If you don't want to drag down your father, you should come and surrender."

The message was signed off with 'Ma'.

Damn Constable Ma. It's likely if you caught my father when you're doing a porn sweep, but there's no way he touched drugs, who framed him?

It was followed by another message:

"Come alone to the first streetlight on Xinhua North Street before 9, I want to talk with you. Don't be late."

It was still signed with a 'Ma'.

What does Constable Ma want to do, does he want to make an exchange with me for my dad? But with his character, if he thinks my dad is guilty, he won't ever let him go, right?

Anyway, it was not the time to continue celebrating Gong CaiCai's birthday. I stated I had an emergency and had to leave early. Both Xiao Qin and Ai Mi asked me almost simultaneously what had happened.

I said goodbye to everyone as if nothing had happened, and refused Xiao Qin's offer to go with me and Ai Mi's offer to drive me. I headed out alone and took a cab straight to Xinhua North Street.

I called my dad's cell phone several times on the car, but it kept telling me it was unavailable. I couldn't reach him through the hotel's landline either.

Did my dad really get caught? I would like to ask Constable Ma his ulterior motive of meeting with a suspect's son in private.

Xinhua North Street was once one of the most prosperous streets in Dongshan city, but along with the reconstruction of the city, many department stores closed down one after another, leaving only big "demolition" words on the old red walls.

I really don't know what's Constable Ma thinking meeting in this place.

And the first street light specified in the text message was broken. As the sky grew dim, I felt uncertainty welling up inside.

I know that Constable Ma is very punctual, and it is only 8 o'clock. He asked me to meet at the designated place before 9 which made him seem like he had a lot of time to wait for me, but he's usually very busy with narcotics work in the morning and organized crime in the afternoon.

I might have placed too much trust in those text messages. The contents and tone may be consistent with Constable Ma's character, but it really could have been anyone.

Right as I was about to leave, I noticed four tall and sturdy men walking towards me from both ends of the street. They were each wearing a ski mask like a bank robber and carrying a baseball bat.

It's my enemies, but I don't know who. I've made enemies with many teenagers before but none of them ever hired grown men as thugs to create a fake text to lure me out&. it has to be someone who knows me well, who was the one who sold me out?

The attacker's bat struck the post of the street light with a clang. I dodged while asking them their identities, but since they were wearing masks, it meant they had no intent of revealing themselves. They were completely silent while attacking me like they were all zombies.

I was heavily outnumbered and they had weapons. Even someone like me who isn't that smart knows to retreat first.

I stared into the eyes of the tallest masked man and sent him killing intent with my eyes.

Of course, you can't actually kill people with your eyes. I just wanted to test if they were professionals.

However, he didn't show any response to my killing intent, but was rather indifferent.

It was extremely unusual. Due to over 100,000 years of hunting instincts, men will always get excited in fights no matter how weak the opponent is. But my opponent was completely apathetic like he was a walking dead.

Wait, don't tell me they are actually zombies? I'm not an alien orphan nor have I been bitten by a mutant animal, so it's not necessary to send zombies to deal with me. Since I didn't know their backgrounds, there's nothing to be ashamed of from running away from four adults, so I turned and ran.

Although their expressions were apathetic, their movements weren't sluggish. The four men arranged themselves in an orderly fashion and blocked my escape routes from all directions.

The wind pressure created by the bat swept past my head and the side of my body. I broke out into a cold sweat as I dodged left and right and exhausting myself.

"Who the hell are you people?" I asked again, but no one answered.

Another swift and merciless blow came at me, although it didn't hit me, it still grazed my pockets. I hope my phone did not break.

Wait, I can use my cell phone to call for help. If I call Peng TouSi, he can take down anyone regardless if it's 4 adults or 8 zombies. I shouldn't have tried to act tough, if I listened to Ai Mi and brought Peng TouSi with me, I wouldn't be in this predicament.

But there was a deeper reason for refusing Ai Mi's offer and it was because I thought it was Constable Ma who invited me out here. If Ai Mi was here with me then it might have been awkward if she might my dad since she was his ex-wife's daughter.

But now the situation is completely different, it was a trap. I didn't even have time to take out my phone and make a call against the four masked men.

"Hey, hey, what's your emergency?"

The phone in my pants suddenly asked loudly in hands-free mode.

I was stunned and didn't immediately react, then the voice said again.

"110 is not a joke, if you call 110 and it's not an emergency, then it is a waste of national resources. It's a serious matter and you may be found liable for&."

Eh, when did I dial 110? I always lock the phone after I use it, so there's no chance of accidentally dialing the police. Did the swing of the bat earlier accidentally brush against the phone and dial 110 with one in 100,000 odds?

Although I couldn't believe it, I couldn't pass on this god given opportunity. I did my best to answer the 110 operator and said:

"I, I have an emergency. I'm in a dangerous situation where I'm being attacked by four masked men with baseball bats! I'm at Xinhua North Street, you'll have to collect my corpse if you don't send someone fast."

The operator may have received too many false alarms, because he didn't believe me and asked, "Why are they attacking you?"

As if to verify my words, the four masked men launched a new round of attacks. The bats collided with a brick wall and let out an unmistakable ring. I dodged while frantically yelling at the operator:

"Now do you believe me? I'm dead if you don't send help."

The operator then believed my words and instructed me: "I'm immediately sending people over, hold on."

Although the situation hasn't changed, I was much more confident with police assurance and I bellowed at the four masked men.

"I don't care who you are, but the police are coming, so get ready to eat lead."

Although I know not all police officers carry guns, it's always good to scare the criminals.

The result was better than I expected. The four masked men exchanged glances and easily gave up and retreated.

The police arrived on scene as the last masked man disappeared into the night. I later learned that the nearest police station was less than 100 meters away, that's why the policed arrived so fast.

There were traces of the fight left at the scene which proved I didn't lie. According to regulations, I had to go to the police station to record a statement. They asked me if I knew their identities, I could only say my luck was bad and ran into a rebel youth motorcycle group.

They weren't really a motorcycle group since they didn't even have motorcycles.

I was in deep thought on my way home after the police let me go.

First, I contacted my dad again, and this time I was lucky enough to get through to his cell phone. He said he was getting harassing phone calls two hours ago, so he turned it off.

As for the matter of being caught with drugs, it was completely false.

I really can't figure it out.

The person who lured me out with a fake text message must be someone who knows me very well. He even deliberately harassed my dad on the phone and confirmed beforehand that he was not at the hotel, making me believe that my dad had really been arrested.

And it definitely wasn't a simple prank. The four adults looked like they spent at least half a year in the gym to get their physiques. Someone who has those kinds of resources is definitely not just trying to prank me.

However, the most puzzling thing for me was the call to the police.

I have never won a lottery in my life. Even the number of times I've won those another bottle prizes in soft drinks can be counted on one hand. How can someone who has such shit luck make a lucky call to 110?

I would have died today without the call to the police.

I can even say that I was actually saved by my cell phone.

Although I was walking down a brightly lit street, I was only 50 meters away from my neighborhood before I was struck by fear.

The mental patient Fang Xin once predicted: my phone will save my life.

Doesn't today's events prove his prophecy?

But, that's& impossible. Something this unscientific changes my view of life.

Fang Xin also once said: if I don't go to him for help, then someone I love will die&

I always took his words as nonsense, but I don't know after what happened today.

That night at 10 pm, I sent a text to Xiao Qin and asked if everyone got home safely. Xiao Qin said everyone got back safely because the class leader instructed everyone to call her after arriving home to make sure they were safe.

I still didn't feel reassured, so on the next day June 27, I used the last day of the break to call all my acquaintances I could think of. Although they felt strange for suddenly receiving my call, none of them suffered the accident Fang Xin predicted.

Except for one person.

The one who was in a bad condition was Li CunZhuang.

Although he suffered a lot of injuries after protecting Shu Sha at the river, he made a complete recovery soon after.

I haven't seen him since last Friday, but I didn't take it too seriously. Anyway, since his academics have always been poor, it was normal for him to cut classes. He had too few points allocated to intelligence, so I'm afraid further education isn't a reasonable future plan.

However, today when I called my acquaintances one by one, and when it was Li CunZhuang's mother's turn, it was obvious something was wrong based on her tone like she was trying desperately to suppresses her pain.

"Auntie, tell me the truth, what happened to ZhuangZi."

For Li CunZhuang, who has a mean face and has a hard time expressing himself, I was one of his few "friends". Although I had a hard time setting boundaries with girls, one of my rules for friends was that I would never desert them.

Li CunZhuang's mother hesitated for a while before she held back her tears and said, "Ye Lin, if you have some time, come and visit Zhuang Zi at the hospital&"

My heart skipped a beat.

Li CunZhuang had strong muscles and bones, so he would never be sent to the hospital for ordinary injuries. If I took into account his mother's tone, then something big must have happened.

I immediately took a taxi according to the address provided to Dong Shan city's brain hospital.

I knew it wasn't a good situation when I saw the hospital sign from a distance.

The brain hospital. Did Li CunZhuang get into a fight again and ended up with a serious brain injury?

I arrived in front of Li CunZhuang's room while smelling the scent of disinfectant in the hallways. The first person to welcome me was Li CunZhuang's father, while his mother was sitting on a bench, wiping her tears with a handkerchief.

"Sigh&."

The first thing he did was give a long sigh.

"Ye Lin, you also know Zhuang Zi doesn't have many friends at school, so we didn't tell the truth to his school about his condition. Anyway, even if we can cure him, I'm afraid he can't attend school anymore&"

"Uncle Li, what's wrong with Zhuang Zi? Please tell me."

I finally heard some ominous words.

A brain tumor.

Starting last week, Li CunZhuang suddenly started seeing doubles in his left eye. It got so serious that he couldn't hold anything or walk properly and he had to cover up his left eye to adapt. Finally, his dad brought him to the hospital for a full examination.

The ophthalmologist was quite experienced and after listening to the symptoms, he immediately suggested Li CunZhuang to get a brain CT scan The results came out that afternoon and it was a brain tumor. The results were the same with an MRI. According to the specialist, the tumor was large and in a bad spot where it could cause the vessels to rupture, so they had to perform surgery as soon as possible.

Li CunZhuang parents were shocked by this sudden news. They asked their acquaintances to help transfer their son to the city's brain hospital that specializes with brain tumors. But the chief physician was still not optimistic about the success rate of the surgery, and according to his words, "I can't even guarantee if he could make it off the operating table alive."

From the nurse's conversations, Li CunZhuang's parents heard "It's in a terrible spot, so even if the operation is successful, he will turn into a moron". When Li CunZhuang heard the words "moron", he was so angry that he threw things at the nurses, and his parents could only shed tears inside when they tried to discourage him.

Since the operation was so dangerous, they asked if there was any possibility of conservative managements. The answer they received was, "Your son's condition is very unstable. One an artery ruptures, even if he doesn't die, he will be paraplegic."

Buddhists say, "All things are unpredictable." Who would have thought that Li CunZhuang, who was as strong as a bear, would face a life and death test all of a sudden?

I took a deep breath and the air in my lungs felt heavy.

Damn what a melodramatic development, I never liked watching tragedy dramas. Damn it, Li CunZhuang how can you die? That psycho Fang Xin predicted that the person I love the most would die& the one I love the most isn't Li CunZhuang! Fang Xin can go eat shit and the one who gave Zhuang Zi a brain tumor can go eat shit!

Because Li CunZhuang became more irritable after being diagnosed and loved to smash things, the hospital arranged a single room for him, of course, it was more expensive.

I walked in just as Li CunZhuang getting angry because he couldn't read the two words on the IV bottle and angrily threw the folding chair towards the door. I used Yin Yang Sanshou to distribute the force, then I took the chair and walked to his bed and sat down.

"It's& you."

A sluggish yet intimate glimmer flashed through Li CunZhuang's right eye.

"Yes, it's me." I tried to remain natural and chatted with Li CunZhuang despite the stinging in my chest.

During our conversation, I realized that Li CunZhuang didn't know about his own condition. It wasn't difficult to hide it form him because of his naturally low intelligence. But even Li CunZhuang could tell it felt different this time.

"Ye& Ye Zi, I feel like I can't use any strength&"

You can't use any strength, but you could throw the chair that high?

"Some& of the nurses talk behind my back and say I'll turn stupid after I get cured. But I'm already stupid, I know I'm stupid but I just don't like it when someone says it right in front of me&"

"If& if I become even more stupid, will I not even recognize myself anymore?" Li CunZhuang raised his head in bewilderment, "I wouldn't be able to remember you, and I might even forget my love, Shu Sha& I can't accept it&"

Although I didn't not want to use the proverb "words of a man on his deathbed always come from the heart", but it really described the current Li CunZhuang.

"Ye& Ye Zi, please don't despise me after I turn even more stupid& can you continue to be my friend? But if I actually forget Shu Sha, please don't remind me of her again. I'm already ugly enough and I don't want Shu Sha to see me in an even worse state& you have to protect her in my stead&"

Damn it, what& demoralizing words. Have you seen any Korean dramas? It's only beautiful woman who suffer unhappy fates, it's not the right time for someone as ugly as you! You should keep living!

After saying a lot of comforting words to Li CunZhuang, which I didn't even believe, I walked out of the room with my thoughts in disarray.

On the way back from the bathroom, I saw Li CunZhuang's father talking to the chief physician. The physician was a bit up there in age and had a forehead full of confident wrinkles. His glasses were as immaculate as his white coat.

"Chief Han, will the success rate be a bit higher if it's at a larger hospital in Beijing?"

Li CunZhuang's father held on to a ray of hope.

Chief Han pushed the bridge of his glasses and said proudly:

"There's not a single brain surgeon in the country who can give you any guarantees. Zhao ZhongXue is an expert in the field at the 301 Hospital in Beijing, but he's my student and isn't even as experienced as me."

Seeing that Li CunZhuang's father was still hesitant, Chief Han aggravated his tone and said.

"Even if you run all over the country, you won't find a higher level of treatment than this hospital for brain tumor surgery. If you really care about a tiny bit more success rate, then you can go to the United States to see a doctor. The United States is indeed more experienced than us in this area, but you would need to apply for a medical passport and take a flight over. Who knows if there would be enough time, unless you can get a famous American surgeon to come to China to operate&"

His words gave me a sudden realization. I could not resist the joy in my heart and ran forward to hold Chief Han's arm. I shook his hand while saying:

"Thank you, thank you for reminding me. You're a savior, I know what I have to do now."

I turned to Li CunZhuang's father and said, "Uncle Li, don't arrange a surgery for Zhuang Zi today. I have to go somewhere, but I will give you an update latest by tonight. Can you trust me?"

Uncle Li hesitated, "Even if you we're doing the surgery here, you need at least three days of preparation time. Ye Lin, what are you are going&"

"Anyway, I will give you the news tonight, just wait for me."

I waved my hand and ran out the hospital, only realizing halfway that running was prohibited and changed to a brisk walk.

"What's wrong with that young man?" A young nurse who saw me shaking hands cordially with Chief Han and mistakenly believed I was one of his acquaintances.

Chief Han frowned, "I don't really remember him& maybe he's a patient I've treated before. But it seems like there was still some residual effects."

After leaving from Dong Shan City Brain Hospital, I went to the VIP building of the Qing Zi Academy to meet with Peng TouSi.

China was a nation of science, how can I believe in the supernatural and go to the Dong Shan City Psychiatric Hospital and find Fang Xin to "change my destiny". Besides, Li CunZhuang isn't the one I love the most, that I'm confident on.

In order to get the best treatment for Li CunZhuang's illness, the most scientific and rational choice was to go to Ai Mi and let her use Ai ShuQiao's network to contact a brain surgeon to come to China and operate on Li CunZhuang.

"Can it be done?"

After I met PengTouSi alone in the guest room, I got straight to the point hoping to get his help.

"Madam Ai ShuQaio does know a lot of elites in the medical world, she has even netted some of them to act as full-time physicians in her own company. She sometimes even offers medical bribes to mafia leaders& letting her people save their lives is a better favor than anything else&"

"That means it's possible to transfer a specialized physician to operate on my friend."

I threw my hands down on the coffee table in excitement.

"Lin, you calm down, we need a better reason." Peng TouSi said cautiously as he sat on the couch with his fingers interlocked.

"A better reason?" I didn't understand.

Peng TouSi lowered his voice, "Think about it, if Madam Ai ShuQiao learns why you need a brain surgery specialist, she might coerce you into agreeing to something you don't want to do."

"Then, that can't be helped." I said anxiously, "If it can save Li CunZhuang's life&"

"What if Madam Ai ShuQiao asked you to rape a female classmate before she would send a doctor over?"

"Um&" I was at a loss for words, "Then what should I do?"

Peng TouSi was right. If Ai ShuQiao knew the importance of the surgery, she would only send a doctor if I met one of her conditions.

A conservative estimate was that Ai ShuQiao also wanted to lead me down a path of crime so we could conquer the world while exploiting each other.

"Lin, what do you think about this." Peng TouSi gave me an idea, "Miss Ai Mi is taking a nap now, but once she wakes up, go and beg her by saying there's something wrong with your brain and you need an operation. Hopefully she can get a surgeon from the United States&"

"Hey." I was mad, "Who has something wrong with their brain."

"It's just an example." Peng TouSi waved his hand, "I'll use the medical equipment in the VIP building to create a fake brain CT scan for you. You could say you got cerebral edema from a fight, as long as you're willing to beg Miss Ai Mi, she will definitely agree to your request."

"Cerebral edema?" I frowned, "Does that even need surgery?"

Peng TouSi smiled, "Don't worry, Miss Ai Mi doesn't have that much medical common sense. As long as you lie and say there's something wrong with your brain, she will definitely save you."

Peng TouSi worked fast and quickly gave me a fake brain CT scan. The cerebral edema was created with the shadow of half a banana. It was really unprofessional and I hope Ai Mi wouldn't be able to tell.

20 minutes later, I went to Ai Mi's bedroom, lowered my head in an undignified way and said, "I& I seem to be sick&"

Maybe it's because I didn't look sick because my words didn't attract Ai Mi's attention. To my surprise, she didn't look like she had just woken from a nap. She looked very clear-headed, and her panting and the redness of her cheeks indicated she had just been in a dangerous situation.

"Good job, manservant."

Ai Mi inexplicably complimented me.

"Eh, what did I do." I still hadn't given her the fake scan with the banana yet, so I don't think she's mocking me.

Ai Mi shook her feet excitedly as she sat on the princess bed covered with a purple canopy.

"Hmph, remember I told you before that I wanted to take a look at Peng TouSi's surveillance room?"

"Oh& I think so, but you didn't have the key."

I remember Ai Mi was trying to get into the surveillance room to see if there were any footage of room 101 locked in the steel cabinets. Then she could speculate where the cameras were installed in the room based on the footage and thus remove them all, but because Peng TouSi always watched the key, so there hasn't been a good opportunity for a while.

"Haha, manservant, you won't believe it. I was lying in bed, tossing and turning because I couldn't sleep, then Obama actually sneaked in with the key to the surveillance room in his mouth to exchange for food."

I looked at Obama who was lying down in the corner while gnawing on a steak. It looks like he had his wish fulfilled and made an equivalent exchange.

Damn, the dog is like a god. He was able to see through Ai Mi's mind and found a way to steal the key from Peng TouSi. Peng TouSi would have never expected a dog to steal from him.

"So you went to the surveillance room, did you find any evidence there were cameras in this room?"

"Well& I originally didn't have enough time, but it's a good thing you came over and distracted Peng TouSi. I wasn't able to find the footage, but I did find this."

Ai Mi took out a thick paper bag from behind her and proudly showed it off to me.

"Tsk, it's pretty heavy." She threw the paper bag on the bed and all the documents inside poured out like a white peacock opening its tail.

Almost all of them were in English except for one that was written in Chinese. It was a receipt from the children's center in Dong Shan City's Yining District (also known as the special education school). Peng TouSi donates half his income every month to that cash-strapped school, which was something I already knew about.

That means the paper bag was filled with Peng TouSi's personal documents. I suddenly had a bad feeling and said to Ai Mi:

"These things seem to have nothing to do with the security camera. Let's not look through Peng TouSi's private items, it's rude&"

"Where does a bodyguard get personal privacy?" Ai Mi said unreasonably, "If you're my subordinate, then you have to give up personal privacy and focus on protecting me. The same goes for you, now come and help me look for traces of security footage."

I had a request for Ai Mi, so I could only aimlessly rummage through the various English documents. Actually, with my English level, I was probably causing more trouble than helping.

But by a freak coincidence, my eyes fell onto a printout with a strange table drawn on it. There was a double helix structure representing DNA drawn in the upper left corner, while the left part of the table seemed to have Ai Mi's English name written on it.

In the right half of the table, an "L" was faintly visible.

I felt my heart skip a beat.

Maybe it was the word "Lin Ye", aka the English spelling of "Ye Lin". Was this the paper that proved Ai Mi and I were related?

Peng TouSi once told me that the test results were locked in the cabinets of his office. So his office is the surveillance room? If it's something that important, make sure to lock it up properly!

Although I've thought about confessing our brother-sister relationship to Ai Mi, but it might be too much of a shock to have the evidence suddenly appear in front of her. Will she even be able to accept reality when she sees the lab results?

I pretended to inadvertently pull the sheet away and planned to quietly put it into the 'worthless' folder that was full of stuff Ai Mi already checked.

Not sure why, but Obama suddenly howled towards the sky. I was feeling guilty and the sheet slipped from my hands and fell onto the bed.

I reflexively grabbed it, but my overly exaggerated actions made Ai Mi suspicious.

"Hey, manservant, what's that in your hand?"

"Nothing, it's nothing&" I backed up while thinking that if Ai Mi came over to grab it, I would tear it up and eat it rather than giving it to her."

I don't think there's anything wrong with revealing our brother-sister relationship, it's actually good for me since we can both get along more naturally. But since Li CunZhuang needs a surgeon, it's not a good idea to have Ai Mi suddenly accept her new identity and add more variables to the field.

"It's& not something for good kids to see." I started to move away from Ai Mi's bed while holding the lab results.

Ai Mi's nose twitched, then she ordered in a high-pitched voice: "Hand it over, it's Peng TouSi's privacy and not yours. Even if it was your privacy, I still have the right to see it whenever I want."

If all else fails, retreat. I turned around and ran towards the living room, but heard an "ouch" from behind me. I subconsciously turned around and found that Ai Mi had fallen off the bed with her golden ponytails sprawled out across the carpet.

"Hey, are you okay?" I turned back with worry not expecting Ai Mi to get up with a smirk on her face. She wasn't injured and deliberately yelled to get my attention.

I was angry and was about to tear up sheet in my hand when Ai Mi waved her hand at Obama and ordered.

"Grab that sheet of paper for me and I'll give you permission to not diet for a month."

The black and white dog pounced liked lightning and instantly tore the lab sheet into two halves. Only a small piece was left in my hand. The majority of it was in Obama's mouth as he wagged his tail to Ai Mi for credit.

I couldn't stop it. Ai Mi sat cross-legged on the carpet and took the lab results from Obama.

Her ice-blue eyes swept up and down and she was immediately filled with doubt.

"& confirmed that the two parties are indeed half-brother and sister&"

Ai Mi translated the contents of the lab results to Chinese as I facepalmed.

"Who and who are brother and sister?" Ai Mi's voice suddenly became ethereal and the room resounded with an echo of her voice as if it were a deep mountain valley.

I was silent as Ai Mi read the lab results over and over again. My silent reaction made her tremble even more.

"Who took my DNA without permission." Ai Mi's voice gradually got louder and it was full of anger and fear, almost approaching the level of a scream, "Why is my name written on it?! And who is this 'Lin'?!"

Obama was shocked by his female owner's abnormal condition. He may be highly intelligent, but he still couldn't understand what was going on and only barked at me.

"What's going on?" Peng TouSi came inside when he heard the racket. He saw Ai Mi sitting on the carpet and the DNA test sheet in her hand. He drew a cross in the air with worry.

"Oh lord, I can't believe I lost the key."

"So it was you." Ai Mi's frail body trembled as she cast an indignant glance at Peng TouSi, "Who is this 'Lin'? Was it the Korean guy that I did a commercial with last year? I'm going to have my mom catch him, torture him, and ask him why he used fake DNA to impersonate as my brother. He is trying to promote himself, right? His eyes are so small that he can't even see, how does he look like my brother&"

"Miss Ai Mi, you have to remain calm." Peng TouSi closed the door to the room and said calmly, "I was going to tell you about it one day, but since you learned about it today by accident, I suggest you not run away and accept it calmly."

"The truth, what truth?" Ai Mi hysterically pulled at her hair and it seems she intentionally tried not to look at me.

"Actually you already know the answer in your mind, don't you." Peng TouSi continued to guide her, while Ai Mi's eyes gradually filled with fear.

"All along, you have been treating Ye Lin as a manservant&"

Peng TouSi deliberately stressed the word "Lin".

"And the proud Ye Lin allowed you to call him that, and willingly let you order him around. It wasn't because he coveted your money or anything else&"

"I'm not listening, I'm not listening, I'm not listening." Ai Mi covered her ears and yelled out loud in protest.

Peng TouSi still finished his words.

"It's because you and Ye Lin have the same mother."

"He is your half-brother, and that is the truth."

"Lies, lies, lies, lies, all lies. You're all lying to me!"

Ai Mi denied it much more than I expected.

Obama began wailing in an untimely manner and made it more chaotic.

"This fake lab test, I won't fall for& these tricks!"

Ai Mi screamed as she tore the sheets into pieces and scattered them around her feet.

"Ai Mi, calm down and listen to me&" I felt I couldn't stay silent any longer.

"A prank." Ai Mi had tears in her eyes, but her lips began to tremble and curl upwards, "It has to be a prank. You heard yesterday that my birthday was April 1st, so you wanted to prank me. I won't fall for it, I'm going to deduct your wages for doing this prank, I mean it."

"That American Express card has long been cancelled by Ai ShuQiao& cancelled by our mother&"

Since it had already progressed to this point, I didn't think I needed to hide it anymore.

"Wh- why?" Ai Mi's thoughts were delayed. She wanted to keep up with my reasoning while denying the reality in front of me.

I shrugged, "It's probably because he doesn't like her ex-husband's son."

Ai Mi pursed her lips nervously. She placed her hands on her knees and evened out the creases on her rainbow stockings.

I'm sure she's already heard rumors that her mother has been married before.

I took advantage of Ai Mi's silence and carefully presented her with the truth.

The book called "The Jewish Persuasion" that my dad used to keep on his desk once said that to convince someone, you have to start with the simplest facts. Make sure the other party says "yes" first, and then work towards your goal step by step.

So I asked, "Ai Mi, do you remember when you asked me to find a substitute for you when your mother asked you to practice Chinese characters? And she found out about the last time, but you weren't held accountable."

Ai Mi furrowed her tiny brow and craned her neck, "So what if I do?"

"Because that time, I temporarily asked my father for help, and your mother recognized the handwriting of her ex-husband."

Ai Mi's expression was clearly shaken, and I continued to strike while the iron was hot.

"The American Express Black Card was frozen immediately after. The reason was simple, your 'mother' didn't like her abandoned son and she didn't like seeing me use her baby daughter's unlimited overdraft card."

"Nonsense." Ai Mi seemed to be in a heated debate with me, "Mom only blocked the card because she didn't want a lowly manservant to use it, and you can't prove that the card is really no longer valid."

Peng TouSi, who was standing by, interjected, "That card has indeed been cancelled. If Miss Ai Mi doesn't believe me, I can contact Commissioner Wang of American Express to testify."

Ai Mi glared indignantly at Peng TouSi and it looked like she wanted to bite something to vent her anger.

These days, I have been called "inferior manservant" or "lowly manservant" numerous times and it was about time to act like her brother.

With this in mind, I straightened my back, and said calmly:

"Ai Mi, do you still remember how Obama was really intimate with me the first time we met? To this day, he still only allows me or you to pat his head. Isn't it because we're related and we have the same smell?"

Obama looked at me stupefied not understanding that I had just used him as evidence.

Ai Mi sneered, "Even if Obama is close to you, it only proves that you are related to him. Why would that make you& my brother."

I smacked my lips and said, "I am your brother."

Ai Mi, who was lying on the edge of the bed, reached out for the pink phone under her pillow. She pressed the keys while saying:

"I'm not falling for it. If you're courageous enough, you should confront my mother directly."

"Miss, please don't dial that number." Peng TouSi stopped her in a hurry.

Ai Mi proudly stopped moving for the moment. She wiped away the teardrops on the corners of her eyes while saying:

"So you were lying to me and now you're afraid."

I was laughing at Peng TouSi's spinelessness in my mind, but then I realized if she talked to Ai ShuQiao, she would realize I had exposed the relationship and it would obstruct my plans of getting a doctor. My friend's life is at stake here.

So I acted as spineless as Peng TouSi and begged Ai Mi to not make the call.

"Hmph, do you think I won't call just because you begged me?" Ai Mi looked like a victorious general pondering how she should deal with her prisoners of war.

Peng TouSi spoke after a brief pause, "Miss Ai Mi, if you make the call, Ye Lin's life may be in danger."

"What? Why would the manservant's life be in danger?"

"Because& your mother, Madam Ai ShuQiao, she&" Peng TouSi lowered his voice, "She warned Ye Lin to not disclose his relationship with you or she would dispose of him&"

Huh, Ai ShuQiao did hint at that possibility at first, but ever since I gave up my life to save Ai Mi, Ai ShuQiao has began to try and bribe me instead. As long as I listen to her, she may even allow me to reconcile with Ai Mi. I don't think she would kill me even if she found out I revealed the secret to Ai Mi.

But Ai Mi shouldn't make the call if we want a doctor transferred here, so it's reasonable for Peng TouSi to lie.

"More nonsense." Ai Mi stood up and crossed her arms, "According to you guys, Ye Lin is my mom's biological son, right? Why would a mother kill her own son?"

That's because you don't know about Ai ShuQiao's ruthlessness. In order to achieve her own goals, she would even use her 4-year-old daughter& Your grandfather was poisoned by her plans and you yourself unknowingly became a murderer. If she knew about it, then her spirit would be broken, right?

"Because Madam Ai ShuQiao didn't want Ye Lin to affect your celebrity career."

Peng TouSi replied smoothly with a convincing half false and half true statement.

On a side note, they always say women are better at lying than men. Peng TouSi was able to gain Ai ShuQiao's trust and lie to Ai Mi without a script. Does it have anything to do with the fact that he is gay and a bottom?

I chimed in, "Basically it means mother thinks I'm a nasty relative who's approaching you just to get favors."

"Are you?" Ai Mi asked seriously.

"Of course not." I said, "After we've interacted that long, didn't you realize I couldn't be moved with money?"

"No." Ai Mi said in a very exasperated flat tone.

"That's right." I had an idea, "I have photos in my dad's old photo album. If you see it, you will understand the relationship between your mom and my dad."

"Pictures with clothes on?" Ai Mi asked.

"Of course it's with clothes on."

"Hmph, even a picture of them cuddling together with no clothes on doesn't prove anything."

"I& can find their marriage certificate."

"It's long been expired and it could be a forgery." Ai Mi thought she had seized the flow of the debate and became aggressive.

"No need to go to all that trouble, Miss Ai Mi. If you want proof, I have it here with me."

Peng TouSi took his military style cell phone out of his suit and started playing a recording.

"& you have to know that only my son has the guts to commit crimes."

"How about it, I'll give you a chance& Ye Lin, do you want to be my son again?"

Isn't& isn't this when I spoke to Ai ShuQiao on the rooftop of the VIP building with Peng TouSi's cell phone? Peng TouSi actually used recording software to record our conversation and save it on his phone. The conversation was irrefutable evidence and this time Ai Mi had nothing to say.

Ai Mi turned silent as expected. Her shoulders were slumped like all the strength was drained from her body.

"&& Although you have always maintained an intimate relationship with Ai Mi, you didn't tell her you were related to her. Why, are you afraid of my punishment?"

Peng TouSi's recording wasn't played in chronological order, but it didn't affect its credibility. Ai ShuQiao's unmistakably confident tone of voice wasn't something anyone could imitate.

"Turn it off, I don't want to hear it, turn it off&"

Ai Mi screamed out frantically.

Peng TouSi complied and turned off the recording. Then he patted me on the shoulder, signaling that he was going to leave me and Ai Mi alone in the room for a while.

When he left, Obama didn't like the heavy atmosphere in the room, so he followed Peng TouSi out.

Thus Ai Mi and I were the only ones left in room 101 of the VIP building.

"Haha, haha, hahahaha." Ai Mi suddenly threw back her head and laughed. I couldn't see her full expression because she covered her eyes with one hand.

"Ai Mi, I know it's hard for you to accept it all of a sudden&"

"Shut up, do you think I would call you brother?" Ai Mi removed her hand from her face and I saw a pair of bloodshot eyes caused by her tears and anger.

"You're a liar. When didn't you tell me earlier about our relationship?"

She yelled at me hysterically.

"I had my own troubles&"

"When was it&" Ai Mi asked in a depressed and angry tone.

"When?"

"When did you learn about it?" Amy growled, "Did you already know we were related when you said you loved me?"

"It's a pure and innocent love between siblings." I explained.

"I'll pretend this never happened." After taking a long time to adjust her breathing, Ai Mi deceived herself and ordered, "Continue to be my manservant, you only need the identity of a manservant&"

Pretending it never happened, what a childish idea. Do you think it's like a wife finding out about her husband sexting another girl then acting generous and saying,

"I'll pretend it never happened if you don't do it again"? We're brother and sister, it's not like it will go away just because you refuse to accept it.

"That's absolutely not okay." My attitude gradually hardened, "It might not have been the best time, but since you know the truth, it's better for you to accept it. My feelings for you won't change&"

"But my feelings for you&" Ai Mi suddenly shouted. After she knew she blurted out something she shouldn't have, she fell silent for a while, then changed her tone and said, "There's only feelings of a master and servant between you and me. I don't want a sibling relationship, you should just remain as my manservant."

I was angry at Ai Mi's unreasonableness. If she's going to deny our sibling relationship, then what's the point of all my previous efforts.

I got heated up and began to speak louder.

"Hey, can you not be so stubborn. Did you forget how I risked my life to save you? I can throw away my life, but I just want you to call me brother, is that an unreasonable request?"

"It's unreasonable, too unreasonable." Ai Mi clenched her fists and shouted at me.

I took a deep breath in an attempt to calm my mind, but failed.

To show I would never back down on this issue, I took a step closer to Ai Mi and looked down at her. She also looked at me like she was accepting the challenge and that she was even angrier than me.

"Ai Mi, are you going to call me brother or not."

I couldn't help but use a threatening tone.

"No, I'm not." Ai Mi stiffened her neck and headbutted me.

"You&" I subconsciously clenched my right fist out of anger.

Ai Mi, who noticed it, wasn't afraid. Instead, she brought her body even closer to me. She placed her hands at her waist and tilted her head.

"Hmph, you lowly manservant, are you going to hit your master? If you have the guts, then hit me, hit me!"

I unclenched my fist and put it down. I wasn't going to hit my sister, it was only a subconscious reaction in the first place.

I closed my eyes tightly in annoyance and squeezed out many wrinkles between my brows.

"Ha, since you're not capable of hitting me, why don't you get on your knees and beg me?" Ai Mi said sarcastically, "All you have to do is press your head against the carpet and beg me sincerely, then maybe I'll call you brother."

"Remember to say 'Oh Great Miss Ai Mi, please grant this favor to your lowly manservant. Call me brother, so that I may die with content'."

"But you can't get a single word wrong, how about it?"

Who would agree to such a humiliating condition. If I have to act slavishly to get you to call me brother, then I would rather not.

"Ai Mi, stop throwing a tantrum like a child. We could only continue our relationship if you first admit our sibling relationship&"

"What do you mean?" Ai Mi interrupted me, "Are you threatening me? Are you saying you won't see me again if I don't call you brother?"

I was going to nod, but seeing the fear and loneliness flickering in the depths of Ai Mi's eyes, I had to change my words and said:

"I don't mind being called a manservant, or rather, I don't mind being called that way because you are my sister. I won't let other people call me that way&"

"So I don't mind if you call me manservant outside, but you have to call me brother when it's only the two of us, must be called my brother. It's the only reason I protect you and care for you or are you going to deprive me of that too?"

Ai Mi hesitated a bit when she heard my sincerity.

Then she shook her head violently like she was trying to reject one of her thoughts.

"Let's, let's make a deal." Ai Mi shouted. It was a familiar statement that couldn't help but remind me of her mother, Ai ShuQiao.

"Ye Lin you.. will continue to be my manservant. And I won't call you brother when we're alone&"

"Hey, that's the same as before, right?" I spat.

"Don't interrupt, I'm not done yet." Ai Mi waved her small fist angrily, "If& if you're okay with that, then I won't give you any hard work in the future, basically you don't have to do anything."

"I& I'm still not seeing any benefits."

"How are there no benefits?" Ai Mi had a red face, "You don't have to work for the rest of your life. All you have to do is eat with me, play with me, and I will raise you& is that not enough?"

Huh, although she's young, she's learned a little of Ai ShuQiao's seduction skills. She wants me to give up my dignity and live off my sister the rest of my life. It seems like it would be an easy and comfortable life.

I let out a sigh.

"Ai Mi, do you still remember the second time we met by chance at the supermarket? You were going to buy the chips in my hand for a lot of money, but I didn't take your money& from then onward, you probably felt I was quite different, someone who couldn't be bribed by your mother. I'm still that same person and I won't be bribed by you either. "

Ai Mi couldn't hide her disappointment.

"But." I added, "I can serve you better, more attentively, more desperately than a manservant, on the condition that you just call me brother, is it really that difficult?"

Ai Mi was dumbfounded by my question, but she remained undeterred and continued to bargain with me:

"Then& continue to be my manservant and I will still provide all your needs. Plus, if you perform well, I will& call you brother once, how about it?"

Based on her expression, this was already the biggest concession she could make.

"No. If even the word 'brother' becomes a reward, then what would my status be?"

"You're a manservant~~" Ai Mi shouted impatiently.

"That's the problem." I shouted back, "You can use me like a manservant, but you have to call me brother. I'd rather have that than be treated like a prince, only to be called a manservant."

"Why do you care so much about the name?" Ai Mi was so angry and anxious that she was about to cry out again.

"Because that's what I deserve to be called." I refused to give in either.

"Let's play rock-paper-scissors." Ai Mi suggested, "If you win, I'll call you brother, otherwise you'll be a manservant for the rest of your life."

Ai Mi said with a self-loathing tone.

"That's ridiculous." I waved my hand in refusal, "How can you treat a brother-sister relationship like child's play?"

Actually, another reason I refused was because I have bad luck. I usually only had a 25% win rate at rock-paper-scissors, so I didn't want to lose my chance at being a brother because of my bad luck.

"Why are you so stubborn?" Ai Mi's face had turned red with anger and she was breathing heavily.

"You're the one who's stubborn, right?" I retorted.

"I've decided." Ai Mi suddenly said loudly, "I'll still call you manservant since I'm used to it. Besides, weren't there movies where the brother acted as the sister's servant? Although they were born from the same mother, there's still a hierarchical difference&"

Her words pierced through my heart like a sword.

My tone quickly became colder.

"What do you mean, do you think you're more noble than me? Do you think the difference comes from having a different father?"

Ai Mi didn't immediately notice my abnormality, still feeling good about herself, said:

"Of course, America is more developed than China. So, of course, my American father compared to your Chinese father&"

That's one point I couldn't stand, I have no intention of comparing America and China, but you can't insult my father. He especially can't be insulted by you, the child of his ex-wife and her eloper.

"Ai Mi, I don't care if you say anything else, but if you say your American father is better than my dad and your looking down on him because of it, then I demand an apology."

"Why would I apologize?" Ai Mi still did not realize the seriousness of the situation and was still peeved at me.

My tone became as cold as falling into an ice cave.

At the same time, my anger had burned out the last trace of reason in my mind.

"If you don't apologize, then I have to assume that our relationship is over, and you don't need to call me brother anymore."

After saying these words, I turned around and left.

Ai Mi froze in place and watched me walk out of her bedroom.

My chest was filled with anger, so my steps were swift. There was a rapidly expanding distance between me and Ai Mi seemed to indicate an insurmountable gulf between us.

I had my back to Ai Mi, so I couldn't see her expression, and she didn't make any sounds either.

Soon, I crossed the living room and walked next to the main entrance of room 101, which Peng TouSi had just left from.

I will also leave, but unlike him, I will not come back.

It's fine to say I was too hot-headed, but I have my own lines that can't be crossed. The only thing that worries me was I didn't know how to reply to Li CunZhuang's parents. I was so confident and filled them with hope, but I couldn't achieve my goals.

My hand gripped the door handle. Strange, it was clearly midsummer, but the handle was ice cold.

"Clack", the sound of the doorknob turning rippled through the silence of the room.

Then another sound rang out behind me. It was the sound of a young girl running desperately across the carpet so eagerly that she almost fell over.

Before I could turn around, Ai Mi had caught up with me. She pounced on me from behind and wrapped her arms around my waist.

Her petite body was pressed against my back. I felt the warmth of her body compared to the cold doorknob and could even hear Ai Mi's frenzied heartbeat.

"Don't go, please don't go. I'll call you brother& I'll always call you brother."

Although I didn't turn around, I could tell her face was covered with tears based on her voice.

I turned my face and looked at Ai Mi whose face was ruined by her tears. I could not help but feel love and compassion and I gave her an understanding smile.

"Brother is a bad person& the worst."

Ai Mi wiped her tears on my clothes. Her hair was messy, her little face was red, and she was full of childishness. I felt her current state was a hundred times cuter than on stage or in front of the camera, no, a thousand times cuter.

Despite the shame, the only thought that occupied my mind was: this life was worth it.

"A neurosurgeon, why would you need one?"

After her emotions had calmed down a bit, Ai Mi sat on the sofa in the living room while holding a stuffed dolphin in her arms, puzzled by my request.

After a lot of drama, she finally admitted our sibling relationship. But she still wasn't quite used to this sudden change, so she still often calls me "manservant" during our conversations. It was only when I narrowed my eyes to point out to her she called me wrong, did she reluctantly call me brother with a pout.

"So& your brother's friend has a brain tumor and needs a highly skilled surgeon to save him."

Since Ai Mi was always reluctant to call me brother, I had to refer to myself as her brother since I was determined to be one.

"What friend?" Ai Mi looked at me with vigilance, "If it's the violent girl, just let her die."

Was it a misperception, but why do I feel that Ai Mi's dislike for Xiao Qin has increased after learning that we were siblings.

"It's not Xiao Qin, it's a guy from my school."

"Why are you doing him such a big favor, do you owe him money?"

"I don't think you can just leave someone to die."

"Hmph, a good Samaritan. You don't usually come to me to make reports, but you come when you're friend is in trouble. Do you only know my worth when you need me?"

"That's not true." I frowned, "Usually, even if I come over often, you don't have time for me. Saving a life is better than anything, so will you help your brother?"

"I'm not going to help." Ai Mi pressed her little chin against the back of the plush dolphin while crossing her legs.

"You were just using despicable means to make me call you brother, and now you're begging me for a favor& I'm not that good-tempered."

Despicable means? I wasn't pretending earlier when I was going to leave. If you didn't run over to stop me, I might have never come back.

But on the flip side, if Ai Mi wasn't sure if my actions were real or fake, it meant she cared about me enough to stop me.

"Just call a doctor over." I unconsciously softened my tone.

Ai Mi switched to pressing her cheek against the plush dolphin and ignored me.

"I heard from Peng TouSi that your mother's company has a lot of skillful physicians, can you borrow one of them? Ever since you drove your personal doctor away, Peng TouSi has been acting as the doctor, but he's not a professional! You should just keep the borrowed doctor as your personal doctor."

Ai Mi made a face and stuck her tongue out with a "I hate you" look.

"Then what should I do to have you bring a doctor here."

I had no choice but to ask in a defeated tone.

Ai Mi tapped her chin with her index finger as she looked up at the ceiling. After thinking for a while, she said mischievously:

"I'll do you a favor if you get under the carpet."

"Eh, as long as I get under the carpet?"

"And roll yourself up with the carpet like a Mexican burrito."

I hesitated, "Uhh& is there a connection between& me turning into a burrito, and you hiring a doctor?"

"No connection, but I will be happy." Ai Mi said bluntly, "You made me suffer by forcing me to call you brother, so I won't help you if you don't let me release my pent up resentment."

"As long as I roll myself up, you'll get a doctor and you won't back out?"

I confirmed.

"I always keep my word, manservant& brother, are you going to do it or not. If you don't want to, then I'll go back on my word right now."

It's fine, I could just take it as playing with my sister.

I went to the edge of the room and laid flat on my back. Then I lifted the carpet that was underneath me and did a quick roll until the carpet was wrapped around me.

"Is this okay?" I asked Ai Mi, looking up from the carpet.

Ai Mi shook her head and said, "No, it's not tight enough, it's too loose."

I squirmed like a maggot until the carpet wrapped even more tightly around my body, damn it was hot.

"What about now?" I asked.

"Hey, show a little more dedication, okay?" Ai Mi said without even looking, "Roll yourself around two more time. You have to be wrapped up tight to the extent that you can't get out without help."

I had no choice but to roll around two more times until the thick and heavy carpet incapacitated me.

I stared sluggishly at the ceiling chandelier as I struggled to catch my breath, and asked again, "Now it should be fine?"

Ai Mi tossed the plush dolphin onto the sofa, then she walked towards me with brisk steps.

Hey, don't walk this way so casually, can't you see I have a low field of view right now? Since your skirt is so short, I would be able to see everything under the skirt, don't get any closer.

I thought Ai Mi would stop by my head, but she didn't and stepped over my head. I was too shocked I couldn't close my eyes in time, and as a result, I saw my sister's pink panties under her skirt.

After Ai Mi stepped over my head, she stood on top of my belly like it was natural. But since there were several layers of carpet, plus the fact she was light, I didn't really feel much pressure.

Ai Mi, who was lacking athletic genes, stretched out her arms to maintain balance. After getting used to it, she stood on my belly and said to me condescendingly:

"Hmph, you think I won't be mad anymore because you rolled yourself up? Do you think it would be that easy? I'm going to punish you!"

She said as she jumped up and down like she was on a trampoline.

Damn this kid really knows how to fool around. Your brother's stomach is about to explode! Good thing there's carpet in between and I could just barely hold on if I flex my abs, but it's still uncomfortable.

Ai Mi kept jumping up and down while yapping.

"Damn manservant, do you think your status changes because you're my brother? I'm going to trample you to death."

Ai Mi happily jumped up and down. I endured the shocks on my belly as I closed my eyes in resignation.

It's not really painful, I mainly closed my eyes so I wouldn't be looking up under her skirt.

Ai Mi bounced twenty times or so before she got tired. She stood still on my belly to catch her breath, then she shifted her feet around to find a better position.

No, not good, don't step there with your feet! There might be a thick carpet in between, but that's where my little friend is! It feels weird having it brushed with my sister's feet.

Ai Mi didn't realize it, and prepared to jump again after a short rest.

Wait, don't jump! My abs can block the impact if you jump on my stomach, but my family member down there doesn't have any muscles! Not to mention the fact my eggs are also there, do you want your brother to be a chicken without any eggs?

"Ai Mi, stop, stop!" I said in a hurry, "Not there, if you want to keep playing, change a spot. Come a little forward back on top of my belly."

At first, she didn't understand my words, but then she immediately covered her mouth and laughed and said:

"Huh, so that means this isn't your belly. Then where exactly is it and why can't I jump on it."

"You can't because it's dangerous and a life is in danger."

Ai Mi became smug when she saw my forehead covered with sweat.

"So, it seems like I'm standing on my bro-ther's baby. And my bro-ther seems like he's enjoying it and thinks his sister's feet is very comfortable&"

"Who's comfortable, I'm afraid! Also, what's up with the uncomfortable pause between the word brother?"

As if dissatisfied with what I said, Ai Mi used her left foot for support as she grinded the spot underneath her right foot like she was crushing a cockroach.

Hey, hey, my little friend isn't a cockroach. It might not look cute, but it isn't a pest. If you keep rubbing it with your foot, it will turn even uglier.

Out of revenge, Ai Mi kept stepping on me viciously while enjoying my expression.

"Hmph, you're not allowed to command me even if you're my brother. I don't care what conflicts you have with mom, but you must always be loyal to me."

It's not that I didn't think about flipping my body around and shaking off Ai Mi, but for one thing the carpet was wrapped too tightly and I had trouble moving, and for another, I was worried that Ai Mi would fall down. Even if she doesn't get hurt, she would get angrier, and then my previous efforts would have been in vain.

At this time, Ai Mi's cell phone, which was still on her bed in her bedroom, suddenly rang.

"What a bummer, who's calling me right now."

Ai Mi jumped off me and the opposing force made me roll my eyes in pain.

"A date? Keep dreaming, go and eat shit."

From the tone of her voice and contents of the call, I could deduce it was Kyle who had called.

"Also, speak to me in English in the future, you're speaking in a different dialect and I can't understand you."

"What, you can re-learn Mandarin for me? That's not necessary, but please hurry up and go die for me."

Ai Mi used her poisonous tongue to lecture Kyle as she walked back and sat on my stomach, using her brother as a cushion.

After hanging up the phone, Ai Mi turned her head to look at me who was already red in the face and dripping with sweat.

"Well, I'm a little less angry now." Ai Mi said, "You smell so sweaty, go to the bathroom and take a shower."

"So the matter of getting a doctor&" it was still my main concern.

"Well, since you went through all that effort, I promise you I will try to get a doctor within three days. But let me be frank, they might be a first-class American doctor, but I'm not responsible if they can't cure your friend."

I was able to calm down with Ai Mi's guarantee. After another discussion with Peng TouSi, we decided to have Ai Mi personally call Ai ShuQiao. She would lie and tell her mom she was missing a personal doctor and needed her mom to send over one of her doctors who is skilled at brain surgeries.

Peng TouSi didn't seem particularly surprised we were able to resolve our conflicts peacefully. In his words, "Although you guys don't have similar appearances, you have much more in common with each other than one might think."

Is that true? I do know that we both have a fear of heights and like to hug things when we sleep&

Everything went smoothly, Ai ShuQiao easily agreed to Ai Mi's request. As for matters related to American doctors coming to Chinese hospitals and operating on patients for free, Peng TouSi was responsible for handling all related matters. Since there were many precedents during the Sichuan earthquake, it would not be particularly difficult.

"I have to be straightforward, the doctor Mom sent over is a bit strange, so you should be prepared."

"How strange." I asked curiously, "Even stranger than Peng TouSi?"

Peng TouSi said with discontent, "Hey, I'm standing right here."

Ai Mi frowned slightly as she tried to recall her memories about the doctor as if it caused her a lot of headaches.

"His name is Yu SuiLiang, a Chinese American with a green card. I met him twice when I was a kid, he was a very strange guy&"

"Uh& I think it's common for talented people to have strange behaviors, but how's his medical skills?"

"You don't have to worry about that, of the doctors in my mom's company, Yu SuiLiang is the best doctor's (sigh) classmate."

And I'm the neighbor of the friend of the aunt of the chairman. Invite the best doctor, I don't want his classmate.

"Hey, don't look down on people! Yu SuiLiang has a double doctorate in medicine and engineering. His goal in life is to create a cyborg&"

This sounds like it's going down the route of Frankenstein's monster! I want a doctor to cure Li CunZhuang, not to transform him. Does Ai ShuQiao not have any normal people around her?

"Actually, he was only recently hired at my mother's company. He previously worked at a charity foundation, but when he was doing aid work in Angola, he implanted chips into the body of rats. It made the group up and run around crazily causing widespread panic, so he ended up getting fired&"

"Since there are strict medical laws in the U.S., Dr. Yu felt like his hands were tied and couldn't exhibit his abilities to its best, so he already wanted to come back to China. There was no way he was going to miss this opportunity&"

I was worried, "Don't tell me he only wants to transform others, but doesn't actually know how to treat people."

Peng TouSi replied on Ai Mi's behalf, "Dr. Yu's surgical skills are first-rate, he once performed brain surgery on a two-year-old child, which caused a huge controversy at the time, but&"

"But what."

"But if you injured your arms or legs, definitely don't go to him for treatment. He will try every possible way to persuade you to amputate your limbs and replace them with his high-tech prosthetics. He calls it 'advancing the evolution of new human beings'&"

I was completely speechless.

So the reason he was returning to China was to carry out human experimentation!

I better keep my distance from Dr. Yu. I just hope he can cure Li CunZhuang's without making any other modifications.

Otherwise, it would be too frightening if Li CunZhuang woke up from his operation with the ability to fire lasers from his eyes.

After things were basically finalized, I called Li CunZhuang's parents and told them that an American surgical expert would fly to Dong Shan city in three days to do free brain surgery for Li CunZhuang.

Of course, I played down my own role in the conversation, saying that an American Foundation heard of their difficulties and had taken the initiative to send a doctor.

Li CunZhuang's parents were skeptical as they had not requested assistance nor did they belong to a family in financial difficulty, so they could not have attracted the attention of an American charity.

Peng TouSi took the phone from my hands and began to dupe them. In short, he said that the American Foundation wanted to expand its influence in China. They heard from Ye Lin that your son was sick, so they thought it was just the right opportunity. The follow-up matters would be negotiated between him and the hospital, and everything would be done in accordance to regulations. When the time comes, all they had to do was sign the consent form for the surgery.

"Ye Lin, you& actually know experts in the US? Young people nowadays really can't be underestimated."

Li CunZhuang's father said to me over the phone.

"Regardless of the final outcome, I have to thank you in advance for running around for Zhuang Zi. I think it's a blessing from our ancestors for Zhuang Zi to have a friend like you."

Hey, that's something you generally say to your daughter-in-law, don't say it to me. It made me remember Fang Xin's prophecy again which said "the person you love most will die".

In order to cure my friend's sickness, I can roll myself up in carpet then let Ai Mi jump on top of me, but Li CunZhuang isn't the one I love the most.

But in retrospect, I still can't explain that night. Why did my phone automatically dial 110, it always felt very mysterious, and I still haven't found a scientific explanation.

I had a good night's sleep that night.

Two problems were solved at once. I was able to get a doctor and also clarify my sibling relationship with Ai Mi.

Although there were some bumps, it went better than I thought. It felt like tomorrow would be another day brimming with sunshine and hope.

Then tomorrow came.

The three days of vacation we had due to the high school exams occupying our classroom was officially over. Which meant from Friday onward, we had to attend eight days of classes in a row. There wasn't a single student without complaints and it felt like the cruel life as a third year student had come earlier.

"I'm so happy I could see Ye Lin again."

Xiao Qin said to me cheerfully. It seems that her menstrual cramps were almost gone and it wasn't a problem anymore.

But I covered the bottom right corner of my desk in embarrassment.

If you ask why, it's because the student who was taking the exam in my seat left a very dirty drawing with a ballpoint pen.

Why couldn't they just focus on writing their exam? Is it because they usually don't study seriously which lead to the same bad habits when writing the exam? Even if that is the case, you should at least try your best to fill in your exam and not waste time.

Damn, the examinee might not have been good at exams, but their drawing skills are off the charts! They easily sketched the outline of two naked cartoon-style girl with a ballpoint pen. One of the girls had her legs spread in an M shape, shamelessly displaying the content between the legs. The other girl was holding up her heavy chest with her hands and she had a look like she wants her appetite to be appeased.

It's at the level where it can be published into an H manga. There's no point going to higher education, might as well move to Japan to develop and you might make a name for themselves.

The worst thing was that the two naked girls were drawn with a ballpoint pen. It was etched into the wood and couldn't be erased with an eraser. I guess I have to use the Swiss Army knife that I have been hiding.

Xiao Qin should stop looking this way, I don't want her to see such a humiliating painting.

I took a sigh of relief when the class finally ended and Loud Mouth called Xiao Qin to go to the washroom together. I took out my Swiss Army knife from my bag and wanted to scrape off the naked girl's drawing on my desk.

But I was caught off guard, right when I moved the paper away, Xiao Qin came running back. She jumped right in front of my desk and was able to get a good look at the drawing.

"Eh." Xiao Qin froze.

Did she freeze from shock?

"Eh eh eh eh eh."

Xiao Qin was astonished.

"Ye Lin students actually draws so well. I didn't know about it at all."

I wasn't the one who drew it. It was a depressed senior who couldn't answer the exam.

"This body& it's almost on the same level as Celery-sensei."

No, I'm pretty sure it's far above Celery-sensei's level. I'm not exaggerating when I say these two naked women are vivid to the extent that you can directly jerk off to.

Xiao Qin suddenly became a little discouraged, but it had nothing to do with her drawing skills.

"So Ye Lin students likes this style& but I can't copy the one on the left for the time being&"

The one on the left, the one holding the two balloons? Yeah, you can't copy it for the time being and you can't copy it for the rest of your life, but Gong CaiCai has potential&

"If Ye Lin classmate likes the one on the right, I can do it&"

Xiao Qin said with a red face.

The right one with the spread legs? I'm not going to be able to focus in school if you keep talking about H stuff.

I pulled Xiao Qin aside and used the Swiss Army knife to scrape off the naked woman on the desk leaving unsightly marks, but it was much better than the original.

But the class leader witnessed me destroying public property.

"Ye Lin, what are you doing?"

The class leader entered from the back door just in time to see me making the last cut to the desk.

"Destroying desks and also bringing such a long knife to school&" the class leader glared at me and reached her hand out to me, "The desk matter will be dealt with later. First give me the knife, dangerous things must be confiscated immediately."

What? The knife was a limited edition diplomatic gift from Wu Sheng. It's an upgraded version of the Centurion and you can't even but it if you had money.

As if reading my mind, Xiao Qin blinked and said to the class leader:

"Um, I brought the knife from home, Ye Lin classmate was just playing with it. My mom will scold me if it's confiscated, so please be lenient and let me off the hook this time&"

"You said you brought the knife with you?"

The class leader's dark pupils flashed with suspicion.

"(@O@)~It's true, believe me. I took it out of my mother's cabinet, if it was confiscated, I wouldn't be able to explain to my mother."

The class leader thought about it, since she knew Xiao Qin's mother was an MMA champion, it wasn't odd for Xiao Qin to like martial arts, so she believed it.

"Let's not talk about how it's a prohibited item at school, but how can a girl carry a knife around with her."

Sometimes I felt like Shu Sha was the teacher in charge of class 2-3.

"Um&" Xiao Qin hesitated, "I have to defend myself since it's so chaotic outside. What if the principal called me to go with him to a hotel or something&"

The class leader felt awkward hearing Xiao Qin talk about this topic, especially in front of me.

"Our principal won't do that."

Theoretically, the class leader is correct. The old principal who's nearing retirement is always muddled and occasionally likes to joke around, but will never overstep his bounds with students. The vice principal was bent on getting to the top and was extremely rigid. He would love if every student in 28 Middle turned into monks. Basically, neither of them are deranged enough to book a hotel room with a middle school student.

"Class leave, even if it's safe at school, I can still meet scum, bullies, or gangsters on my way home from school, so I need something to protect myself."

The class leader half narrowed her eyes and lowered her voice.

"If you want to defend yourself, you don't need a knife at all, right?"

"Yeah& hehehe&" Xiao Qin, who was seen by the class leader using martial arts, could only laugh foolishly.

"Since I was exposed, I have to tell the truth, actually&"

Xiao Qin gave me a weird look.

"Actually, I stole the Swiss army knife as a gift for Ye Lin classmate, because he has always liked knives&"

That statement was obviously more credible, because the class leader nodded along while listening.

"But it was like Ye Lin classmate was possessed once he got the knife. He began cutting the desk and I couldn't stop him."

Xiao Qin made an expression as if to say "I was worried about him".

"Not only did Ye Lin classmate scratch the desks, he also threatened he would stab anyone who doesn't listen to him. He would also cut the face of any girl who doesn't accept his requests&"

According to you, I would be the scum or hooligan you need to guard against, right?

"I was kind enough to give him a gift, but didn't think he would us it that way. I was worrying about how to take it back, but it's a good thing you came over. Class leader, please help me get my knife back, so he wouldn't use the knife to do anything bad anymore."

Xiao Qin's words were earnest and her expression was lively which made the class leader feel very sympathetic towards her.

"Ye Lin, have you heard that saying before."

"Which saying?"

"Money doesn't change a person's nature, but only makes a person's strengths and weaknesses become more apparent."

"Who said that, but I don't think it has anything to do with my knife."

"Class leader, class leader." Xiao Qin interjected, "Look at how Ye Lin classmate always say it's his knife, he must not want to return it to me."

The class leader continued, "There's also an old saying that goes 'a person with a weapon will have thoughts of killing'. Ye Lin, you already had a tendency towards violence, so you're not fit to have the knife."

The class leader ordered with a non-negotiable tone, "Return the knife back to Xiao Qin and tell her to hurry up and take it home, and there better not be a next time."

I wanted to defend myself, but on second thought, I realized Xiao Qin only told so many lies to help me prevent the Swiss Army knife from being confiscated.

So I retracted the blade dejectedly and reluctantly handed it to Xiao Qin.

Xiao Qin took the blade happily and put it into her own bag.

"Make sure to put the knife away properly and don't take it out at school. Bring it home quickly after school, okay?"

"Mm, mm." Xiao Qin nodded her head at the class leader's instructions.

The class leader returned to her seat when the bell rang.

I waited for half the class until I felt it was safe. While the biology teacher was talking about the "racist" customs of the kangaroo colony, I said to Xiao Qin:

"Hey, can I have my knife back now?"

"What?" Xiao Qin held her textbook in a disciplined manner and pretended she didn't hear me well.

"Knife, give me back my Swiss Army knife." I repeated a little impatiently.

"Ye Lin classmate's words are so strange." Xiao Qin muttered, "It's obviously my knife."

"The class leader isn't here, so you don't have to act anymore."

"I wasn't acting, it was originally my knife. I wanted to give it to Ye Lin classmate as a gift, but you used it to do bad things, so I had to take it back. Let me think& I'll put it together with brother Optimus Prime."

So that's your plan! You always take the things I like away from me. Do you think you can have my heart just because you have my treasures?

I couldn't make too much of a move during class, so I endured until the end of class, before continuing to ask Xiao Qin for my knife.

"Give my knife&" Xiao Qin jumped up and ran towards the back of the classroom before I even finished my sentence.

Huh, I thought she would have stopped me, but she gave up so easily. Did she rush to the washroom because of her menstrual pain?

So I bluntly sat down on Xiao Qin's chair and began to go through her bag. I remembered that the knife was hidden at the bottom of the bag.

"Ye Lin, what are you doing?"

The class leader's angry voice rang by my ears.

I raised my head and saw the class leader's angry face. Next to her was Xiao Qin, who was putting on an act.

So Xiao Qin didn't run out of the classroom, she went to tell on me. She had a "the class leader will back me up" look on her face.

"Going through a girl's bag, do you have any shame?" The class leader had an acerbic tone, probably because she thought that Xiao Qin, who was still in her menstrual period, might have some private items in her bag.

"I, I just want my knife back." I explained with a red face.

"Class leader, I'm not wrong, right? Ye Lin classmate still says that the knife is his." Xiao Qin pouted and slandered me from behind the class president.

I was furious, "It was mines originally."

"Is that so?" The class leader said coldly, "I was only lenient because the knife was Xiao Qin's. If it's yours, then I have to confiscate it now."

She said as she stuck her hand out, "Give it to me."

Give it my ass, I didn't even find it yet. I thought Xiao Qqin was covering for me out of good intentions, but I didn't think it was to embezzle my personal property. She managed to trick the class leader and put me in a difficult position.

"I, I'm not looking for the knife. I wanted to go to the bathroom and I'm just checking if Xiao Qin had any tissues in her bag."

I said a sentence in embarrassment and headed to the washroom.

"If Ye Lin comes to you again and asks for the knife, come tell me and I'll help you."

I heard the voice of the class leader and Xiao Qin from behind me.

"Thank you, I knew the class leader is the best. I was willing to give the knife to Ye Lin classmate, but he went crazy when he got the knife&"

Don't pretend to be a good person, you're the one who's crazy! You're trying to take away the things I like just like with brother Optimus Prime. You're a demon, a fiend!

In the next few classes, I found a slot where both Xiao Qin and the class leader were away and went through Xiao Qin's bag inside and out. I didn't find anything but a few ultra-thin sanitary napkins, the Swiss army knife must have been hidden somewhere or she was carrying it with her.

When school was over, I couldn't resist and asked her directly.

"Where did you hide the army knife."

"Hey, it's a~ secret." Xiao Qin replied joyfully.

"You're carrying it with you, aren't you?" I looked Xiao Qin up and down and tried to guess her hiding place.

"Stop~ looking at me with those lecherous eyes~~~" Xiao Qin giggled, "If you want to know where the knife is hidden, why don't you just search me? Hint: it's hidden in an unexpected place."

Hmph, do you think I'm afraid to do a body search? Compared to almost crossing the line with you before, a body search is simple. Let's see first if it's on your waist&

I never expected Xiao Qin to scream out 'Yah' in the middle of a self study session right when I touched her waist.

The whole class turned in shock to look towards Xiao Qin and me, and they all saw me withdraw my hands.

"It looks like Ye Lin still didn't chance. My impression of him got slightly better after he led the basketball team to victory, but didn't expect so soon&"

"Touching a female classmate during class, I think that's going overboard even if you're childhood friends&"

I was inevitably glared at again by the class leader.

I had to wait until the end of the school day, but the class leader protected Xiao Qin from me as if I would rob Xiao Qin of her knife when I got a chance.

If there really was a chance& of course I would grab it, otherwise it will disappear like brother Optimus Prime with no hopes of returning!

After watching the class leader head to the bike shed, I waited a while before running towards the same subway station Xiao Qin was heading to.

Give me back my army knife! I'm not going to allow you to increase your collection. I must intercept you before you reach the subway station and take back what's mines!

Made in the USA
Las Vegas, NV
19 November 2024

12157690R00160